PITTSBURGH SERIES IN

Composition, Literacy, and Culture

David Bartholomae and Jean Ferguson Carr, Editors

The Emperor's New Clothes

Literature,

Literacy,

and the

Ideology of Style

Kathryn T. Flannery

University of Pittsburgh Press
Pittsburgh and London

Published by the University of Pittsburgh Press, Pittsburgh, Pa.
15260
Copyright © 1995, University of Pittsburgh Press
All rights reserved.
Manufactured in the United States of America
Printed on acid-free paper

Designed by Jane Tenenbaum

Library of Congress Cataloging-in-Publication Data

Flannery, Kathryn T.
    The emperor's new clothes : literature, literacy, and the ideology
of style / Kathryn T. Flannery.
        p.   cm. — (Pittsburgh series in composition, literacy, and
culture)
    Includes bibliographical references (p.   ) and index.
    ISBN 0-8229-3799-9. — ISBN 0-8229-5525-3 (pbk.)
        1. English prose literature—History and criticism—Theory, etc.
    2. American prose literature—History and criticism—Theory, etc.
    3. English language—Style. 4. Canon (Literature) 5. Literacy.
    I. Title. II. Series.
    PR751.F58 1994
    828'.08—dc20   94-24999
                                                                  CIP

A CIP catalogue record for this book is available from the British Library.
Eurospan, London

*To my mother, who taught me to read
between the lines*

CONTENTS

Acknowledgments   ix

Introduction: Style as Cultural Capital   3

1   *Prosa Oratio:* "All Men's and Every Man's Best Style"   33

2   The Charmed Circle, Part 1: Literature and Literacy as Instruments of Culture   66

3   The Charmed Circle, Part 2: The Pedagogues   92

4   "Eliot's 'Axe to Grind'": Locating Origins   133

5   The National Prose Problem   174

Postscript: Classroom Dialogue   199

Appendix   205

Notes   209

Bibliography   219

Index   235

ACKNOWLEDGMENTS

This project grew out of a commonplace book entry—a note on decorum—from a Milton seminar I took with Bob Hinman. He remains for me the model of the teacher-scholar: he invited me into the capacious library, gave me room to work in my inefficient, circuitous way, supported what I found, and respected where we diverged. Along the way, from that commonplace book entry to this book, I have been fortunate in the many folks who have talked out parts of this project with me—especially, early on, Steve Carr (who always seemed to see something there when I couldn't), Jim Knapp, Paul Bové (even, or especially, when we disagreed), and Hugh Kearney; and more recently, Gene Kintgen, Pat Brantlinger, Don Gray, Mary Burgan, and Barry Kroll, all of whom generously read portions of the manuscript at various stages.

Smart, theorized, reflective teacher talk with Jerry Harste and Carolyn Burke has been a refreshing tonic. Thanks to the patience and good humor of undergraduate and graduate classes, I've had the opportunity to work out what is at stake in considering the historical intersections of literature and literacy. I have learned much from J. Arthur Bond, Lewis Roberts, Suzanne Henry, Kathy Egawa, and Beth Berghoff, whose collective intelligence and cross-disciplinary dexterity have been sustaining. Dean of the faculties at Indiana University, Anya Royce, through her support of a faculty seminar in cultural studies, made possible a portion of the research, and a departmental pretenure leave gave me precious time to finish the manuscript. Librarians at the Lilly, Newberry, and British libraries were all helpful in locating peculiarly catalogued textbooks and pamphlets. The readers for the University of Pittsburgh Press have offered particularly thoughtful commentary for which I am most grateful.

Finally, this book would not be without the friendship and rare collegiality of four people. Dave Barholomae has had a vision of the whole for far longer than I have and the capacity to show me how to bring it off. Jean Carr has modeled for me what intradisciplinary boundary crossing can be. Mariolina Salvatori, in her intellectual rigor and rare teacher sense, has been there with much needed conversation. And, never least, Jim Flannery has had the bravery to remain in-house counsel extraordinaire.

The Emperor's New Clothes

Introduction
Style as Cultural Capital

What is involved, here, is neither the acceptance of some
static historical "inheritance" nor the simple substitution of
a preferred alternative, but a continuous transformation, a
"rewriting," of what we have received in terms of what we
have to do.

Janet Batsleer et al., Rewriting English

Literacy . . . is always embedded in some social form, in
conventions such as letter writing, charters, catechisms,
business style, academic "texts" etc., and it is always learnt
in relation to these uses in specific social conditions. These
conditions include theories of pedagogy and practices of
hegemony that help to determine the meanings of literacy
for particular practitioners.

Brian Street, Literacy in Theory and Practice

Several years ago, E. L. Epstein declared style to be "less a fact of
the history of culture than of the history of psychology" (xi). In this
book, I reverse the order of Epstein's claim, reasserting the importance of understanding written style—specifically prose style—as
cultural capital, a commodity differentially legitimated, controlled, and distributed among members of a given society.[1] What
counts as style, what counts as valued written form, is part of and
derives its meaning from a matrix of elements that comprise a
given culture. The material arrangement of words on the page has
no essential or intrinsic meaning apart from a given culture, apart
from the conventions for reading and writing. Style is thus not a
natural exhalation of either the individual or the nation. It is, as
Quintilian put it, necessarily schooled. And schools, Henry Giroux

reminds us, "are not merely instructional sites but also sites where the culture of the dominant society is learned and where students experience the difference between those status and class distinctions that exist in the larger society" (5–6).

My interest in the question of style as cultural capital grows out of my reading and teaching in what are often institutionally separate areas of practice: late Renaissance prose, especially the part stylistic reform played in both the rise of science and Reformation politics; composition studies, in particular what appears to me to be the odd conjuncture of a liberatory (but not therefore revolutionary) rhetoric and the privileging of a normative, hygienic prose (clear, concise, forceful, and sincere); and cultural theory, with its emphasis on the ways in which the "structures of the social world are not an objective given, any more than intellectual and psychological categories . . . [but are] produced historically by the interconnected practices—political, social and discursive—that construct their figures" (Chartier 13–14).

In reading about late English Renaissance prose style and in reading contemporary discussions of style, I found myself trying to figure out what other people have been seeing when they see something they call *style*. Much like the little boy in the crowd who could see only the emperor's underwear and not the golden threads that the adults were so ready to praise, I could not fit the descriptions to texts. What exactly is a close, naked, natural style? What *is* sincere style? What *is* masculine style? Stanley Fish has already argued that stylistic analysis is inevitably interested, that it is never simply a matter of describing, however technically sophisticated linguistically, what is empirically there on the page to see. Style is always a kind of excuse for some evaluative agenda (cf. *Is There a Text*). Fish is content to leave it at that, to deconstruct the formalist claim to objectivity as always already interpretive and leave style talk as if in a theoretical heap like an unraveled sweater. But style talk persists.

Richard Ohmann has approached the question of style in terms of ideology and pedagogy. Puzzling over the persistence of the writing teacher's maxim to use definite, specific, concrete language, Ohmann sees a "well-defined ideological pattern." In teaching such a stylistic maxim, one is also, he argues, teaching ahistoricism, empiricism, fragmentation (an obscuring of the situatedness of things and the "social relations . . . embedded in things"), solipsism, and denial of conflict (387–88). Ohmann thus goes a bit further than Fish in naming what's at stake in at least one kind of style talk. In his essay, "Use Definite, Specific, Concrete Language," however, Ohmann does not say whose interest such an ideology serves, though one might surmise from his other writings that he would argue that such an ideology is supportive of an "establishment," those entrenched and antidemocratic interests that have much to lose if schools are to teach something other than the present order. While, certainly, there is no simple conspiracy, no cabal of English teachers who want to freeze the youth of America in a sort of blindly happy presentism, nor even a cabal of politicos from the Right or the Left who pull pedagogical strings to lead students astray, one might begin to look at what ideological projects such conceptions of style are used to support, and here I find a compelling analysis in Brian Street's critique of what he calls the autonomous model of literacy.

Street offers the work of Angela Hildyard and David Olson as a strong version of the autonomous model, of that conception of literacy that assumes it to be a "neutral technology that can be detached from specific social contexts" (1). Street contends that Hildyard and Olson find support for this conception of literacy in the English essayist tradition, and they locate the origins of that tradition in the 1662 charter of the Royal Society. That charter sets as one of its aims the development of a writing style approximating "mathematical plainness," with "all amplifications, digressions and swellings of style" to be avoided (qtd. in Street 39). Street argues that the Royal Society is thus used—erroneously— as "evidence of the logical and socially detached nature of language" (39). The Royal Society's *desire* for—more than their success in producing—a language that could operate as pure denotation, without history, without figuration, as unmediated sign of the natural world, is translated into a paradigm for the operation of all language—transhistorically, transculturally—and then used as the gauge by which to measure all literacy practices.

But why turn in particular to the Royal Society to find an origin for a normative literate practice? Street suggests that the Royal Society has come to stand for objectivity. In attempting to justify the valuing of a particular kind of schooled literacy, Hildyard and Olson want to argue that such literacy makes possible certain kinds of thinking that are superior to that which is possible in oral or inadequately literate cultures. As Street reads them, "The result of acquiring literacy, they conjecture, 'is not an ordinary language . . . it is the language of analytic thinking and explicit argument and it is the tool that has been adopted by science and philosophy and to a large extent by the formal school system'" (Hildyard and Olson qtd. in Street 40).

In such an admittedly reduced form, the argument for an autonomous model of literacy seems at best to stretch the limits of acceptable generalization; at worst it appears, in Street's terms, "parochial and ethnocentric" (40). One literate practice—the Western "essay-text form of writing" with its emphasis on formal conventions of explicitness and objectivity—is made to stand for and serve as the standard for literacy in general, as justification for public expenditures for compulsory schooling and for global literacy campaigns. But the example of the Royal Society charter—that originary text—Street argues, can be used to challenge that position it is meant to support. He goes on to deconstruct the argument by rehistoricizing this originary moment. He points out that "the origins and development of the Royal Society of London, far from demonstrating the objectivity and truth of scientific inquiry, is a classic example of the extent to which such inquiry is contingent on social pressure, political interests and the nature of the institutions in which it is conducted" (39). As I discuss more fully in chapter 3, the Royal Society's project for the reformation of language, explicitly acknowledged as deriving from Francis Bacon's program (if not, as many have argued, from his example as a writer), was part of a larger polemical stance, a positioning of the new science in opposition to the old. Street describes the society's charter as a "political weapon in the battle for status and funding," and he emphasizes that it "is not to be taken simply at face value" (40).

While Street acknowledges that societies certainly have constructed "devices for specialising and separating out levels of meaning"—in this case, developing conventions for a plain or transparent style—"this does not mean that they ever achieve in reality the claims that they make about such discourse." The British Baconians "make ritualistic claims for objectivity that function more to support their own ideology than to convince a sceptical reader of the 'truth.'" Certainly, writers of any philosophical persuasion do not "have a monopoly on such claims; they are a part of oral practices too" (41).

Street's discussion makes clear that style talk plays a rather important role in sustaining a model for a literacy that helps to support a certain kind of cultural hegemony both within national boundaries and without.[2] Innocent-seeming value terms (be "clear, concise, specific, concrete") are thus a part of an effort to define not only what is culturally superior but also what is fully human. Those who do not master and display the culturally valued behaviors are then labeled as cognitively deficient—as with the student in the classroom, or primitive—as with the citizen of a nonwesternized culture. The student and the primitive (in Goody's unfortunate and telling term, the "savage") are thus more readily made the objects of efforts to control and colonize, to make orderly and docile.

The very persistence of style talk—as a way to read and a way to write—suggests that the manifestations of the ideology of style and the interests that ideology serves are not single but multiple. The same style or, put differently, the same stylistic designation serves different masters. It is overdetermined, and its very resistance to a single definition makes it more malleable and enhances its utility. Style has been a notoriously slippery term. As Edward Corbett explains in his *Classical Rhetoric for the Modern Student*, "famous definitions of style, like Buffon's 'style is the man,' Swift's 'proper words in proper places,' Newman's 'style is a thinking out into language,' and Blair's 'the peculiar manner in which a man expresses his conceptions,' are apt, but they are just vague enough to tease us out of thought and just general enough to give us a sense of style without giving us a clear definition of it" (26). Or, as William Brewster wrote earlier in the century, "Whoever will be at pains to peruse the numberless definitions of the term *style* will in course of time perceive that [Robert Louis] Stevenson states the difficulty; whether or not the reality of style lie 'too deep in nature and too far back in the mysterious history of man,' it is certain that the larger number of definitions of the term, as well as the essays on the subject, even if they abandon practical details in the search for principles underlying a body of phenomena, rarely succeed even in approaching an explanation of the idea of style" (ix). We know it when we see it, but what is it that we are seeing? And perhaps more importantly, what does focussing on style as a formal feature of texts or as neutral linguistic practice allow us not to see?

This book is intended as an exploration of not only the said but the unsaid of style talk and as a consideration of the processes by which the apparently same stylistic designation has served rather different ends. To situate this approach more concretely, I begin with three instances of what I am calling *style talk*, instances I am reading as culturally isomorphic, to borrow Katherine Hayle's term: first, a construction of a literary genealogy of style; second, textbook constructions of a hygienic style; and third, legislation to mandate style. Each shares in common the simultaneous assumption of (as a given) and the need to argue for (as embattled) a standard, best, normal (and normative), plain style.

I

The first instance involves the appropriation of two late Renaissance writers as exemplars of style.[3] Style has served as one way to ascertain a literary genealogy, to establish a pedigree for present practice, linguistic practice certainly but cultural practices more generally. Style thus has defined what has been (and how to read what has been) but also what ought to be produced now as legitimate heir to a literary (national) inheritance. Tony Bennett and Renée Balibar have each argued for the importance of seeing the relationship between canonization and nationalism. In a study of the production of literary texts for educational use, Balibar has shown how the restricted use of privileged texts within the educational system in France was a tactic by which the middle class "created and reproduced for itself a position of supremacy in language" (Bennett, *Formalism and Marxism* 158–59). Balibar studied the uses to which texts "under the name of 'George Sand'" were put. She compared an edited passage from *The Devil's Pool*, which served as the basis for grammar exercises in French elementary schools, with the apparently same passage in a critical edition (29–30, 35), in order to investigate the process by which certain texts become literary and to what ends.

Balibar has argued that in nineteenth-century France the categories *literature* and *nonliterature* marked the difference between writing and nonwriting, between reading and nonreading, reflecting the separation between the literate official language of the court and the illiterate spoken language of the people. While there is nothing comparable to the French Academy in England or the United States, there was nonetheless a similar development in the shifting uses of the terms *literature* and *literacy*, as Raymond Williams has pointed out (*Keywords* 183–88). *Literature* designated writing that was available simply by virtue of being written to the literate, who were by definition those who could read (Bennett, *Formalism and Marxism* 158). Balibar's interest is in what happens when literature no longer marks the difference between those who can and cannot read and write. How, in other words, are "certain writings (readings?) . . . singled out, valorized, and recognized as literary in modern society where literature is no longer a question of a social category openly denoting a privileged access to reading and writing" (Balibar 28).

Balibar finds that the passage from *The Devil's Pool* produced for children is edited to model a more linguistically limited writing than what one might find in the critical edition. Not a very remarkable occurrence, one might say, to produce a children's version that is more apparently accessible. Balibar's point, however, is to defamiliarize such familiar practice, to suggest that making accessible is teaching a particular kind of simplified language use: the audience—children, students, ordinary adults—are considered incapable of reading more linguistically (and conceptually) advanced texts, and a pedagogy that might engage an audience in complexity is not imagined.

Children were not always confined to age-specific materials but have at different times and in different cultures learned to read with adults and older children what adults and older children read (consider, for a contemporary example, the children in Shirley Brice Heath's account of Trackton residents). More importantly, for my purposes here, the process of appropriation and reproduction that Balibar is discussing is not confined to children but is indeed the very process by which texts are made to signify in the world—how they are produced for consumption through editorial and pedagogical practice. That process helps shape and reinforce a national language and a particular version of the national culture, at the same time that it is shaping a conception of the reader as inadequate. The text under the name of "George Sand," edited for grammar school use, helps to consolidate and perpetuate a particular kind of linguistic hegemony; that is, the linguistic structures (and strictures) learned from lessons based on such a text are intended to be taken up by the reader as normal and right. Such a production does not preclude other uses, of course. As David Cressy, Natalie Zemon Davis, and Harvey Graff have found, in separate social histories, the desired results from the spread of literacy—whether to socialize the poor, to produce honest and industrious workers, or to create a knowledgeable citizenry necessary for a democracy—have not always been what is actually achieved. The literacy achieved by the masses may not be in fact precisely the literacy wished for by social planners, teachers, or government officials—for good or ill. But the more uniform a pedagogy, and the more widespread the practice, the more effective it is in limiting what appears possible and the more successful it is in establishing what is "normal."

What is chosen as acceptable literature to be taught—how far back one must go in the historic past before the works can be made to be literature—says something about not only the mythic nature of national language, but the extent to which literature designates a series of isolated artifacts (Williams, "Base and Superstructure" 14–15). The origin of English prose style has traditionally been located in the late English Renaissance, with the strengthening of the vernacular and the displacing of Latin on multiple fronts (religious, political, and pedagogical), but—importantly—the texts to be made useful for present purposes first must be removed from that cultural context.

T. S. Eliot, that great and self-conscious canonizer, provides a representative instance. In 1929, Eliot introduced Richard Hooker and Francis Bacon to a BBC radio audience as the fathers of "the philosophic prose style." Eliot was quite clear about his intentions. He wanted to establish for a broad audience the origins of a prose style he claimed had made possible everything from typewriter manuals to scientific and philosophic treatises. Because Eliot had earlier declared his loyalties in *For Lancelot Andrewes: Essays on Style and Order* (1929) as a classicist in literature, a royalist in politics, and an Anglo-Catholic in religion, he provides a rather explicit case of interest in naming a genealogy of style.[4] He makes visible an interestedness in fact that almost disappears from view in the anthologies and rhetorics by which students are taught style. Eliot, a high modernist, standing at the entryway to modern disinterestedness, provides an appropriate place to look at one kind of style talk—the canonical, literary history–making kind. I want to make it clear that I am not treating Eliot as an origin for a practice. Indeed, as chapter 2 shows, the reading he offers of Bacon's and Hooker's places in literary history would have been familiar already in the nineteenth century. His ordinariness, in fact, combined with his visibility in passing on tradition—one might say his pedagogical role—leads me to choose him as a sample. Additionally, his status as a transatlantic literary figure opens up a space to begin to consider the complex ways a decidedly *English* literary history has been redeployed in the American context.

Eliot's address—what might have been a specialists' lecture—was broadcast over the remarkably ordinary mass medium of radio. His address on the religious controversialist Hooker and the Renaissance polymath Bacon was one of a series he gave on English writers, and it was printed in *The Listener*, a BBC publication. There it sits side by side such other radio presentations as "Scotland and John Knox," "Clear Thinking and Disarmament," and "Reforming Men's Dress." The radio audience could have tuned in to household hints on home dyeing, bookbinding for the amateur, a discussion between Vita Sackville-West and Harold Nicolson, or a travel narrative, "From Nile to Niger." Or they could have heard Eliot expound on prose style, a topic he acknowledged might sound rather forbidding if one were expected to attend to either the philosophy of Bacon or the theology of Hooker.

Eliot reassures the listener that he has no intention of discussing either. That Bacon and Hooker are the "fathers of modern philosophy and theology respectively is not the point with which [Eliot has] to deal: [his] point . . . is that they are the fathers of the modern abstract style." He intends to consider "the two men as great prose writers, and indicate their contribution to the English language which we use to-day." Through this rather unremarkable comment, Eliot offers to do what English teachers and literature anthologies traditionally have done as a matter of course: ostensibly set aside matter in order to concentrate on manner. He proposes to discuss a kind of writing we all make use of "either when we write or in much that we read." "Any kind of argument," Eliot contends, "legal, political, or general; any kind of scientific exposition or explanation, from the theory of relativity to how to clean a typewriter or oil a motor car, owes something to Bacon and Hooker" ("Genesis" 907). Putting aside for the moment the odd—un-Eliot-like—utilitarianism of this pronouncement, one might note the process by which two canonical figures familiar to most English schoolboys and anthologized for college students on both sides of the Atlantic are thus further domesticated, brought into the parlor, oddly dehistoricized, and sanitized of any controversy with which either writer might have been associated, so that they can be made contemporary and instructive.

Eliot was not breaking new ground in choosing Hooker and Bacon. Most nineteenth- and early twentieth-century handbooks yoked the two as representative late Elizabethan prose stylists, sometimes as *the* representatives (see chapter 2). Hooker was already assumed to be a writer of moderation and Bacon was the epitome of a scientific clarity. Following established practice, then, Eliot chooses Hooker and Bacon because of their historical importance. But in a move characteristic of canon formation, he then removes them from any partisan arena into the realm of literature, that is, into the recently (since the nineteenth century) narrowed realm of "well-written books," of aesthetically valued writings (Williams, *Keywords* 186). Once operating as literature, such works could be valued for themselves, without apparent reference to any other worldly concerns (despite the claim that such works have had practical consequences in everyday life—typewriter manuals, for example). And yet this very freeing of what are now literary objects allows them to be redeployed in support of conceptions of a literacy—in support of what ought to be valued in writing, what ought to be taught, how and to whom—and more generally in support of a conception of a specifically English national language and culture. Thus the freed artifact is more readily captured and put to use.

Having reassured his listeners that he would not pay attention to either Bacon's philosophy or Hooker's religion, Eliot nonetheless makes clear that his choice of Bacon and Hooker as fathers of a widely used modern style is predicated precisely on his valuing their philosophy and religion: "They were the fathers of modern philosophy and theology respectively," a point with which he does not intend to deal because the claim is assumed (at least rhetorically) to be uncontestable. The matter that has been put out of play is in fact central to his argument about style. He states later in the address that "nothing is more dreary, or more deadening . . . than to read 'for the sake of the style' some book on a subject about which you care nothing" ("Genesis" 907). Similarly, in a discussion of "Prose and Verse" from *The Chapbook* (1921), Eliot remarks that "you cannot get the pleasure of the style unless you interest yourself in something more than words" (7). In his radio address, in fact, Eliot does not use the technical language of the handbooks to analyze either writer's diction or sentence structure or preference for one sort of figure of speech over another. Rather, discussing them generally as writers allows him to make more prominent the unsaid content of their writings, to merely assert, as if it were a statement universally accepted, that what they had to say is worthy of attention.

Behind this move stands Eliot's larger mission to establish the relationship between certain cultural values conveyed by a certain kind of language use and the maintenance of an orderly society. Grafton and Jardine, linking Eliot and F. R. Leavis as "twentieth-century guardians of European 'civilisation,'" suggest that they have contributed to the mystification of arts education—"a connivance in overlooking the evident mismatch between ideals and practice—which has clouded our intellectual judgement of the progress and importance of the liberal arts" (xv). At least part of what is at stake for Eliot is the maintenance of a humanist ideology. In defining "What is a Classic?" for example, Eliot asserts that "maturity of mind, maturity of language and perfection of the common style" are the primary features. Grafton and Jardine see the implications of such a definition to be that, since "eloquence is synonymous with maturity[,] recognition of that eloquence on the part of modern Europe [to which they link North America] is equivalent to confirmation of contemporary values." That is, not only is it supposed that certain values make possible a certain maturity of language (say, the notion of the civic ideal in the Roman Empire making possible the maturity of the Latin language), but our current recognition of that language would be confirmation of our sharing in the values that made that language possible in the first place (xv). Grafton and Jardine go on to argue that in fact there is no essential or material match between the valuing of a language and the exercise of the values that made it possible.

The oddity of Eliot praising Hooker and Bacon because their prose made possible typewriter manuals may be a function of this apparent mismatch. What, after all, is the relationship between humanistic ideals and typewriter manuals? In a Clarke lecture delivered in 1967, Leavis addresses "Eliot's 'Axe to Grind', and the Nature of Great Criticism," offering some insight into the odd conjuncture of humanism and manuals. Leavis is concerned to defend Eliot's notion of "dissociation of sensibility"—that phrase that marks, according to Leavis, a seismic shift occurring at some point after the Restoration, "when England achieved and put into general use the norms of a prose of common currency—lucid, logical, business-like and idiomatic" (94). Eliot's own dating of the shift is not so clear, nor for that matter are his accounts of the apparent causes of this definitive dissociation. Leavis, whose politics and literary theory did not entirely coincide with Eliot's, was less interested in attacking Puritans, and thus had more at stake in locating the move to the modern in the Restoration.[5]

In magisterial fashion and with more than a touch of irony, Leavis observes, "When we ask how it was that modern prose appeared so decisively in the first decade of the Restoration, with an effect of having prevailed over-night, the answer is an account of the total movement of civilization that then after twenty years of civil war and Commonwealth, made itself felt as the decisive start of a new age, and the sure promise of triumphant human achievement" (94). Lest anyone mistake what one is to make of this "sure promise," Leavis asserts that "all the forces of change that had been at work through the century had come together to inaugurate the triumphant advance toward civilization, technological and Benthamite, that we live in" (95). The "sure promise" is a rather sorry promise to the extent that it leads, in Leavis's view, to a spiritually vacated utilitarianism. In a telling "digression" from his defense of Eliot's "dissociation of sensibility," Leavis adds that recent suggestions (from Lord Snow in particular) for educational reform that would have science students attending English literature lectures and humanities students attending lectures on science "can only play a part in destroying education" (96). The "dissociation of sensibilities," as Leavis offers it, is the "process . . . by which the most essential differences between the distinctively poetic use of language and the prose use are being eliminated"; it is the failure to see the difference between *"presenting* or *doing* and merely telling, between evoking the concrete and describing discursively" (96–97). The proposal to mix the study of science and literature is thus a latter-day sign of such dissociation of sensibilities, clearly the child of the technological and Benthamite civilization we live in and that, for Leavis and Eliot, we should resist.

For the purposes of his BBC talk, Eliot seems to have situated the dissociation of sensibility sometime after Hooker and Bacon, suggesting something rather different than a celebration of technological culture. Indeed, his linking of Bacon with Hooker seems to be an effort to retain Bacon as a predissociation Elizabethan and rescue him from the ways in which he was, especially from the nineteenth century on, claimed as a proto-utilitarian. For Eliot, one does not have to read either Hooker for his theology or Bacon for his philosophy as long as one understands that they are both classics. Both Hooker and Bacon model paradoxically *in embryo* a mature, modern English prose style and also, at the same time, a mature, modern Englishness—a stylistic and cultural homunculus, as it were.

Eliot's discussion of style, as his flexible and ideologically marked periodization suggests, always hinges on something other than style, as Stanley Fish might say: on Hooker's position as a father for high church Anglicanism (Eliot explicitly identifies himself with the high church position) and on Bacon's status as the first essayist in English and the first English philosopher to see the future as shaped by experimental science. Stylistic interestedness also depends on the assumption that the work of such figures as Hooker and Bacon were always literature in the narrower twentieth-century sense of the term, or that their literariness is now more evident because partisan bias finally can be stripped away to reveal the true nature of the object—assuming, that is, as E. D. Hirsch does, that "meaning remains the same" if readers try to operate "beyond predisposition and preference" in order to discover the constant meaning of the text ("Politics of Theories" 236). The sanitized text then can be used more readily, in Renée Balibar's terms, to support a conception of a national language and a national culture—*as if* they were both above political dispute.

Hooker's position as a disputant, a controversialist in a long and often bloody religiopolitical battle, is muted here (as it often is in canonical treatments of his prose), constructing him as someone who dealt with a philosophical and legal question with admirable moderation and more than ordinary skill. Bacon's large, fragmentary corpus is reduced to a few key texts that make it more likely that one can argue for Bacon's unified rhetorical practice and less likely that readers would see either any revolutionary potential in his work (cf. Whitney 135) or any conflict in his contradictory desire for a language that would be plain enough to speak to the enlightened few and plain enough to obscure the truth from the common herd (cf. Stephens 3–4; Briggs). Conflict and contradiction, as Ohmann suggested, are reduced to something more like a watered sherry version of academic debate, so that what Hooker has to say about whose version of the Church of England should win out or what Bacon has to say about finding a way to disseminate his biblical vision of the Great Instauration through a *discriminating* plain language is reduced to an intellectual disquisition that any reasonable person may appreciate and by which any reasonable person may be persuaded. In Charles Whitney's terms, "Being a 'master of English prose,' wielding powerful influence on the development of later style and language, consigns the writer to membership in a particular archive of knowledge and subjects him to certain canons of interpretation that . . . render him harmless" (126). I would qualify that assertion by saying that such membership renders the writer only apparently harmless, so that he can be wielded rhetorically in new battles—in Eliot's representative case, in the defense of a particular form of humanism.

A number of studies have read such treatments of style as error. That is, it is an error to read Hooker's or Bacon's late Renaissance styles in terms of twentieth-century conceptions of prose. Such arguments rest on several premises, however, that much recent theory challenges: the premise that there is some privileged original text; that style is an empirically available component of a privileged text; and, granting the first and second premises, that we as twentieth-century readers, free of preconceptions, can access the original style. W. Speed Hill, for example, distinguishes between present practice, which relegates style to secondary status in relation to substance, and the rhetorical tradition, which insisted on the unity of style and substance. Hill sees behind present-day contempt for "mere rhetoric" a Ramist (and therefore part of the Renaissance) conception that viewed style as separable from content. The implication is that since Hooker "himself deplored" the Ramist tradition, we too must abandon such a tradition if we are to read Hooker aright (Preface, *Studies* xiii).

Brian Vickers, among others, has argued a similar case for the need to read Bacon's work according to Bacon's own rhetorical principles (cf. *Bacon and Renaissance Prose*). Such arguments are familiar and perhaps their very familiarity contributes to their persuasiveness. There is clearly a sense of fair play in reading a writer on his own terms. But such arguments in their disinterested attempt to uncover a true reading are unable to acknowledge their own interestedness, or the degree to which the production of Bacon, Hooker, or other canonical figures as literary is already and necessarily a production of a different object than that which worked in the late Renaissance. And perhaps more importantly, in producing a nonpartisan text, such arguments cannot acknowledge or perhaps cannot even know how such a production makes the text available for uses inconsistent with or even contrary to that which is read as authorial intent. Within the terms in which the present study operates, such other uses—contrary or otherwise—are not instances of error. Rather, they are signs of the dynamic of reading, of texts working in the world. To choose from among various uses is not a matter of determining that which is closest to authorial intent (arguably a futile task at any rate) but of understanding what one can of the situatedness, the interestedness of the use. Such acts of interpretation, in Dominick LaCapra's terms, are political interventions.

In the case of Eliot, he turns to the late Renaissance to recover for present use two already canonical figures. The issue here is not that Eliot misreads either Hooker or Bacon, but that he suppresses conflict, decontextualizes, and dehistoricizes, in order to redeploy them as *literary* figures defined in terms of style in the service of a conception of a modern English language and a modern Englishness, and that this activity defines the normal and normalizing process of canon formation.

II

For Donald Hall, "good style, all by itself, *is* good politics and good mental hygiene." In introducing students to his textbook, *The Contemporary Essay,* Hall mentions first the diversity of authors included in the collection. He then suggests the extent to which these diverse writers share fundamental beliefs about writing. They "agree, by and large, to use the concrete detail in place of the abstraction; to employ the active not the passive mood; to withhold the adjective and search for the verb. They agree to pursue clarity and vigor. And most would agree with Robert Graves . . . who said some years ago: 'The writing of good English is a . . . moral matter' " (xv). A hygienic moral style is intended to avoid what George Orwell saw as the "vices of vagueness, triteness, jargon, and pomposity"—flaws that are more than error because they "often . . . serve the purposes of deceit." The student is thus advised to produce a clear prose style because, Hall maintains, not only will it not deceive others, it "will help the writer to avoid self-deceit" (xv).[6]

Efficiency and clarity alone do not make good writing, however. In addition to using concrete, active language, good writing as Hall presents it also taps into "underworlds of feeling" through the work of the imagination. Hall enlarges on Ezra Pound's maxim (which he quotes) that one should close the "gap between one's real and one's declared meaning." This is more than "saying what one means." This is also, it seems, a matter of knowing one's self well enough to know what one's real meaning is and illuminating through the imagination those "dark" places of the inner self (xv–xvi).

Here is a powerful charge to the student, more emotionally loaded than a functionalist argument alone, because in invoking the importance of writing from the wellspring of the self and of drawing from the power of one's own imagination, Hall speaks to key elements—moral, organicist, self-knowing, romantic—in American culture. Not only is the student to ward off political and moral evil through clear, vigorous writing, but she is to come to know the truth of herself and write in such a way that there is resonance between the self and the writing. However compelling a statement of purpose this is, and however explicitly political it is presented to be, Hall's pedagogy ends up oddly vacated of politically useful analysis. To equate style with morality (or hygiene or self-revelation) is to run the risk of forgetting rhetoric. Rhetoric never claims for itself the truth. It announces the craftedness of language, the importance of calculating effects, reading audiences, anticipating what is expected, manipulating the linguistic resources to make words work in the world. Rhetoric is not thereby of the devil's party (unless perhaps in Blake's terms), however much it may appear the spoiler in the midst of the glorious purposes Hall ascribes to writing. Rather, rhetoric is the constant reminder of contingency and history and change. No style, rhetoric reminds us, is inherently good or bad. To wish to simplify matters by declaring that one sort of style is closer to godliness, cleanliness, or truth is to wish for a prelapsarian world, an apolitical world.

Now, few students may in fact read Hall's introduction, though their teachers might. Instead, the students will likely learn about good writing by engaging in the questions and tasks Hall poses at the end of each reading selection and learn about the difficulty of achieving clarity and vigor and self-revelation when they try to write. It is ironic, then, that the strongest lesson to be learned from the teaching apparatus is that form and content are separate; if there is a politics of style in this advice giving, it is a formalist politics where the form has a life independent of the content. Students respond to disconnected, decontextualized essays—"The Psychology of Astronauts," "A Ride through Spain," "Women and Honor: Some Notes on Lying"—by drawing on what is referred to unproblematically as their "personal experience," and that response is treated primarily as an occasion to practice formal "strategies" derived from the reading selections. It does not really matter what the student is writing about or for so long as he tries his hand at following modern masters, whether Adrienne Rich, Stephen Jay Gould, or E. B. White (whose own "most influential writing manual" argues for "plainness, simplicity, orderliness, sincerity"). The essays are treated as if they speak their own text, not as posing problems or raising questions about the world, but as set pieces for students to practice on, and as such, this contemporary collection operates in much the same way as nineteenth-century textbooks (see chapter 2).

Each reading is followed by "questions on meaning," having to do with content ("Do Cowley's remarks about old age reveal anything about how to live when we are younger?"); "questions on strategy," having to do with form ("Cowley ends his first paragraph with a shocking anecdote. What effect does the placement of this anecdote have on the essay?"); "explorations," or suggestions for further reading; "writing topics"; and "books available in paper-back" (a brief bibliography of works by each writer). After Mal-colm Cowley's essay, "The View from 80," the student is asked to note the "variety of methods" used, especially the "powerful anec-dote" closing the piece. He is then instructed to try his hand at a similar essay: "Write an essay in which you develop your argument in several ways as Cowley does, and conclude with a telling anec-dote—something you've read, heard about, or experienced your-self that brings your subject into a conclusive light" (13).

No one would say that such an assignment could not work on some level, of course, or that a student could not learn something of importance about aging and about anecdotes. The point here is to note that, despite the emphasis on the morality of good writing that hinges not only on clarity but on some sort of consonance be-tween self and style, style operates in the lessons as a template that is placed over a personal content. The morality of organi-cism—of closing the gap between one's real meaning and one's de-clared meaning, between the inside and the outside—runs the risk of exposing itself as merely a matter of convention. Or, put differ-ently, sincerity itself is conventionalized. What one reads as sin-cere—or clear or vigorous—is what has been conventionally con-structed as being so. One reads a writer as sincere because one has learned to read such writing as a sign of sincerity. That cru-cial, critical, rhetorical step, however, to move from the exercise of using some other writer's strategies to reading sincerity or clar-ity or vigor as themselves conventionalized strategies does not happen in any visible form in this text. My concern here is not to simply expose inconsistency in Hall's practice, but to suggest that the movement from formal categories to value terms (morality, good politics, hygiene) to a pedagogy that effaces its own politics is paradigmatic of style talk. And style provides the occasion for such a movement in allowing the writer to invoke value terms only to put them out of play.

Wayne Booth and Marshall Gregory also talk of clarity, unity, and forcefulness in their *Harper and Row Rhetoric*. Echoing Eliot's description of the abstract style, they describe the "formal" or "standard" style, a middle style between the colloquial and the literary in their taxonomy, used to do the world's work: term papers, business letters, scholarly books, textbooks, reports, newspaper and magazine writing, all the forms in which "most of the world's written information is exchanged." This style is grammatically correct "even in minor points," avoids slang, "insists on a precise but not technically difficult vocabulary," "shows care in sentence construction, and . . . follows an orderly development of points" (273). More than Hall, Booth and Gregory, following traditional rhetorical teaching, tie such writing to audience and purpose. They are careful to say that the traditional textbook maxim that good writers achieve "unity, coherence, and emphasis" or "clarity" and "forcefulness" is not sufficient to guide anyone in writing because these general qualities do not specify degree: how much clarity and concision versus how much profundity or playfulness? might not emphasis, requiring perhaps multiple iterations, contradict concision? and so forth. Even though they concede that "most good essays, once they are completed, will *seem* clear, unified, coherent, emphatic, and concise," they emphasize that those descriptors do not signal ways to achieve the effect (55, emphasis added). Their conclusion, then, is that one does not learn to write through stylistic rules but through practice in connecting one's purpose to an appropriate means (57).

But despite their apparently greater rhetorical flexibility—indeed, their general theoretical pluralism as signalled in their preface addressed to the teacher ("This book does not preach . . . a given line to the exclusion of all competing ideas, nor does it try to convert all teachers to a single writing 'approach' " [xv])—Booth and Gregory nonetheless offer a package remarkably like Hall's. They too tie the importance of students learning "good writing" to morality, good politics, and mental hygiene, even while their pedagogy also disconnects form from content. Addressing the teacher, they ask, rhetorically, how students can "be helped to see that day-by-day writing practice is not an isolated, discrete activity but an influence on their intellectual, social, and ethical development?" They propose to offer students both "utilitarian" and "intrinsic" arguments—writing well is important to students' success in college and in the working world, but it is also important to them as social beings—their very "concepts of 'self' are grounded in words." Writing, in short, is placed in the "larger context of 'cultural literacy.'" Students, it is hoped, will see that the "character of the world they live in is determined in large part by the quality of discourse shared by its citizens" (xv–xvi).

Addressing the student, Booth and Gregory draw a parallel between physical health and linguistic health:

> To view language as inherited property may be misleading. Language is more like the air we breathe, the medium that sustains our very life. Can you imagine a life without words? Or a world in which most speech was so garbled that only the speakers knew what they meant? Such imaginings suggest that language is more like health than property. We desire physical health because without it most of what we care for in life becomes impossible or painfully difficult. But we also desire health because it is an intrinsic joy—just plain good in itself. Similarly we seek linguistic health—competence and control in our use of language—both because it is useful and because it is enjoyable for its own sake. (29)

It may help, in order to defamiliarize this sort of talk, to keep in mind that this is from a textbook concerned with the teaching of *writing* (not all language use) to *college students* (who have managed to live in the world for some eighteen years or more with some degree of linguistic competence—in fact, greater competence than their teachers or popular doomsayers have given them credit for). The issue here, then, isn't a fear of a literal Babel, unless riding just below the surface is a xenophobic fear of a non–English speaking invasion (something other writers concerned with a literacy crisis sometimes express more explicitly). The issue then must be what counts as genuine linguistic competence. Linguistic health is thus not natural, as the analogy to physical health seems to suggest, but a contested cultural form requiring frequent reiteration of standards and norms to maintain.

One could multiply examples of a moralizing textbook talk joined to a pedagogy that disengages form from content. The point here is not to say that all writing instruction follows this pattern—it does not—or to say that only writing instruction falls prey to this move—it does not. Indeed, one aim of this book is to suggest how English studies (language study, literature, and composition/rhetoric) from the beginning have been marked by such a conception of writing and of reading.

III

A concern for establishing a normative style has not been confined to literary historians or English teachers, of course. Politicians, business people, and ordinary citizens contribute to style talk. The movement to simplify the language of legal documents is a particularly striking instance of the complex functions of style. In the 1940s, the New Deal Office of Price Administration (OPA) found that small businesses needed to hire lawyers in order to understand the laws imposing price controls. The OPA hired Rudolf Flesch (of later *Why Johnny Can't Read* fame) to help them adjust the language of their regulations according to his readability formula so that business people could comply with the law without the burden of legal expenses made all the more painful in a depression economy (see chapter 1). World War II eased the pressure for price controls, and it also took away a major incentive for legal language reform. Not until the 1970s, with an activist consumer movement, was there a renewed interest in plain English legislation (Dickerson).

Under the Carter administration, an executive order was issued mandating the use of "plain English" in all documents produced by federal agencies. Since then, at least half the states have passed or have considered plain language laws requiring simple, clear, and understandable language in insurance forms, consumer contracts, credit documents, and product warranties.[7] New Jersey, for example, requires that consumer contracts be "easily readable," which means that, among other things, sentences should be "no longer than necessary"; double negatives and exceptions to exceptions should be kept to a minimum; and words that are French, obsolete, Latinate, or from Old or Middle English should be avoided (*New Jersey Statutes Annotated*, 56: 12-1 et seq.). The Sullivan Law in New York legislated simply "clear and coherent" language in consumer contracts. Other states mandated that certain Flesch scores (derived from his readability scale) be maintained in legal documents. In Connecticut, this has meant that sentences on the average should be no longer than twenty-two words, and never longer than fifty words; paragraphs on the average should be no more than seventy-five words and never more than 150 words; syllables in words should not exceed 1.55 on the average; and no line should be more than sixty-five characters (MacDonald).

Consumer groups have supported such legislation, arguing that plain language or plain English, because it is presumably more understandable, protects consumers and citizens from shysters, bureaucrats, and a host of other obfuscating bamboozlers who would not know straight talk if they tripped over it. "Bad drafting," in the lawyers' phrase—that is, shoddy composing of legal documents or of legislation—helps create bureaucracies in proliferating paper that requires lawyers to read and interpret; gives the advantage to the wealthy who can better afford legal counsel; forecloses the legal system to those whom it is supposed to serve in obscuring the processes by which citizens are to participate; and clogs the courts with litigation generated out of legal transactions that could have been settled if the legal documents had been done right in the first place (MacDonald). The expense entailed in what columnist Sylvia Porter has called "legal bafflegab" has led some reform-minded lawyers and business people to adopt a "plain English" stance (Mumford). Despite some grumblings about the potential costs in converting old forms to new, as a counsel for CitiCorp put it, "Big Business hasn't suffered" from plain English legislation (MacDonald).

Much of the debate concerning legal language reform appeals to the American desire for straight talk and an age-old suspicion of lawyers as those who, by profession, speak with forked tongue. In some versions, this leads to something very much like a Strunk and White for lawyers. Richard Wydick, for example, offers a list of rules for lawyers to achieve plain English: "Omit surplus words; use familiar concrete words, use short sentences; use base verbs and the active voice; arrange your words with care; and avoid language quirks" (Blake 34). Ronald Goldfarb (a lawyer) and James Raymond (an English professor) offer what Marion Blake calls ten commandments for legal writing: "Write like a human being; think of your audience; do not use jargon unless you have to; forget the windup [and] just make the pitch; avoid purple; write concise, clear, simple words, sentences, and paragraphs; punctuate precisely; use other people's written work incidentally and deftly; check writing authorities; edit one more time" (Blake 35). Such prescriptions are legion.

My interest, however, is less in enumerating prescriptions for clearing out the underbrush in legal language, than with those advocates of legal language reform who are wary of simple prescriptions even while they advocate plain English. Reed Dickerson and Duncan MacDonald, both lawyers who have spoken out in favor of plain English legislation, have argued that the phrase *plain English* misleads to the extent that it suggests a single, ideal way to satisfy the needs of all legal audiences. Rudolf Flesch's *"Reader's Digest"* notion of legal language reform may be appropriate as a standard for "uneducated clients," but a document can meet the requirements of Flesch's or Robert Gunning's readability formulas and still be "gibberish" (Dickerson). The laws mandating reform, as Dickerson and MacDonald see them, are thus primarily symbolic and not, therefore, unimportant to the extent that they provide a necessary legislative jolt urging bar associations and law schools to rethink their practices. The direct, short-term effect, in other words, of the legislation on consumers may be minimal, but the indirect and long-term effect of lawyers rethinking their use of language is potentially enormous. MacDonald compares "plain English" in its vagueness to such other equally vague terms of law as "reasonable man," "good faith," "equal protection," and "due process." "Vagueness" may appear to be the antithesis of the sort of language use "plain English" is intended to signal, but for MacDonald such "vague" terms constitute "legal language at its ethical best," because they are rhetorically flexible enough to work in different circumstances for the good of people.

For the legal profession and for legislators, plain English can signal the importance of considering consumers and citizens, a reminder, in other words, of ethical responsibilities. The hazard is that what (ideally) reminds a public servant or a businessman of his duty may lull citizens and consumers into a false sense of security. MacDonald notes that New York's Sullivan Law in some cases has led only to surface changes—old documents in *"Reader's Digest"* language, on one level more "readable" but still set with contractual "hooks" protecting companies that sold lemons. If, as Terry Mumford has suggested, plain language can lead consumers into assuming that everything is visible, out in the open, and aboveboard, they then are made more, rather than less, vulnerable to shoddy business practices and legislative rough riding. But the desire for straight talk, in fact, may run deep enough in our culture that it is more likely that not only would we be thus snagged by legal hooks but we would demand laws be passed to obfuscate (plainly) the fact of our bamboozlement.

The way out of this Chinese puzzle, for these cautious advocates of legal language reform, is education. Through better legal education and better undergraduate education, they hope (if somewhat wistfully, in the case of the law school professor Dickerson) to achieve what Gene Wilkins has called "consumer guardianship." Wilkins contends that legislating plain English does people a disservice in assuming from the beginning that they cannot use and understand the full resources of the English language. To understand, for example, that the "same set of words creates different relationships among people" is a necessary knowledge, he argues. In Wilkins's terms, a given contract can establish simultaneously a relationship between lessor and lessee, between a lessor and the IRS, between the lessee and a bank, between the lessee and the IRS. Plain language cannot get around the "external context"—what is already in the reader's/client's head, what is already a part of the situatedness of the legal transaction. Nor can it train the reader/client to be always vigilant, however plain-dealing a contract or other legal paper seems to be.

Significantly, the several lawyers I have referred to suggest a great deal about how lawyers learn to write, and yet they do not translate that knowledge into a changed curriculum for legal education (or an undergraduate education that includes writing). Terry Mumford reports on a writing consultant's experience working with a large, prestigious New York law firm. The consultant found that the associates in the law firm had difficulty with organizing, paragraphing, and developing a line of argument, but it was not that they were not bright or that they lacked "basic skills." They were, in fact, intelligent enough to know that they should be writing as lawyers write, and hence they were trying to write the way they thought lawyers write. But that meant that they wrote with the "rhythm of obfuscation." The best and the brightest from law schools around the country, hired by a prestigious law firm, were engaging in a process much like that David Bartholomae has described among those first-year students in college deemed "not well-prepared for college." They write not primarily by rules as many writing pedagogies seem to presume, at least not by the rules of writing textbooks, but by trying to write as they imagine insiders write (cf. "Inventing the University" and "Writing on the Margins"). The legal language reform movement, in attempting to control stylistic rules of the product, fails not only to address the situatedness of legal discourse in terms of the consumer (what is in the reader's/client's head), but also the situatedness of the producer— the nature of localized writing apprenticeship.

IV

The instance of style talk in the law indicates that plain English functions in multiple ways, both revealing and concealing the business at hand. To forget that plain style is not the simple sign of truth telling, as several of the lawyers suggest, is to mislead. Promoting as the ideal a language that disappears is to risk allowing our collective rhetorical (and therefore political) acuity to atrophy. When teachers of English repeat the handbooks' maxims about style, about clarity, precision, concision, and the like, they are presuming for the most part a nonpartisan skill.[8] To teach straightforward English prose is thus to teach a functional skill, something that gets the job done, no frills. But style is never innocent. Historically, when writers have claimed to produce plain language or plain style, they have thereby claimed to speak the truth. Or when they have read other writers as plain, they have thus been claiming those writers as brethren in truth. Plain style has been a way to mark allegiances, affiliations, relative proximity to orthodoxy. And it continues to operate in this fashion as part of what Foucault has called a regime of truth. This does not mean that plain style goes uncontested, or that it does not coexist with other language practices. Indeed, Kenneth Cmiel offers a persuasive case for placing plain style alongside the colloquial and the technical in the modern American context as contemporary forms of the commonplace that together "corrode civic discussion" (260–61). As I discuss in chapters 1 and 2, the plain style (and, Cmiel adds, the colloquial and technical styles as well) is consolidated through the apparently unlikely and unwitting marriage of high-culture academics and progressive politics.

Central to the argument of this book is the contention that style operates and has operated in the scholarly and popular discourse as a displacement for what is at stake in the reading and writing of a given text or what is at stake more generally in defining what counts as literate behavior and determining what sort of education is best suited to the transmission of cultural forms and behaviors. Discussion of what is in the text as a formal property or as an essential characteristic allows a reader to give name to and provide substantiation for an evaluative agenda that would otherwise go nameless, which in fact often must go nameless in the name of objectivity or certainty. Style has thus resided on the boundary between literature and literacy, helping to mark the literary and what would count as literate practice. To study the ideology of style, then, is also to construct an understanding of the relationship between competing and overlapping aspects of the practice of English studies in the academy.

As an English teacher, my most direct concern is with those agendas that promote conceptions of literacy in the guise of universal literary value, reality, truth, or common sense, which are in fact representations of class interest, nationalism, and unacknowledged ideology. While one might understand the desire to create reliable texts, texts one could count on, there is also a way in which such a desire is dangerously naive. Certain meaning requires authority to ascertain that certainty, authority that will control drift, that will reduce the "conflicting ideologies which confuse us and hamper progress," in order to give "direction" (Hirsch, *Philosophy* 3) to our teaching, research, and learning. Such fear of conflict suggests the need to promote homogeneity of purpose and consequently homogeneity of product. The image of that homogeneity derives from a narrow, primarily Western, primarily white, primarily upper-middle-class, primarily male canon (the expression of praise so frequent in the seventeenth, eighteenth, and nineteenth centuries, that a work is characterized by "masculine expression—nothing effeminate about it," still surfaces in discussions of style, sometimes in the barely displaced, metaphoric sense, of praise for a writer's seminal style). The present study attempts to construct a cultural, material history of normative style in order to examine the conflicting interests that support this shifting signifier.

V

The chapters that follow do not presume to offer an exhaustive tracing of the uses of style. Rather, the essays work something like Geertzian postholes, geologic samples that serve to disrupt the linear and progressive histories of prose style and of institutional practice, histories that are used to legitimate practice. And, like Geertzian postholes, these are not random samples. Instead, I was looking for striations (to harken back to Katherine Hayles's metaphor of isomorphic lines that do not necessarily denote causality but rather simultaneity, one striation to another), striations that would indicate some sort of conjuncture, just below the surface or between the lines, of literary practice, pedagogy, and politics (cf. *Chaos Bound*).

The first chapter considers the twentieth-century American plain style movement not only in relation to the academic construction of literary history but also in terms of larger educational reform movements, especially the impact of scientific management or Taylorism. The second and third chapters deal with the nineteenth-century construction of English as a discipline in England and the United States by putting literary histories together with manuals and handbooks and the pronouncements of public figures to suggest the interaction of literature, literacy, and ideology that can be said to have provided a ground for our present practice. Few historical studies have thus far read English as a discipline comprised of the teaching of literacy, literature, and language. Most histories have treated literary study and the teaching of writing as separate. Histories of the rise of literary study have been concerned to show primarily the steps by which literature eventually freed itself from its vassalage to the practical, utilitarian, or instrumentalist teaching of writing. Histories of the teaching of writing have tended to focus on a rhetorical heritage in order to legitimate composition, which is still the less prestigious part of English study. In these chapters, style serves as a nexus for seeing how the teaching of writing and literary study combined in uneasy alliance to make possible English departments. Style also makes visible the ideological interestedness at the heart of normalizing discourses that continue to define what we do.

Chapter 4 follows Eliot's (and Leavis's) lead, returning to the late Renaissance and the positioning of the two so-called fathers of modern style, Hooker and Bacon, in order to reread a moment that has been appropriated as an origin (and justification) for current practice and to suggest what is at stake in such an appropriation. The fifth chapter returns to the present and to the work of Richard Lanham and E. D. Hirsch, both of whom have put style at the center of their attempts to bridge the institutional gap between literary study and composition. Unlike Lanham, who revels in style play, Hirsch renounces his earlier formalism in favor of cultural literacy, and how he does that is particularly suggestive for the study at hand. Both Lanham and Hirsch—writing under the banner of combatting a literacy crisis and in the name of an embattled humanism—provide a place to consider the institutional and larger ideological stakes involved in contemporary style talk.

Throughout the book, the traditional and unlikely figures of Bacon and Hooker provide a semblance of coherence and also a check against arguing too much, either by generalizing too far about a single process or by effacing the potentiality of matter in a formalist's or structuralist's game. I do not want, in other words, to reinscribe these figures as some Renaissance origin for a plain style that sprouts up and grows like kudzu in New World soil. On the other hand, the fact that they have been appropriated in various ways in disparate contexts to serve as exemplars of a normative style signals for me the importance of attending to the double question, not only *why* Hooker and Bacon, but *how?* That other origins can be and have been named and that a given process can be repeated in at least some of its lines with rather different figures (Addison and Steele, for example, or Macaulay) does not efface a certain material specificity that obtains in *these* historical, material choices.

I conclude with a postscript that offers not some totalizing answer, pedagogical or otherwise, to the problem of a normalizing style, but a consideration of where such a study leaves me as a teacher of English: specifically, where it leaves me in terms of how institutional histories reinscribe and make historically or evolutionarily natural the present institutional separation of literature and literacy and how that separation continues to weaken the study of language practices—in the classroom and out. I mean *weaken* here particularly in the sense of undermining the contribution such language study could make to democratic education. Thus, I see this book contributing to a growing conversation concerning postmodern democratic institutions. It is neither possible nor desirable to simply recuperate John Dewey's progressive vision, but it does seem to be the moment—in the midst of, on the one hand, a sometimes alienating critical discourse that too often leads to nothing other than its own reproduction and, on the other hand, a nostalgic return to a humanism that never was—to join with folk as diverse as Paul Feyerabend and Kenneth Cmiel in reconsidering the paradoxical possibilities of a postmodern democracy.

1

Prosa Oratio: "All Men's and Every Man's Best Style"

Language is the most democratic institution in the world.
Its basis is majority rule, its final authority is the people.

Rudolf Flesch, The Art of Readable Writing

For the benefit of businessmen who wanted to learn techniques of clear writing, Robert Gunning, a readability consultant in the 1940s and 1950s, provided a sample of Francis Bacon's prose. The sample appears in a chapter titled, "Keep Sentences Short," and serves to illustrate Lucius Adelno Sherman's theory of sentence length. In the journal, *Nebraska University Studies* (1888), and again in his *Analytics of Literature* (1893), Sherman had argued that the English sentence had decreased in length over time. He calculated sentence lengths from the Elizabethan period to his own day and concluded that the "literary sentence" had shrunk on the average from one-half to two-thirds. Sherman, however, had some difficulty placing Francis Bacon because, according to Gunning, Bacon "was writing 'modern' short sentences three hundred and fifty years ago . . . averaging some twenty-eight words per sentence, less than half that of Milton" (Gunning 45–46).[1]

It might be tempting to dismiss Gunning as a philistine catering to the demands of the marketplace and turn one's attention to more serious, scholarly treatments of prose style, except that Gunning's work was (and is) in fact influential in shaping public perceptions of what constitutes good writing and what, therefore, ought to be taught in the schools. Gunning's was indeed a by-product of scholarly work, operating at the intersection of the scholarly and the philistine. The scholarly treatment of prose, like

33

nonfiction prose itself, has long been of the world, lending itself (or selling itself) to be used in the world. To critique Gunning's use of Bacon's prose on the grounds that it is not scholarly is in a sense scholarship's denial of its own implicatedness, a way to shore up its claims to a disinterested truth, which are, of course, claims to power. The irony of this move—or perhaps the effectiveness of this move—is that the more scholarship can claim to be pure, disinterested, true, the more likely it is that it will spawn Gunnings. But it is also the case that Gunnings spawn scholarship by providing a market for it, a demand, by creating an intellectual climate conducive to the asking of certain questions, or by contributing to a climate in which certain notions are taken to be fact and providing ground from which other questions can spring.[2]

Gunning puts on the same plate the work of a University of Nebraska sentence counter of the 1890s, a snippet of Bacon's essay, "Of Riches," bits of Thomas Paine and Adam Smith, and some common sense, and binds all the ingredients together with the then current research on readability, all for the delectation of businessmen from Borden's, the B & O Railroad, and General Motors, who were his clientele (*Fortune* 134). In so doing, Gunning makes ideological and cultural space for texts so that they will function in particular ways, so that they will exist in relation to other texts, so that they can be consumed in particular ways.

Typically, literary history does not concern itself with the likes of Gunning and his ideological space. Traditional histories of prose style will make claims that canonical figures such as Hooker and Bacon "made possible" the rise of the "modern abstract prose style" (Eliot, "Genesis" 907), but making possible is seen primarily as a linear process by which great works give rise to, influence the creation of, or father other great works, which then, over time, somehow are translated into the common practice of most men, sometimes modified to mean the common practice of most educated men. The rather messy avenues by which the translation occurs have been largely ignored except in cultural history and more recently in cultural studies. Text-based literary studies, for the most part, tend to treat both style and text as ascertainable facts, parts of which can be traced through time, something like barium sulfate that can be seen through the X-ray vision of scholarship, coursing through history's veins. Certainly there have been enough critiques of idealist conceptions of style, of the text, and of history that the arguments need not be repeated here.

But it is not particularly useful simply to dismiss histories of prose style as hopelessly flawed. The example of Gunning Associates is an argument against too easy dismissal. To criticize histories of prose style as idealist is in a sense to continue to operate in an idealist world, where to fault the idea on intellectual grounds is to disarm it. Ideas do not exist exclusively in the academy, nor is their truthfulness determined exclusively according to the rules of intellectual logic. To say, for example, that style is not an empirically available component of a text, as critiques of stylistics would have it, does not explain why communities, however defined, have somehow persisted in seeing style in texts (cf. Stanley Fish). There must be other reinforcements, to use the psychological metaphor, for seeing the emperor's new clothes. A critical history of literacy would need to understand something of the reinforcements, something of the way a literary concept such as style persists, even in the most prosaic of contexts, and how, more generally, texts as exemplars of style are made to function in the lives of ordinary women and men.

Among twentieth-century literary scholars, the works of Hooker and Bacon are considered important historically—they are seen as having played a part in something called history—and readings are often predicated on some notion of the historical milieu out of which the works were created. Primarily, however, when works under Hooker's or Bacon's name are praised as literary, they are praised in terms of style. That is, they may be presented as valuable to us simply because they were able to write well, or because they were able to write well truths of more than momentary import. While their works may come to our attention because they played a part in history, they remain of interest to the extent that they are perceived as raising themselves above the historical moment out of which they were originally created.

The possibility of such perception has much to do with the way in which literary practice constitutes a work and much to do with the ease with which canonical texts lend themselves for use in what might be thought of as nonliterary literacy practices. Thus, for example, while Hooker may have engaged in what one editor calls the "bitterest dispute of his time," that is, the dispute over Elizabeth's policies concerning church governance, he is said to have "interest" for the twentieth-century reader to the extent that his work rises above the controversy out of which it sprang. One anthology introduces a selection from *Of the Laws of Ecclesiastical Polity*, which the editors have titled "On Moderation in Controversy," by assessing the value of the passage for the reader and thereby helping to shape readings of the text *they have produced*:

> Hooker was a close and effective reasoner; he relied not upon the fiery invective or impassioned rhetoric which characterized most disputants of his time, but rather upon a calm, reasonable, tolerant approach. His defense of existing ecclesiastical practices went back to fundamental principles, to a philosophy of nature and of man's place in it, of his relation to God and to his fellow men. It is this world view which makes Hooker's book of interest when the controversy over church organization has long since died down. (Abrams et al. 439–40)

This is from a 1968 edition. A more recent version (1986) of this anthology alters only a few words, referring to "our" relation to God and asserting that "this world view . . . makes Hooker's book of enduring value" (Abrams et al. 1034). The move to universalize—in this case from a core of Christian humanist values—is typical of canonization, as is the move to dehistoricize (cf. Sinfield, *Faultlines* 149–50).

Such an anthology introduction is perhaps unremarkable for its general language. But the very choice of such general words of praise is telling. A reasonable approach back to fundamental principles suggests writing that is sensible, moderate (within "the limits assigned by reason"), and marked by sound judgment and by reasoning that gets to origins, to foundations upon which some structure of thought has been or can be built ("Reasonable," OED; Williams, *Keywords* 252–56). This very yoking of reasonableness with origins suggests structures of thought that are apart from time, existing prior to and long after any historically specific controversy. The 1986 personalizing touch—the use of *our*—is further evidence of the effort to bring the work into the transcendent world of the perpetual and universal present (the literary present). Hooker is thus constituted as literary to the extent that in a moderate manner he gets to basic truths. Such a move depends upon the construction of Hooker's unnamed (and unanthologized) fellow disputants as "fiery" and "impassioned"; as, in other words, unreasonable. Thus, Hooker's historical victory—if one can argue that "his" conception of the Church of England triumphed over presbyterian and other dissenting voices—is sealed through the reiteration of his triumph in "style," seen, now that the controversy "has long since died down," as a triumph of reason over unreason, moderation over fire.

As Brian Vickers has pointed out, Hooker as man of moderation is a commonplace reading. We do a "disservice" to Hooker, Vickers argues, by perpetuating the myth of his "reasonableness, toleration and piety," in part because such praise excites little "pleasure" (Introduction 43). But even if one were to resurrect Hooker as a man of controversy, as Vickers has attempted, Hooker the man or Hooker's words are nonetheless produced for readers such that "controversy" is now "timeless" and can therefore be made part of our time. Vickers, as a rhetorician, is primarily interested in stylistic analysis, ostensibly independent of a concern for "fundamental principles" in Abrams's sense, above. He argues that in order to make a fresh evaluation free, presumably, from myth, of Hooker as a writer, "we must approach him on his own terms, without any pre-formed scheme, and we must . . . relate imagery, or sentence-structure, or whatever aspect we isolate, to the work's overall intention, meaning or function" (Introduction 42).

The primary "function," as Vickers sees it, is exemplified in the rhetorical form of "controversy": Hooker must praise his own party and attack his opponents. Thus, given the prescribed hermeneutics, one must analyze Hooker's style in terms of defense and attack, understanding all the while that the "genre is inherently violent." With such a preparation, Vickers can then go on "with studied impartiality" to "point" to the "energy" with which Hooker writes. Such impartiality is possible because "today not many readers will be offended on sectarian grounds by Hooker's treatment of the Reformers." We are thus, as Vickers would have it, free to appreciate (take pleasure in) Hooker's "energy," the "undignified, uninhibited style; a style which is a weapon," the target of which need no longer concern us (Introduction 42–46).

The energy that Vickers celebrates, according to his own account, was generated out of a particular historical controversy, but all that remains of value to us from that controversy in a literary sense is the energy as residual in style. Style seems then to operate as that which is left after historical specificity in all its partisanship, in all its messiness, has leached out of a text: style produced as oddly neutral, as nonpartisan. Vickers attempts to displace the praise of (mythic) moderation with a praise of energy that is based not on preconceptions but on Hooker's own terms. His practice, however, like Abrams's, simultaneously depends on the historicity of a work and operates as if literary value were free from historical specificity—both in terms of the past and of the present.

A figure such as Hooker is confined primarily to scholarly circles or the occasional undergraduate who happens to be assigned a small portion of the *Laws*. Bacon, on the other hand, is disseminated more widely: bits and pieces of Baconian wisdom operate like biblical proverbs to add weight to newspaper editorials and to provide thoughts for the day on the radio, cartoons for publishers, and epigraphs for popular and scholarly texts. He is frequently anthologized and produced in popular editions of essays, as well as readers, rhetorics, and in handbooks. In much of the pedagogical work, Bacon is treated as an exemplar of style rather than, say, as a philosopher or a scientist. And that style is treated as if it could, in fact, be seen independent of Bacon's philosophy or his science.

Early in the twentieth century, George Saintsbury asserted that Bacon was a "rhetorician rather than a philosopher" (211). Stephen Penrose and more recently Jonathan Marvil have offered similar assessments, but as criticism rather than praise. Marvil argues that "for too long the charm and detached quality of Bacon's style have won him undeserved credibility" (64). Such assessments have found their way into the anthologies as well. Hollander and Kermode, for example, in their anthology of Renaissance literature, are dismissive of Bacon's "great idea for a reconstruction of the institutions by which truths are discovered, recorded, and maintained," claiming that his was "in no way . . . one of the major advances of seventeenth-century science." Instead, Bacon was "a literary intellect whose thought seldom strayed far from the gardens of imagery and symbol in which they flourished" (934). The sort of dichotomy established here between real science on the one hand and gardens of imagery on the other says much about twentieth-century specialization and fragmentation of knowledge and very little about the seventeenth century. But it is a notion expressed again and again—by literary scholars more often than historians or philosophers of science.

Even when a scholar attempts to look at Bacon's writings as entireties, as in the case of James Stevens's useful work on *Francis Bacon and the Style of Science,* the modern polarities force their way into the analysis. Stevens is critical of those who either view Bacon as "the father of the age of reason" or as a "poet and fabulist" and of those who cannot see that Bacon was one of the last to "enjoy the best of both worlds" (171). But this criticism suggests that in the seventeenth century there must have been both worlds, in the same sense that we understand them today, perhaps because they now appear so inevitable. What should be emphasized here, however, is that the context of twentieth-century specialization in large measure produces Bacon as literary in a particular way. If science is defined as twentieth-century science, and as separate from literature, then once science has left Bacon's content behind, the remaining residue of text becomes more clearly literary. Of course, many scholars have thought outside such dichotomies (cf. Gillespie, Perez-Ramos), but the canonical view constructs Bacon as literature such that he can be, oddly, both a so-called literary intellect and wrong-headed. His work can be lush with imagery and symbol, but in terms of the execution of his great idea, he writ no science. It would appear that in the twentieth-century scheme of things—if one can judge from such distilla-tions of canonical wisdom as anthologies—to be literature is a flimsy alternative.

Literary scholars have been generally more comfortable with the *Essays,* where worrisome specialized content rarely intrudes. Filled with "more quotable common sense" (Penrose 207), the es-says, Hollander and Kermode inform us, are "memorable for their crisp, 'pointed' style"; "aphoristic, flexible, far less bound in their structure to the quoted words of other men than even Mon-taigne's *Essais,* they have remained celebrated and widely quoted" (935). It is the supposed generality of the alleged truths contained in the essays that allows them to speak to generation after genera-tion. But it is the curt style that makes them "memorable." The es-says, then, are more clearly literary because they are apparently not tied to a historical moment and their aesthetic function is more clearly foregrounded (Mukarovsky 9–10).

It is perhaps ironic that this last would be the case. If the pointed or curt or plain style is that which most approximates stylelessness (as was the hope or dream of Baconians—a "close, naked, natural way of speaking," Thomas Sprat extolled in 1667), then one might think that such style would disappear to more clearly show the matter. But for Bacon's essays, the style that would efface itself instead announces itself (or is read as an-nouncing itself), in its plainness, as literary. Certainly many writ-ers have remarked on the difficulty of producing and understand-ing what is plain, from the sentence counters Sherman and Rosewell Lowrey to more recent scholars such as Hugh Kenner. But despite such recognition of the potential complexity in plain-ness, more often than not plain is equated with simple, truthful, or transparent. However one reads plainness, it is nonetheless ironic that Bacon, who wrote so many different kinds of works, should be reduced to an exemplar of the *genus humile.* Bacon's nineteenth-century editor, James Spedding, tried to stress how "many-mannered" Bacon was. But the most frequent and most fa-miliar form for which Bacon is remembered is still the essays—and as if they were all of a piece (Wallace 153–54).

But what does such institutional practice have to do with readability, with writing prose in the workplace, and with Mr. Gunning? Returning to Gunning's text will help to show more specifically how what might be called the reduced literary version of Bacon has been made to operate and, more broadly, to suggest some further sense of the interrelationships of literature and literacy. Robert Gunning formed, in 1944, a "business not [previously] listed among more than 20,000 job classes of the United States census." This new work was "readability counseling," whereby research on how and why readers read is adapted to the use of writers in business (Gunning vii). Gunning promoted his book, *The Technique of Clear Writing,* by arguing for his business's primacy but also by acknowledging its indebtedness to the research that preceded him. He was, by the account of contemporaries and later analysts of the movement, an important part of a highly successful, primarily American, readability or plain talk movement in the forties and fifties, which continues to have some influence in academic and popular circles today, most evident in journalism, reading research (especially in the assessment and production of constituent-specific textbooks), adult education, business, and legal writing.

Following on the heels of Louis M. Terman's revision of the Binet-Simon Intelligence scales (cf. *The Measurement of Intelligence*), educational psychologists began studying relative "ease of understanding and comprehension due to the style of writing" in order to choose and produce graded reading materials for children (Klare 1, 37; *Fortune* 133–34). Part of the impetus for such research came from the increased enforcement of compulsory school attendance laws and the perceived need to educate more children from what would now be labeled as disadvantaged or educationally deprived households—including an influx of first-generation Americans. Importantly, the definitions of need and approaches to meeting such needs grew out of the scientific management movement, that amalgam of business interests, science, and psychology that emphasized efficiency through standardization and bureaucratization and sought quantitatively derived "solutions" to complex social problems (Shannon 10–11; Goodman 13, 17).

Certainly, as a number of educational historians have pointed out, there was no single, universally agreed upon approach to educational policy making. At the same time that Terman and the educational psychologist Edward Thorndike were arguing for scientific solutions to the perceived challenges facing American education, other approaches were advocated that at first appear to be in opposition to scientific management. Kliebard, for example, names four groups who were vying for control at the turn of the century: scientific managers, humanists, advocates of a child-centered pedagogy, and social reconstructionists (cf. *Struggle for The American Curriculum*). But what from a distance may appear to be mutually exclusive categories were in fact overlapping and interacting approaches to naming (and one might say constructing) educational problems and attempting to solve those problems. Readability research and the readability formulas certainly grew out of a faith in scientific solutions—and especially a desire for greater efficiency in literacy education—but they also drew on humanist (including literary), child-centered, and even social constructionist rhetoric.

Readability studies were methodologically rather simple. They invariably involved the most elementary of statistical analyses—first counting and then averaging. Readability studies yielded relative word frequency lists that aimed to show how many "difficult" words appeared in literature for children, whether in classics, textbooks, newspapers, reference works, or technical books. Definitions of difficulty were derived from standard word lists such as Thorndike's *A Teacher's Word Book of the Twenty Thousand Words Found Most Frequently and Widely in General Reading for Children and Young People*, lists that were themselves the result of counting. Other studies looked at vocabulary burden, that is, they counted the number of different words within a text; others considered the relative difficulty of words beginning with certain consonants or vowels (words beginning with *w, h,* or *b* were said to suggest ease of reading, while those beginning with *i* or *e* suggested greater difficulty); still other studies counted the number of polysyllables, technical terms, indeterminate clauses, and so on (Flesch, *Marks* 3–5). Such dedicated counting continues apparently unabated, as a cursory reading of some of the 772-odd entries under the 1991 (Silver Platter) ERIC subject heading "readability" indicates (one might compare this number to Rudolph Flesch's count of "nineteen significant attempts to measure readability objectively" from 1923 to 1943 [*Marks* 3]).

The general aim of most of this counting was (and is) twofold: in determining the difficulty of various kinds of materials—the "efficiency and simplicity of use" in materials for students at various levels (Klare 51)—researchers wanted to help teachers and librarians choose "appropriate" materials for a clientele that was constructed more and more in terms of eugenics (Terman and others, for example, believed that mental capacities were inherited and that one could describe relatively discrete categories of learners through the use of standardized intelligence tests [Flannery "Stanford-Binet"]). They wanted to assist writers and publishers in producing more "appropriate" materials for these newly defined learners.

Progressive aims are evident throughout the literature on readability. Writer after writer wanted to increase the accessibility of written materials for learners who were themselves characterized as in need and also, importantly, in some sense fixed in place in their neediness. Thus, at the same time that a desire for educational progress is built into the readability movement—wanting more people to be able to read a more elevated and more elevating kind of literature more easily and with greater understanding—there is also a sense that progress is not about individual mobility between more or less fluid ability groups. Though testimonials of individual achievement (bootstrap stories) are part of the readability literature as they are a fundamental part of literacy campaigns more generally, progress is nonetheless always relative among relatively fixed groups. This fixity is treated as less a function of social structures that hamper educational change and more a matter of what Terman called "mental endowment" (Flannery 1). A teacher or librarian or book publisher might make it more likely that learners considered slow would learn to read thanks to more accessible materials—the "correct stimulus" to "evoke the appropriate response" (Goodman 18)—but because the so-called brightest students were given more complex, advanced, culturally valued materials, from the start they were already ahead in the educational game. Accessible materials in fact helped to mark the gap in what were taken to be inherited abilities.

For the most part, readability researchers did not stop to ask how they might be able to make powerful reading—reading that would make possible the reading of less quantifiably "readable" texts—available to all students across ability (and therefore class) boundaries except as a promised outcome, the reward at the end of a scientifically controlled process of learning. They did not stop to ask whether so much controlled reading might in fact incapacitate readers for that elevated literature held out as the carrot at the end of the stick. When the first principle is efficiency, as it was in scientific management, and efficiency exemplified by the assembly line, it is difficult to conceive of an education that is something more socially responsive than the accumulation of educational nuts and bolts.

Alongside scientific management research aimed at making reading instruction for children more efficient, an interest in the application of readability formulas to adult material developed, initially as a response to adult education needs for the military and such programs as the Works Progress Administration (Chall, *Readability* 153; Flesch, *Marks* 17). Perhaps the most influential study applying readability research to adults was published in 1935. William Gray and Bernice Leary surveyed earlier work in the field in light of newly developed adult reading comprehension tests. Their book, *What Makes a Book Readable*, has as its explicit aim "getting the right book into the hands of the right reader" (1). Although Gray and Leary grant that "selecting a readable book, like defining a readable book, is a highly individual problem [depending as it does] first, upon the reader's interests, needs, and abilities; and, second, upon the qualities of a book that make it readable for him" (230), they nonetheless focus only on those structural elements *in the text* that "lend themselves most readily to quantitative enumeration and statistical treatment" (7). They make it clear that the readability they are measuring is of a very limited sort, applicable to reading defined "somewhat narrowly" as obtaining "a general impression" or "gist" of what is read (1, 8–9), and aimed at adults of limited reading ability. They chose to consider only what was readily quantifiable, because they felt that their study then would be immune to challenges coming from what they call "subjective opinion" (7). The solution they offer to a newly perceived need, then, is admittedly partial, but at least, from a scientific management perspective, it is sure. And that sureness, as they rightly anticipate, will make this solution far more usable and more likely to be disseminated than approaches to literacy education that see literacy in more complex, socially embedded terms.

For all their faith in scientific definitions and constructions of problems and scientifically managed solutions, however, Gray and Leary nonetheless couch their study in the rhetoric of the Enlightenment, with a particularly American and New Deal twist: "In a society like our own some ability to read is attained by all but a small minority. This is the consequence of a long-established belief that literacy is essential to an intelligent citizenry. Social enlightenment, personal advancement, enrichment of experience, wholesome enjoyment of leisure—all are enhanced by the ability to read easily and understandingly whatever interprets and illuminates the phenomena of life" (v). Such faith in the positive role of literacy is not unusual, of course. But it obscures the extent to which literacy has been available differentially based on race and gender, and the extent to which the supposed rewards for literacy achievement have been differentially allocated.

Recent analysis of literacy data in the form of self-reports of literacy achievement from the 1880s to the present suggests that, indeed, rudimentary literacy was attained by most white males and females by the 1920s. But blacks fared less well. In 1920, among the 25–29-year-old population, 12.9 percent of whites had fewer than five years of schooling, compared to 44.6 percent of blacks (Kaestle 125). There was a similar gap between native-born citizens and immigrants. Kaestle notes that "immigrant illiteracy was concentrated among the century's first arrivals and declined rapidly after the restriction of immigration in 1921" (25), suggesting *not* the success of schooling, progressive or otherwise, but rather the impact of class- and education-based immigration quotas. Similarly, as Harvey Graff, John Ogbu, and others have pointed out, literacy by itself was no guarantee that an individual would achieve any of the benefits—personal, economic, or social—often claimed for literacy achievement. The Enlightenment rhetoric so characteristic of literacy campaigns does not take into account significant racial, ethnic, and class biases that are the ground on which literacy operates. Gray and Leary suggest that it is enough to make the materials available; then literacy will happen. But those who fail to take advantage of what is made available to them are thus more easily blamed for what becomes *their* failures.

Gray and Leary do in fact look to socioeconomic conditions to explain what drives their research. Leisure time, which they see as potential reading time, had increased because of the shortening of the working day and of the working week, and because of "technological unemployment" and "prolonged economic distress"— that is, the Great Depression. Adult education, as one component of the New Deal,[3] was seen as having the potential to alleviate economic distress in several ways: by teaching native- and foreign-born "illiterates" as a way to employ teachers; retraining those whose specialized trades were no longer in demand; extending general education for those "dissatisfied with their past attainments"; and guiding adult students "to find a way out of an economic situation they but partially" understood. This latter "way out" is possibly linked, they suggest, to the ability to command and interpret "facts which explain progressive changes and evolving social life in a dynamic world"—the ability, as they see it, to read. To make such reading possible, Gray and Leary contend, a range of books is needed: general information, fiction, travel, biography, history, and so on. Because much of the material of "general adult interest" was judged suitable only for readers "at the top stratum" (Gray and Leary 2–3), new materials needed to be produced. After surveying librarians and teachers and developing a list of factors from the survey that could account for the relative readability of various texts, Gray and Leary settled on what they felt to be the five key elements: number of different hard words (defined as those not included in Edgar Dale's standard reading list of some 769 "easy" words); number of first, second, and third person pronouns; average sentence length in words; percentage of different words; and number of prepositional phrases.

Rudolf Flesch, working out of the Readability Laboratory of the American Association of Adult Education at Columbia Teachers College, began his research with what he thought to be the limitations of Gray and Leary's work. Finding that the Gray-Leary readability formula failed to distinguish adequately between "mature English prose" and "light reading," Flesch set out to develop a formula that was better able to determine what was readable for adults (*Marks* 7–9) and in the process became the great "plain talk" popularizer, turning his dissertation into the best-selling *The Art of Plain Talk* (1946).

Flesch, like Gray and Leary, characterized his project in populist and New Deal terms, arguing that language belongs to the people and that, concomitantly, those who use the language of the people (Franklin Roosevelt was his favorite example) are "for the people." He viewed grammar and rhetoric as the imposition of Greek and Latin norms by teachers who fail to acknowledge that these norms no longer apply to twentieth-century American life. We write stiffly and ineffectively, he suggested, thanks to this inheritance that imposes rigid social standards. American prose, therefore, ought to follow American plain talk, and to this end Flesch published and lectured, teaching, as a contemporary *Fortune* magazine article put it, "a scientific method of achieving plain, understandable prose." This meant that "we should write as we talk; eschew irony, rhythm, rhetorical sentences; substitute concrete for abstract words. Equally we should surcharge our prose with as much human interest as possible" (*Fortune* 133–34).

In his early monograph, *Marks of a Readable Style: A Study in Adult Education* (1943), Flesch considered some objections that had been raised against the word difficulty component of earlier readability formulas, including what would have seemed to have been the serious issue raised by I. A. Richards, who argued that "words shift their meanings under the pressure of their contexts."[4] Flesch does agree that word difficulty is not a meaningful measure of readability for adults: "As a child grows older, as a foreigner learns the language better, or as a person gains reading and living experience, this aspect of reading difficulty becomes less important" (15). But he does not seem to notice what others have seen as Richards's challenge to the "superstition" that there are "proper meanings" (Ricoeur 77)—or, for that matter, the potential challenge from Flesch's own insight into how experience—learning—helps shape what constitutes ease or difficulty.

Reading, for Flesch, is decoding (as it has been for a large and influential portion of the educational establishment). Some sense of what decoding means comes from Edward Thorndike, whom Flesch quotes at length:

> Reading is a very elaborate procedure, involving a weighing of each of many elements in a sentence, their organization in the proper relations one to another, the selection of certain of their connotations and the rejection of others, and the cooperation of many forces to determine final response. . . .
>
> In correct reading 1) *each word produces a correct meaning,* 2) each such element of meaning is given a correct weight in comparison with the others, and 3) the resulting ideas are examined and validated to make sure they satisfy the mental set or adjustment or purpose for whose sake the reading is done. Reading may be wrong or inadequate 1) because of wrong connections with the words singly, 2) because of over-potency or under-potency of elements, or 3) because of failure to treat the ideas produced by the reading as provisional, and so to inspect and welcome or reject them as they appear. . . .
>
> *Understanding a paragraph is like solving a problem in mathematics.* It consists in selecting the right elements of the situation and putting them together in the right relations, and also with the right amount of weight or influence or force for each. *The mind is assailed* as it were by every word in the paragraph. *It must select, repress, soften, emphasize, correlate and organize,* all under the influence of the right mental set or purpose or demand. . . .
>
> It thus appears that reading . . . involves the same sort of organization and analytic action of ideas as occur in thinking of supposedly higher sorts. (Thorndike, "Reading as Reasoning," qtd. in Flesch, *Marks* 21; emphasis added)

One might critique readability formulas for their very formulaicism and simplification. And there continue to be very serious challenges to decoding as the definitive process we call reading (cf. Chall, *Learning to Read: The Great Debate,* 1983). But what is striking in much of the early readability literature is the acknowledgment that formulas are simplifications and that, at the same time, such simplifications are good because the reading is likely to be more efficiently managed as a simplification. As problematically, reading has an odd way of shifting in the readability literature from a text-determined process (words *produce* meaning) to something potentially more interactional (the mind may be *assailed,* but it then needs to *select, sort, suppress,* and so on). The readability literature thus seems to concede from the outset the arguments raised against it by its many critics. Such apparent concession, however, operates as the merest gesture, an intellectual formality very readily swept aside by the "surer" arguments of science. Flesch finds a way to turn even "poetical" descriptions of reading into support for readability's "purely statistical attack on our problem" (*Marks* 22).

Flesch's "purely statistical attack" yielded two formulas for measuring the success of any given passage: one, based on syllable and sentence count per one hundred words, measures "reading ease"; the other, based on the percentage of "personal" words and sentences, measures its "human interest" (*Fortune* 134). He did not argue that such formulas measure anything approximating absolute value, but rather that the formulas provide criteria for grading or producing "a new form of literature for a new type of reader" (*Marks* 40). This new form of literature would likely be a "popular non-fiction book, a 'layman's book' . . . an instrument for the dissemination of knowledge, not for a contribution to knowledge . . . a book for self-education . . . [but not] a textbook" (*Marks* 39). And the new readers would be those who read "confessional, detective, adventure books, and . . . the women's and family magazines" (*Marks* 2). All literature for all readers, in other words, ought not follow the formula. But for the "typical reader of the *Saturday Evening Post,*" who needs to be informed in order to be a contributing citizen, Flesch argues that his formulas will help produce the needed materials.

The confluence of populist talk (anybody can write) and prose jingoism (*American* prose) with scientific formulas no doubt contributed to the popularity of Flesch's work among business-men, journalists, and other mass communicators, appealing to a distinctly American sense of free enterprise and a faith in the rightness of scientific solutions. But it also appealed to a particular sense of literacy, a sense revealed most tellingly in Lymon Bryson's foreword to *The Art of Plain Talk*. Bryson was director of the Readability Laboratory when Flesch was working there and later became educational director of Columbia Broadcasting Service. Bryson speaks of the need that Flesch's book fills:

> There is one thing we can do, and that is to see that a few books on important subjects get written in language that they—these millions of amiable but letter-blind friends—can follow. More than that, we can see that the books they need to read, the documents they have to understand, the instructions that will keep them out of trouble, are written in plain English. . . . There is nothing anti-literary in such a suggestion. In the great stream of English literature there are two lines, one ornate, the other plain, and surely no one will say that Swift was less than Sir Thomas Browne. (x)

If Bryson is attempting to be magnanimous, his rhetoric does him in. Perhaps no one says that Swift was less than Sir Thomas Browne, but because Bryson's rhetoric has made it clear that the amiable millions are in no way comparable to Swift, the Swift/Browne, plain/ornate terms are of no consequence to the argument. There is, indeed, nothing "anti-literary" in Bryson's remarks, because he has constituted two different language worlds, one for the letter-blind, a world of "plain English," which has no need and feels no lack (in its amiableness) of the other world, which is for the likes of Bryson, a world of linguistic noblesse oblige. *Literary* as employed in Bryson's remarks is a category of exclusivity: there are those of us who are fully literate as signalled by our ability to compare Swift and Browne—to "get" the literary comparison, the order of which he reverses as if it were a test (ornate is to plain *not* as Swift is to Browne)—and then there are the millions who need to be instructed plainly, in Bryson's patronizing terms, *to keep out of trouble*. Bryson's remarks suggest the underbelly of good intentions, the lurking elitism of Flesch's populism.

It is into this odd margin between the populist and the elitist, between the prosaic and the literary, the popular and the scholarly, that Robert Gunning Associates enters, offering a humanistic genealogy for a scientific management explanation of readability. Language may be democratic, according to Flesch, but the Fleschian premise of Gunning's book is that ordinary folk need to be taught how to use the language that is theirs, via both scientific formulas and quotations from canonical figures who, as historical beings, were hardly "folk." Gunning does not constitute Francis Bacon (or any other canonical figure, for that matter) as an historical figure in his role, for example, as lord chancellor. Rather, Bacon is produced as a modern, ahead of his time, in terms of word count. The signification of word count, as invariably with formal features, however, has to do with meaning. In Gunning's argument, Bacon's word count is evidence that he, Adam Smith, and Thomas Paine "were men more interested in communicating facts and ideas than in self-expression. Naturally the two go hand in hand, for it is impossible to wrap an idea or fact in language without leaving your mark on it. But emphasis on self in expression accounts for a deal of fog in poetry, music, painting, and business letters" (Gunning 47).

While managing rather neatly to associate the one-time lord chancellor with two figures evocative of American free enterprise and free speech, Gunning stays very much within the commonplace or canonical reading of Bacon: the writer (ostensibly) more interested in matter than words; the essayist who, in contrast to Montaigne, withheld himself; the manly man of the world who in caring more for facts than wrappings, who *in withholding himself,* fathered a style. But the canonical reading as employed here, as well as by many rhetoricians and popularizers since the seventeenth century, ironically ends up caring more for words than matter, caring more, that is, for Bacon's style than his musings on the perils of riches. Such a canonical reading lends itself, then, to the production of a text under Bacon's name, which serves to charge the businessman to Keep Sentences Short! even while the snippet begins "I cannot call riches better than the baggage of virtue" (Gunning 45–46).

In a sense, Gunning's production of a text under Bacon's name as exemplar of a particular stylistic feature has little to do with the production of the 1607 or 1625 essays titled "Of Riches." The earlier essays functioned on multiple levels, not the least of which was as the literary—in the more inclusive Renaissance sense of that term—and popular production of a man of prominence and notoriety. Gunning understandably exhibits little interest, scholarly or otherwise, in the historically privileged essays, but rather produces as his text a "new," shorter text, with different punctuation that generally leads to shorter sentences (and hence supports his case more easily) than would be found in either the 1607 or 1625 essays. And yet his new production is significant for his argument to the extent that it passes as an historical artifact. Gunning constitutes the Baconian text as an historical and literary artifact ("literary" now in the restricted twentieth-century sense) that will function as a stylistic exemplar. Gunning's Bacon is no less real than the 1607 or the 1625 essays, and is more likely to be the Bacon that is known by the average person, more akin to the various and most widely disseminated productions of texts under Bacon's name current in readers, rhetorics, anthologies, and general histories presently available; and, as argued earlier, is dependent upon the canonical and therefore scholarly readings of Bacon. But it is also a clearly limited text, a version of Bacon such that he was valuable to modern businessmen to the extent to which he serves as an early version of themselves, a straight shooter who wrote shorter sentences than Milton.

If one were looking for the missing link in the genealogical chain that is supposed to lead from the prose style of the Lord Bacon to the writing style of typewriter manuals (T. S. Eliot's example), then one might propose Gunning as a candidate for that position, except that in making Bacon's texts available to a wide audience Gunning has, necessarily, constituted a new text. Gunning's text "by Bacon" is produced such that it functions in ways radically different from the 1607 or 1625 texts. Gunning's production is dependent upon the earlier texts, of course, but it is also fundamentally other. The genealogical explanation works, then, only if changelings are a normal part of the chain. Or, put differently, Lord Bacon "made possible" present-day typewriter manuals to the extent that Lord Bacon's prose was produced for the Gunnings of the world to be made available as certification that if one wants to communicate facts and ideas, one ought to keep one's sentences short.

Gunning's work in its very cultural embeddedness is no aberration. He was part of a much larger readability movement, which was itself part of the larger scientific management movement, that shaped and continues to shape educational practice at all levels of schooling. Further, his turn to the canonical literary figure, his reliance on a literary history to justify his "scientific" practice—borrowing on cultural capital, in other words—is also not at all unusual in this or earlier centuries. Editors and anthologizers of Bacon's work and other canonical writers from the seventeenth century on produced various texts to be used to improve everything from letter writing to morality and to support particular scientific and religious attitudes and institutions. Producers of these texts often as not stated or implied—as does Gunning—that they were preserving the true spirit or intent of the author. But the process of production—even production under the aegis of an author—is such that, whatever the spirit or intent of the author, the text enters into a network of affiliations—in this case, a network of educational affiliations that help to define reading and readers—that allows it to be consumed (or impedes consumption) in ways that may or may not have anything to do with the author's spirit or intent. In fact, the editorial practice of establishing the text "as the author wished to have it presented to the public" (Tanselle 172–73) is itself a limiting production, an attempt to confine consumption to a reading dependent upon a conception (reading/interpretation) of the author, as opposed, for example, to a reading that might attempt to take into account the "dynamic social relations which always exist in literary production" (McGann 81).

Gunning's production of a text under Bacon's name operates within a network of affiliations that includes the readability movement, positioning it between the marketplace and the academy. The readability movement in general began in the academy and, after having been nurtured in the marketplace, returned to

the academy. Such a commonplace movement, most visible perhaps in the hard sciences, is from the academy's perspective (and
particularly in the humanities) necessarily invisible, and yet it has
to do with, in fundamental ways, the constituting of academic
practice, the constituting of the object of study. Gunning and the
readability movement are important in their specificity, important
in a political sense for their helping to sustain specific pedagogical practice; but they are also useful as an illustration of what I
would argue is an ignored but constituting and general part of literary and literacy history.

While educational and industrial psychologists attempted
what *Fortune* called a sort of "prose engineering" (133) for the amiable millions, literary historians were composing the last (to date)
of the great sweeping histories of English prose, dominated by the
work of Morris Croll, who formulated the notion of the fundamental anti-Ciceronianism of modern prose style, and Richard Foster
Jones, who linked the rise of modern prose style to the rise of science. While there are significant differences between the two positions, both nonetheless situated the beginnings of modern prose
style in the seventeenth century, both saw the modern as characteristically plain (though *plain* signified rather different formal and
semantic properties), and both often treated the same figures—
Francis Bacon among them. Croll and Jones were not pioneers in
arguing from these shared premises. As the quotation from Bryson
suggests, the plain/ornate dichotomy had circulated in literary historical circles long enough to become commonplace. What is important, however, is that despite a long-running Croll-Jones debate,
which continued to attract a few hardy souls into the 1960s, the
fundamental terms of the argument went unchallenged, so that
when readability returned to the academy, or perhaps more accurately when the child of educational psychologists found a new
home in English departments, the language, at least on the surface, was also at home.

Further reinforcing the comfortableness of readability in
English departments was the continued pressure to turn out literate freshmen. One can read complaints in every century about
the thick-headedness of students learning to write. The com-

plaints and concerns about illiteracy are not new, but with the increasing numbers of students entering college in the fifties and sixties—and with the cold war pressure to stay ahead of the Russians—the complaints became grounded in the perceived reality of larger numbers of less-well-prepared students entering the academy—comparable to the perceived pressures on elementary education in the twenties. Throughout this period (and even with a few straggling examples into the present), rhetorics and readers were produced following classic principles oft quoted from Ben Jonson's *Timber:* "For a man to write well, there are required three necessities: to read the best authors, observe the best speakers, and much exercise of his own style." The maxim that immediately follows this and that places matter before manner is not quoted, however (122). The best authors, from the textbook editors' perspective, are always from the modern canon, which in the fifties and sixties meant Francis Bacon forward, with the heaviest concentration from the nineteenth century. Occasionally an editor will offer "a wider domain than the plain or encyclopedia style" (Staffard and Candelaria vii) but, if for no other reason than the constraints of space, selections never exceed essay length—and sometimes not even complete essay length—and, again, of "necessity" are chosen to be more "accessible" than "challenging." The continued presence of the scientific management principles of efficiency and accessibility are uncomfortably apparent here.

One might not expect canonical figures to figure in a scientific management schema. But as with Gunning, Bacon qualified for use in freshman readers on several counts. Even if one were to eschew plainness, one might anthologize Bacon because, at least, his essays are short and, conveniently, several have to do with student life. "Of Studies" and a translated portion of *Novum Organum* on the idols of the mind are the most frequently anthologized texts under Bacon's name, with portions of *The Advancement of Learning* or the Salomon's House section from *The New Atlantis* appearing almost as often.[5] One rhetoric-reader, *Twenty Lessons in Reading and Writing Prose* (1955), offers a text under Bacon's name titled "Vicissitudes in Wars" that, while the editor acknowledges it to be "from" the longer essay "Of Vicissitude of Things" (1625), nonetheless is treated as a complete argument, the "scope" and "plan" of which can be ascertained, the editor asserts, from the "first" sentence. This text is promoted as exhibiting "clearness, economy, and strength," setting a standard that "we might well aspire to emulate." "A study of Bacon's prose," the textbook's author goes on to urge, "is a good corrective for vagueness and diffuseness in composition" (Davidson 105, 108).

Texts under Bacon's name were generally deployed this way: following the pattern Balibar describes in nineteenth-century France (see the introduction), an altered text, though it may be acknowledged as altered, is treated as a whole text, a true text from which lessons can be drawn. Content is not irrelevant, exactly; selections are chosen because they might hold some interest for the student. But content is treated in a generally simple sense as a single theme or subject that can yield a relatively uncomplicated moral or simple idea. The primary function of the selection, however, is as exemplar of style, which may lead to some rather odd choices. Late English translations of Bacon's Latin works are treated as having the same validity as an English original to serve as exemplars of English prose style. Hence the frequent use of the "idols of the mind" portion of the *Novum Organum*, translated by others than Francis Bacon but treated as an example of *his* style. As with Gunning's production of texts under Bacon's name, the textbooks' Baconian texts are true and real. In a very real sense, such texts serve to displace privileged originals, functioning in the textbooks and for the majority of their readers as *the* text. The literate elite—historians of prose, for example—may read a greater variety of texts under Bacon's name and may have a different, more complex notion of what one might learn from those texts, but for the great unwashed mass of freshmen, a clear, economical, and rather limited Bacon is *the* Bacon for purposes not unlike the purposes of Flesch's *The Art of Plain Talk:* writing modeled after the textbooks' Bacon may not be as "persuasive and lofty in its influence as the . . . King James . . . Bible," as one textbook author puts it (Davidson 108), but it will presumably help in Bryson's sense "to keep [freshmen] out of trouble."

Given, then, the confluence of a history that argued for a plain modernism and a demand for and already established practice of disseminating plain prose to academic initiates, it is not surprising that readability would find a home in English departments. But it is also not surprising that the concept would be deployed in slightly different ways. Readability as it was applied to writing was the pragmatic offspring of a marriage between science and literary history. English departments have in a sense attempted to return the child to its roots, attempting to make readability both more scientific and more historical in order in part to make it more useful, more workable, but also to make it more palatable to a particular kind of literacy.

A *Fortune* magazine review of the readability movement offers a nonacademic view of what was at stake for the academy. The review was first published in 1950 and was later anthologized in a text for freshmen titled, significantly, *Toward Liberal Education* (1957). Although *Fortune* speaks favorably about the aims of readability—agreeing that fog and gobbledygook obscure too much of the language that is part of everyday life—the editors suggest that it is a sign of the failure of schools that such a movement is needed at all. "Patently, something is very wrong with the teaching of English when graduates so fail to grasp the fundamentals of good English that they feel they must learn a separate kind for everyday life—and a rather bobtail one at that. The fault may be, as some have claimed, that our academic English courses are still set up on the implicit assumption that their function is to provide a schooling for those who are to be novelists, poets, and scholars. Perhaps it is for this reason that the word 'literary' is increasingly used as a term of opprobrium" (*Fortune* 137). *Fortune* is not subscribing to Bryson's noblesse oblige version of a literacy designed for the amiable millions, but it is arguing for a middle style appropriate to most Americans. If one stumbling block has been the emphasis on literary writing, then the other stumbling block, from *Fortune's* perspective, is the equally destructive, exclusive emphasis on the functional.

The magazine quotes Edward Kilduff of New York University's School of Commerce, who argues that "the most effective kind of English composition being taught . . . is the realistic, practical non-literary American type" to be found in specialty courses, business writing, engineering writing, and the like (*Fortune* 137). But *Fortune* fears that such specialty courses mark the "breakdown of the humanities," the breakdown of a "common" language that is held by all. What is needed is not, they argue, more applied courses but "better basic ones," courses that teach not the slavish application of rules but the *"awareness* of good English." What this good English is, of course, is not explained but presumed. We ought not "forswear all the richness of our language" (138) in favor of some fraudulent plain talk, some "illusion of simplicity" (*Fortune* 137). *Fortune* argues that following formulas to write "downscale," to "shoot beneath the target" as the plain talk movement advocates, would lead eventually to an atrophied language (136) or, worse yet, a disembodied language separated from the "ethical," from "ourselves, our positions, our relations with those about us" (137).

In a sense, *Fortune* carves out for itself—and others in the business of mass communication outside the academy—the rich middle ground between the "functional" and the "literary," which has been left unmanned by the academy. If the schools fail, it is the "moral obligation" of those who write advertisements, who speak on radio and TV, who produce movies, to offer audiences "the best we [can] give them" (*Fortune* 136). These audiences as characterized by the magazine are not the letter-blind millions. They are capable of responding to the best. But it is clear that there is still the distinction between the audiences as consumers and the producers of the language that is to be consumed. The producers are the keepers of the best. They know how to produce the best. Consumers are intelligent enough to recognize the best, but are dependent upon the producers to give them the best. Speaking of the man in the street, *Fortune* observes:

> We should long since have delivered ourselves of this oaf, for in reality he does not even exist. He is a self-perpetuating stereotype, the reflection of the lowest common denominators we have been looking for. In creating him we have done not only ourselves but our audi-

ences a disservice, for though they will respond to the tawdry, they will also respond—as many a book, speech, ad, and movie has demonstrated—to the best we give them. But they cannot if we abdicate our moral obligation to give the best that is in us. (136)

The editors of *Fortune* create the middle ground perhaps, as is ideally true of all middle grounds, to preserve the best of both extremes, in this case, to have a functional literacy where literacy has not sold out to functionality, where it maintains its humanistic roots, and where literacy loses some of the taint of literary exclusivity. But it is a middle ground designed for general audiences. The guardians of the middle ground, the producers of the best, have to have a knowledge, an intimate familiarity with the literary in its more exclusive sense, if for no other reason than to presume good English. *Fortune*'s editors believe they do not have to talk down to audiences, but they also believe they ought not foist the likes of Sir Thomas Browne on them. To think thus, one must know both talking down and Thomas Browne. *Fortune*, like Bryson and Flesch, defines and defends as its own a privileged literacy that allows it to produce the middle ground appropriate to constituted audiences, an audience very similar to the middling classes constructed as in need of a plain English in the nineteenth century (see chapter 3).

In the academy, the functionalists continued (and continue) to be a strong voice in determining pedagogical policy. But there has also been the ongoing attempt to promote the kind of middle ground that *Fortune* advocated, a middle ground that would continue to draw from the best that men and increasingly women have thought and written but in such a way that it would be functional, with functionality more broadly conceived. Thanks to the push in the sixties and seventies for readers and rhetorics that contained materials relevant to students' lives—"selections that would illuminate the contemporary American scene" (Levine and Coulette ix)—canonical prose writers of the past appeared to almost entirely disappear. Francis Bacon, who had been an important figure in the construction of English as a discipline and had been used as a teaching tool for some time, was represented in forms longer than the epigram only rarely after the sixties.

In Donald Hall and D. L. Emblen's *A Writer's Reader* (1979), Bacon's essay "Of Marriage and Single Life" is preceded by a brief sketch identifying Bacon as "a father of our written language, often counted with Jonathan Swift among the greatest makers of English prose" (24). Ironically, however, the essay is followed by the statement that "most modern readers find Bacon's compressed style difficult" (25), suggesting perhaps that this most modern of plain stylists (as defined by Gunning) has become for modern readers so astringently plain that he is now obscure (or in Bacon's terms, the modern common reader is not the appropriate reader for the truths to be found in his essays). Perhaps this perceived difficulty accounts for the more typical and far more reduced form of Bacon's writings to be found in Young, Becker, and Pike's *Rhetoric* (1970) in which they mention "Francis Bacon's discussion of the art of communication" and include the briefest of quotations from the unnamed "discussion" and later arrange a writing assignment around part of a Baconian maxim (241, 271). In this latter instance, Bacon has been produced as a kind of touchstone, a producer of maxims and writer of essays not to be read but rather to be remembered as having been read.

Through the sixties, seventies, and eighties, fuller works under Bacon's name appear to have had little play in composition classrooms. The network of affiliations—readability research linked to educational and industrial demands for an American kind of literacy—had shifted, so that texts such as Gunning's Bacon or the Bacon of *Twenty Lessons in Reading and Writing Prose* have been far less likely to be produced. More recently, perhaps as a response to the call for a turn away from process approaches, the renewed interest in a connection between writing and reading, cultural literacy and the western canon, Bacon and other older canonical writers have reappeared in readers (see, for example, Lydia Fakundiny's *The Art of the Essay*). But whatever the visibility of canonical figures in textbooks, for the advocates of the middle ground the canon continues to provide support for a particular conception of prose style; that is, writers conceived of as canonical, whether anthologized or not, continue to influence pedagogical practice by creating a genealogy for a normative style. Freshmen and businessmen may not always be deemed interested or capable enough to read pre–twentieth-century writers of prose, but the premises upon which rest notions of acceptable prose style derive in part from conceptions of the history of prose style, conceptions, that is, of what constitutes the modern prose canon—and that history remains the story of a progressive plainness. Selections are likely to be drawn from what is said to be accessible. Efficiency of use is still a dominant value. Thus, collections of readings for undergraduates, with few exceptions, tend to avoid the sort of prose that does not readily yield a quantifiably testable response or a clear, concise student essay.

Not all teachers of composition read pre–twentieth-century prose. But many theoreticians of composition pedagogy do, or depend upon those who do. In a real sense, then, the likes of Bacon and other canonical prose stylists continue to exist in the support literature as authority for pedagogy. Thus, to take one example: E. D. Hirsch, in *The Philosophy of Composition*, used histories of prose to support his conception of "relative readability." Hirsch constructs a genealogical and progressive chain of ever more efficient style in order to promote a Spencerian conception of literacy.[6] Hirsch does not concern himself with individual figures within the larger histories but relies instead on the conclusions that ostensibly grow out of the cumulative pattern of canonical figures. Like Rudolf Flesch, Hirsch has added his voice to popular as well as academic debate concerning the causes and cures of the latest literacy crisis. And like Flesch, Hirsch argued for a certain kind of readability as the standard by which writing can be taught and judged. But while Hirsch expressed admiration for Flesch's work, he nonetheless saw Flesch's formulas as too limited (*Philosophy* 83). Hirsch proposed instead a sort of middle-ground readability that speaks to the kind of concerns expressed by the editors of *Fortune* in the fifties. In his *Philosophy* and in his later formulation of "cultural literacy," Hirsch brings together the functional and the literary—in particular, his own intentionalist critical theory—interweaving linguistics, psycholinguistics, and readability research with histories of language and of prose. Hirsch constructs an intricate argument, one represented as scientific and

historical, to support what might be called his humanistic functionalism.

Hirsch proposes to provide a common ground upon which
policy makers and teachers of composition can stand and thereby
resist "the conflicting ideologies which confuse us and hamper
progress" in teaching and research. Just as earlier readability researchers and consultants characterized their project as a distinctively American prose revolution, so too Hirsch explains his purpose as ideologically crucial. In the rhetoric of his text, there are,
on the one hand, the conflicting ideologies that "always [hold]
greatest sway where knowledge is least" (*Philosophy* 3), and, on
the other hand, there is the "authentic ideology of literacy [that]
inheres in the subject itself, and should guide our teaching of it"
(*Philosophy* xiii). The structure of Hirsch's argument—that is, that
it argues from certain historical tendencies—is considered by
Hirsch to be Marxist. But he quickly dissociates himself from "political Marxism" by arguing that "the fallibility of Marxism is not
in the structure of its argument" but in "its premises." "The validity of all such historical theses about goals," Hirsch asserts, "depends at least in part upon the validity of the facts adduced in
their favor." The goals Hirsch proposes for the teaching of composition rest, he argues, upon "careful empirical support." Hirsch
believes that the empirical evidence he has "adduced and interpreted" raises his argument "above mere ideology" (*Philosophy* 4).
What is at stake, then, in Hirsch's text is more than merely composition teaching and research; it is a conflict between the forces
of error in the form of ideological conflict and the forces of validity in the form of authentic, inherent, unitary ideology—this latter
ideology used in the kinder sense of the science of ideas.

That error is associated with conflict (and Marxism) and validity is associated with common ground, with unity, is not new.
Multiple tongues, after all, have been a sign of the Fall (as Bacon
and Hooker remind us). But such an opposition does lead to a
reading—or is intertwined with a reading—of "empirical evidence" such that conflicting evidence, if acknowledged at all, is
argued away as "anomolous" (*Philosophy* 56). What will constitute empirical evidence will be that which fits a linear, unitary pat-

tern. In its barest outlines, this is the paradigmatic move of canon formation, but it is also a fundamental move in the historical construction of literacy. Hirsch chooses as correct those histories of language and of prose that show a tendency toward progressive change, toward ever greater *communicative efficiency* (*Philosophy* 52–71)—a concept that can be read as an elaboration of the argument offered by the earlier sentence counters and can be seen as an offspring of the scientific management movement. Like the earlier sentence counters before him, Hirsch discounts as "irregularities" those texts that do not fit the picture of linear progression (*Philosophy* 56).

Thus Hirsch supports and perpetuates the kind of reading of histories of prose that Gunning made use of in producing a text under Bacon's name that teaches readers to keep sentences short. Hirsch does not charge teachers to instruct pupils in the art of composing short sentences. He does argue, however, that "assuming that two texts convey the same meaning, the more readable text will take less time and effort to understand" (*Philosophy* 85). Students should be taught "communicative efficiency," however. Given Hirsch's beliefs that different language can convey the same meaning and that the reader's mind has universally, transculturally, and transhistorically the same limitations (*Philosophy* 65–67), it is reasonable to assume, then, that one can read texts from the past and evaluate them in terms of "relative readability" to see whether they fit the "universal" tendencies of language toward the "shortening of unresolved stretches of discourse" (*Philosophy* 71). It is also reasonable to assume that a normative prose style can be naturally derived from this history to be taught to students.

One could challenge Hirsch's assumptions about meaning and mind. One could challenge the logic of his argument, his selection of data, his dismissal of conflicting material. All of which would be of some importance, even now that Hirsch has disavowed what he terms his earlier formalism. But what is important for the present discussion is the way in which Hirsch affiliated himself (and continues to do so despite his disavowal) with a powerful ideological network, and by so doing helps to perpetuate the network. He brings together beliefs and "facts" that were well established, in fact commonplace, in the first half of the twentieth century, as the previous discussion has shown. As did historians of prose and readability researchers in the fifties, he depends heavily on nineteenth-century philologists and linguists, and particularly on the father of sociology, Herbert Spencer. While he makes some use of more recent material, the work of psycholinguistics, for example, he positions himself primarily within a pedagogical, philosophical, economic, and political network that grows out of nineteenth-century beliefs about language (and behind that, beliefs about the social order)—a network that values efficiency, especially when it comes to administering large, complex bureaucracies, in this case educational bureaucracies in the name of access—making learning of a limited sort available to more people but making it available in such a form that the educated thereby help contribute to the social stability and order.

Hirsch speaks of some of his conclusions as appearing almost "self-evident" (*Philosophy* 55), and they appear so because they are part of a system of beliefs and values developed out of the nineteenth-century debates over the institutionalization of English teaching, beliefs and values associated with writing pedagogy and the dissemination of literacy to a newly conceived general public, a system that helped shape what constitutes style, what is valued as style, how one reads style, how one produces what sort of style (if any— since in some instances to produce with style is not a universal right). Hirsch relies on the self-evidentiary quality of histories of prose and also helps perpetuate those qualities, thus helping to make possible practices such as Gunning's.

When Robert Gunning produces a text under Bacon's name he does so within a network of affiliations—educational, governmental, economic—that helps to define style and reading and writing in particular contexts. Gunning cannot control all readings of his respective texts, nor does the network function as some monolithic or conspiratorial structure that can insure a universal but limited consumption of these texts. In fact, Gunning's production of the text may serve to alter the network, by shifting definitions of *plain* and shifting readings of Bacon as plain. Gunning's plain does not mean quite the same thing as Hirsch's. But the val-

ued space already made for the term, and the continued maintenance of that space, help to contribute to the sense that twentieth-
century plain talk is the same as seventeenth-century plain style,
that history puts its imprimatur on our current practice. Francis
Bacon wrote of choosing to take up language that he had inherited while recasting it to new use. In a sense, the process by which
Bacon or other canonical writers come to us is as taking up what
was previously valued, taking the language of valuing and recasting the valued object, perhaps recasting so radically that what was
valued is no longer valued. But the illusion is that the object of
valuing remains the same, or that the signification of the terms of
valuation are the same. In large measure, Bacon comes to the
twentieth century as a valued object. The uses to which such valued objects are put, in whose interests they are made to operate,
however, differ, as is evident in the debates over the institutionalization of English, as the next chapters will show.

The often unwitting collusion of literary and literacy practices
and traditions in the service of solving the literacy crisis may
seem tame enough. To make a greater range of reading material
available to a broader reading public and make mastery of writing
skills a possibility for more learners are worthy goals. The readability movement, however, settled for too little, for a building
block notion of literacy's component skills and a rhetorically and
politically naive plain style, populist in intent but ultimately cor-
rosive of public discourse, as Cmiel has argued. Readability in its
various guises constructs the average reader/writer as requiring
simplification, as unable to deal with complex sign systems in
situ. Learning theorists and language philosophers from Lev
Vygotsky and John Dewey to Paul Ricoeur, Jerome Harste, and
Carolyn Burke have challenged the bases on which readability
theory and practice rest. But our collective ideological investment
in efficiency, order, and control help to reinforce and maintain a
practice that even the supporters of readability acknowledge as
a simplification.

2

The Charmed Circle

Part 1: Literature and Literacy as Instruments of Culture

The student will not wisely ignore any book which has been
admitted by recognised authority within the charmed circle.

Sidney Lee, The Place of English Literature in the Modern University

A literature which is represented by such writers as
Shakespeare and Milton, as Pope and Wordsworth, as
Bacon and Hooker, as Gibbon and Burke, is a very serious
thing . . . and . . . regarded as an instrument of culture, it
is—if studied in a liberal spirit—of the utmost importance
and value.

John Churton Collins, The Study of English Literature

Teaching English to the English (or to the English-colonized and
English-speaking) was not a nineteenth-century idea, but the institutionalization of English teaching as a university subject legiti-
mately could be called a nineteenth-century process.[1] Several
forces converged in the nineteenth century to produce a discipline
that largely displaced the classics in England and the United
States, redefining what a college or university education would be,
and, not incidentally, consolidating a corpus of texts that came to
constitute true literature, a charmed circle including Hooker's and,
more prominently, Bacon's works, that came to comprise a literary
history, a genealogy for a normalizing but bifurcated literacy.

The formal introduction of such modern subjects as English
into the academy is often characterized in twentieth-century histories of the teaching of English, and was praised by some nineteenth-
century moderns, as the triumph of the forces of liberalism,

democracy, and progress over traditionalism, aristocracy, and stagnation (e.g. Altick, Applebee, McMurtry). Confining a study of the origins of the teaching of English to the ideas of various writers who played a part in the creation of the new discipline has led to such narratives of progress or, more recently, to attempts to reclaim some figure from the past to serve as progenitor for some current (better) practice. If, however, the ideas that float Laputa-like over the ground of practice are tied more directly to that practice, the narrative becomes more complicated and the origins for present practice become muddier. The liberal program was not in simple opposition to tradition and certainly not in simple opposition to a class order designed to control access to education and through education, jobs and social standing or power. Indeed, the institutionalization of English studies was dependent on tradition even while it served to alter it and helped shore up a social order even while it was associated with reform. In a very real sense, the creation of a new subject helped preserve and perpetuate a particular conception of a single, common linguistic heritage in England and the United States, while it helped to create the sort of conception of literature as oddly decontextualized and depoliticized, that would make possible the use of texts evident in the readability literature. The varying deployments of Hooker and Bacon in the course of the creation of English as a university subject is a particularly telling instance of how structures of power are strengthened and altered through the discourse of change.

Terry Eagleton has argued that "literary scholarship . . . was for the most part born in the service of an urgent ideological project: the construction and refurbishing, in nineteenth-century Europe, of the various 'national' cultures and lineages" ("Ideology and Scholarship" 124–25). The consolidation of a literary corpus and the construction of a literary genealogy were part of this larger ideological project, concerned with defining what literary series would best represent and reinforce appropriate or desired versions of the national culture. Naming a literary series is not sufficient in and of itself, however, but must be accompanied by—or, more appropriately—arises alongside and interacts with an educational apparatus for cultural dissemination and control. Canonization contributes to and is simultaneously shaped by pedagogical practice. Constructions of what constitutes literature affect what constitutes literacy and literacy education.

Pedagogical practice in England and the United States can be read in part through ordinary grammars, manuals, composition guides, and examination papers, as well as in the pedagogical theorizing of a host of writers. In such materials one can see the proliferation of normalizing structures out of diverse motives, driven by conflicting aims.[2] Examinations and their accompanying guides, justifications, and critiques are a particularly useful place to look in order to consider the complex forces contributing to the construction of a discipline.

William Collins and Sons was one of several English publishers in the latter part of the nineteenth century supplying a still new market with inexpensive manuals and guides aimed at preparing the student for matriculation exams, examinations for degrees, and civil service exams for various government jobs. If "an essential article of the Victorian faith was . . . examinations," as one contemporary put it, then such ordinary and yet virtually invisible objects as Collins's textbooks served as the catechism (Kellett qtd. in Roach 3).

Volume 1 of Collins's School and College Classics series, published between 1873 and 1879, is devoted to thirty of Bacon's essays. For each essay in this pocket-sized volume, the editor, Henry Lewis, supplies annotations explaining vocabulary and usage and appends an analysis or outline of the essay's main points. For Bacon's "Of Discourse," for example, Lewis glosses some twenty-two words—this for a relatively short piece of writing—words from "discourse" and "honourablest" to "would" and "he," the latter to indicate Bacon's use of a "repeated nominative" that is, "strictly speaking, not grammatically correct" (Lewis 187). The analysis or outline divides the essay into two parts: first, "Good conversation is marred . . . by [the] desire to cultivate readiness rather than judgement [and by] the tedious and ridiculous reiteration of remarks already well known and looked for"; and second, "Rules for good conversation" include the importance of not monopolizing the talk and the importance of avoiding talking too much about oneself or about "personalities" (Lewis 190–91).

The apparatus surrounding, indeed almost overwhelming, Bacon's essays is consistent with the instruction given to examinees from midcentury onward about what to read and how to read it in order to pass the various exams. And Bacon was a frequent subject upon which to exercise students. Study manuals often emphasized grammar and rules of composition and set students to work on excerpts from the great men of letters. Reading literature was a means, perhaps as one guide put it, "the most pleasing and efficient means," of developing greater proficiency in language and composition (Dodds, *What to Read* 11). This is not to say that the student was not advised to attend to the greatness of the truths to be found in the literature, but greatness and truth would not be on the test. Whatever the prominent writers of the day might say in support of teaching English, about how it would raise the spirit and exercise the higher faculties or refine and invigorate the national character, English studies were intertwined with an examination system that served to discipline students and job seekers, placing them more firmly and explicitly in a social hierarchy in terms of that most intimate and, one might say, most human attribute, language.

By the end of the nineteenth century, "a rich profusion of examinations throughout the civil, military and educational systems of Europe and North America . . . bore witness to their enormous social prestige and professional importance" (Macleod 3). Early in the history of American universities, students were examined much as they were in Europe, for participation in church and state. And the primary basis of evaluation was sheer quantity of information with the stated purpose of determining a student's ability, his mastery of information, and of motivating him to strive for honors. Harvard set the standard for most American universities when, after the Civil War, entrance examinations in English were instituted, first an oral and then later a written screening of students' use of English. Students were to attend to "correct spelling, punctuation, and expression, as well as legible handwriting" as they responded to composition topics drawn from set literary works (Applebee 34–35). Adams Sherman Hill, who was responsible for teaching composition at Harvard in the

latter part of the century, believed that the examination would encourage students to become familiar with esteemed literature and
thereby acquire not only a taste for good reading but a facility
with "better methods of thought and better forms of expression"
(Applebee 35).

In addition to establishing norms for good taste and proper
expression, such examinations in Europe and America came to be
used more and more to classify and categorize the learner in relation to himself (often tied to expectations based on family background and "potential") and to a conception of a group, a measuring based on what one historian of testing calls "an almost
fanatical belief that minute distinctions can be made" (Smallwood 104–10), culminating in the highly standardized examinations we live with today. Indeed it is difficult to think outside of
such a system of classification and categorization because so
much of current practice, current life, is predicated on using tests
to construct standards by which individuals will then be made visible. As Foucault puts it, a disciplinary apparatus such as the examination " 'makes' individuals" (*Discipline and Punish* 170).

In his very helpful essay on the English examination system
and the "schooling of science," Keith Hoskin, following Foucault,
sees the examination as a new means of "correct training" (213).
Foucault names two forms of disciplinary power: "hierarchical observation," by which those upon whom coercion is applied are
made "clearly visible," and "normalizing judgement," by which individuals are differentiated from one another according to a delin-
eation of the "frontier of the abnormal" and thus the demarcation
of the normal (*Discipline and Punish* 171, 183). Hoskins sees these
forms of disciplinary power merging in the examination:

> The examination is transformed; from being the final proof of com-
> petence at the end of one's apprenticeship in knowledge, it becomes
> a constant observing presence in educational practice, a regular
> means of testing performance and keeping students "up to the
> mark." In its modern institutional form it makes possible the control
> of the student through a system of "micro-penalty," of constant good
> marks and bad. Since the school becomes "a sort of apparatus of un-
> interrupted examination" the student is placed in a whole field of

surveillance; thus in this respect the examination is an exercise in hierarchical observation. (214)

For the Victorians, the examination system was not simply confined to formal schooling. It extended the disciplinary mechanisms of formal schooling to "capture" those who were self-taught (cf. Gibson's *London Matriculation Course*) as well as the already schooled job seekers. Thus, not only is there an extensive "archive"—to use Foucault's term—an accumulated record of "good marks and bad" that serves to define and demarcate the individual while in school, "introduc[ing] individuality into the field of documentation" (*Discipline and Punish* 189), but that archive is extended further into adult life. As, Hoskin argues, "the examination becomes an exercise in judging the individual while simultaneously generating a measure of the overall 'standard' of performance; it 'normalizes' at the same time as it makes each individual into a case with a case-history" (214). And in normalizing it further standardizes and narrows the avenues by which people learn.

One nineteenth-century manual writer, Richard Dawes, saw the examination system as a "wholesome and conservative" mode of administering public patronage. While he thought that examinations had their flaws, the improvement over the old, corrupt system of handing out government jobs would be felt as an improvement "more or less . . . by all classes of society" (viii). Indeed, one of the strongest arguments for competitive, open and, increasingly, written examinations at all levels of Victorian life was that they would democratize a system that had previously privileged the few (Roach 9). Examinations were part of both middle-class and radical educational reform movements from the late eighteenth century onward, aimed at raising standards, encouraging greater effort among the populace (including fostering "good sportsmanship"),[3] and attempting to insure that individual talent would be rewarded (Hoskin 215; MacLeod 1, 3). Examinations were intended to make rational and visible the process by which people were educated and admitted to jobs. As with other progressive movements, however, built into the process and particularly apparent in the English language and literature portion of examinations was a classification system that defined the individual's place in society through a closer scrutiny of the individual language user and greater systematization of what constituted literature and normal literate practice.

In an earlier manual, *What to Read, and How to Read It; or Hints to Candidates for the Government Civil Service* (1858), a "London schoolmaster" advised the reader that it was "absolutely essential that the candidate should manifest a correct knowledge of the construction of his own language, which he will be required to exhibit in the parsing and paraphrasing of sentences, the derivation and inflection of words, and the production of an original paper, probably a letter, upon some given subject" (Dodds 11).[4] While criticisms of teaching writing through abstract rules of usage can be found at least from Milton forward, they have made little dent in practice—or in the deeply inscribed faith even those who are excluded by it have in the truth of grammar. It is thus not very remarkable that, as in the passage above, language can be somehow one's own and yet the rules governing correct use of that language come not from one's own use or even from collective use but from a literary construction, a literary history. The distillation of literary history can be found in inexpensive grammars such as Latham's, Morrell's *Essentials of English Grammar*, Trench's "transmutations of and progress of the language," or G. C. Craik's edition of Shakespeare's *Julius Caesar* with its "good etymological notes"—all books the schoolmaster recommends. But, the schoolmaster warns, the distillations will not really be enough; proficiency in English composition is best achieved through the "patient study of the best authors." Addison in the *Spectator* and Knight's *Half Hours with the Best Authors* would be a start, augmented by Reid's *Rudiments of English Composition* and Cornwell's *Young Composer*.[5] Such works provide the tools for turning verse into prose (a frequent exercise in composition) and composing a précis of prose passages, activities designed to test a specifically schooled use of language (Dodds 11–13). Composing as a test subject was thus primarily a matter of displaying "correct" usage.

The several guides for students wishing to enter London University offer a similar picture. George Bede Cox compiled London matriculation papers in English through the 1870s, publishing them along with model answers in 1882. He comments that "papers on English Language set at the London Matriculation Examination have ever proved a difficulty to the majority of candidates. Though candidates may have acquired a fairly large amount of information in the subject from standard works, yet they have found a difficulty in applying their knowledge to the questions set" (Cox 1). He notes that the tests presuppose a familiarity with grammars such as Morris's, Adams's, Bain's, or Mason's. But his own guide does not discuss principles of grammar; rather, like some modern examination guides, he models appropriate answers without any explanation of why a particular answer is appropriate or correct. Many of the questions are drawn from literature, but always with the focus on grammar: "Discuss the grammar of these sentences: 'Who'er I woo, myself would be his wife'—Shakespeare; 'He would have spoke'—Milton; 'O thou my voice inspire / Who touched Isaiah's hallow'd lips with fire'—Pope" (Cox 54). Or, the answers are expected to make at least cursory use of literary history. Thus, with the question, "Explain as precisely as you can, the origin of the genitive in 's, of the plural in s, and of any other plural forms in English nouns," the answer suggested makes reference to, among other things, the "false theory of the origin of the suffix -s, which prevailed from Ben Jonson's to Addison's time, namely that it was a contraction of *his*" (Cox 74–75).

Few of the questions require composing anything more extensive than a short answer or analysis. Students are asked to outline an English language pedigree through its Indo-European or "Aryan" roots or to break down a selection from an unidentified literary work in such a way as to exhibit its "component elements in a simple form." For these later questions neither Cox's nor Barlet's guides to the London matriculation examinations provide much help. The best that the guidebook writer John Gibson can offer to "aid those students who read by themselves in preparation for the exams" is sympathy and the advice to practice. The English language, he says, "is what may be called an un-get-at-able subject. The papers set in the examination vary so much in general character and in detail, that it is difficult to know exactly what will be wanted. We may, however, be pretty safe in assuming that analysis will be required; and hence we should practise this from time to time, according to the system laid down by Dr. Morris" (11).

The student thus should pay particular attention to syntax, the connection of English with kindred languages, pronouns especially in reference to suffixes and original form and meaning, case forms, and he should read plenty of English to enhance his ability to spell. Gibson's last bit of advice is to attend to tidiness: "You cannot be too careful in sending up well-written, neat and workmanlike papers" (12).

The many how-to manuals hold out the hope that one can in fact study English grammar and composition in a relatively short period in order to pass a test. And yet, at the same time, the manuals make very clear that anything approximating full literacy will require more than what a manual has to offer: it will require "patient study." The London schoolmaster in *What to Read* warns his readers against cramming. Indeed, a constant complaint throughout the nineteenth century was that students were not studying to learn but cramming to pass a test. Literature, the schoolmaster says, is "the most uncrammable" of subjects. One cannot "prepare . . . for papers, the especial object of which must be to bring out the *well-informed* man—the man of extensive and thoughtful reading" (Dodds 41). Here in miniature is a central conflict characteristic of nineteenth-century educational debates, between practical education on the one hand and liberal education on the other. English literature and language were associated with the new subjects, with science, with technology, with preparation for particular professions. Yet the liberal orientation to language teaching arising out of the classical curriculum inevitably colored the teaching of English as well. An education was

> liberal so far as it concern[ed] itself with the good and the cultivation
> of the pupil; valuing any accomplishment it may give him, for the new
> perceptions it opens out, for the new powers it confers, or for any
> other good it may do the man, and not regarding the work produced:

Liberal Education would like to make a man an artist, that he may have a delightful occupation, and acquire an eye for beauty and for truth; she would like him to paint well, because this would shew the possession of such an eye and many other qualities as well, but she would not care much about the pictures themselves; she would not care a bit whether his pictures were valuable or not. (Latham 4–5)

Such an education assumed, however, a "certain independence of means." In fitting the man to no particular job, the liberal education, initially at any rate, was most suited to those who did not need to work or whose future employment was secure. Qualities such as "openness and generosity of spirit—traits of the gentleman as handed down from the courtly literature and ideals of the courtier of earlier times" were removed from their specific historical conditions, dissociated from the economic and social inequities that helped to make them possible, and read as signs of a moral conduct (Sanderson 1–2). It was certainly true that the liberal curriculum had been in fact the avenue by which men came to positions in the church and to public school headmasterships. And apologists for a liberal education, John Henry Newman not least among them, came to argue that a liberal education in preparing students for no particular vocation was in fact all the more "vocational" because it was better suited to train the mind to approach problems in any field (Sanderson 2–3).

No manual could substitute for a liberal education defined not simply in terms of curriculum but in terms of social status. English was indeed an un-get-at-able subject to the extent that the definition of its mastery was tied so intimately to class. Thus, rather than insuring that anyone who passed the test would be equally well qualified for a government job, the examinations could register only a minimal level of cultural capital. The self-taught examinee could not acquire what either leisure, social standing, or access to a proper education could supply. Reading Hallam's *Literature of Europe* or Chamber's *Cyclopedia of English Literature* or any of the hundreds of textbooks and manuals published from the midcentury onward could at best provide only a "mechanical grind of deadening fact and superficial understanding" or a "chronological series of facts and dates with potted biographies of the principal authors" (Palmer 47–48). Put very concretely, the examinations did not insure equal access to higher education or government jobs. The Indian Civil Service examinations, for example, planned and administered by Oxford and Cambridge dons and public servants who were graduates of Oxford or Cambridge, were thus closely tied to the traditional curriculum. These also were considered the most difficult, and in some sense the most prestigious, public competitive examinations (Sanderson 3). And, not surprisingly, they "were generally won by Oxford or Cambridge graduates, and often these had already carried off prizes at their universities" (Montgomery 30).

The success of these Oxbridge graduates was further proof of the value of a liberal education: "The administration of post-mutiny India and of the nascent welfare services at home seemed ample proof that an apparently useless non-vocational form of education did train practical minds who could turn their studies to account for the benefit of their own careers and of society at large" (Sanderson 3). Other candidates would take the less rigorous examinations for Home Civil Service or for entry into the army for which they could—and in large number did—prepare by attending a "crammer" or special course rather like familiar courses today preparatory to college entrance or law school exams (Montgomery 30). The sort of education that would produce "the man of extensive and thoughtful reading" was still limited to the few, and more importantly, the concept of what extensive and thoughtful reading consisted of was defined not by the writers of manuals or through cram-course curricula, which were for the most part reflections of well-established cultural norms, but in the universities and among the men who participated in the many educational commissions that helped shape educational practice in the nineteenth century. Thus, even when very explicitly intending to open access and challenge class privilege, examinations presumed a bifurcated literacy: the literacy possible to achieve by studying manuals or taking crammers and the literacy possible only through patient reading.

The manual writers (as well as critics of the examination system) argued that disconnected grammatical detail and sweeping literary histories could not substitute either for reading the "authors themselves" (Dodds 42) or for the experience of actually composing something more extensive than an outline or short answer. Most histories of the development of English, themselves predicated on the importance and value of a liberal education, reinforce this sense that the authors themselves were the antidote to the grammatical Gradgrindery evident in too many manuals. D. J. Palmer, in his "account of the study of English language and literature from its origins to the making of the Oxford English school" (1965), devotes a chapter to "The Muse in Chains." His argument is that pedantry shut out any consideration of the creativity or beauty to be found in the works. The "authors themselves" were equivalent to the Botanist's specimens or the Anatomist's bones (Dodds 42), natural objects that spoke their meaning free of interpretation; but the teaching practice as exemplified in the examination system was viewed as interfering with what would have been the natural process of reading a freely available meaning. According to this argument, there was an opposition between the version of English language and literature to be found in the manuals and that to be found among the more "enlightened" advocates of the teaching of English.

Among other things, telling the story in this manner is a way to derive prestige for English studies from a privileged subject matter—the authors themselves, the great men of letters—and from an often unacknowledged aristocratic conception of literate behavior, rather than from either the mass of students or the actual practices upon which the aristocratic practice is said to rest. Modern teachers of English might well want to dissociate themselves from what is often constructed as nineteenth-century pedantry as well as from what is read as the philistine nature of examinations. And as in more recent histories of the teaching of English, one might want to dissociate oneself from the messiness of class-marked liberalism. But telling the story this way also cuts us off from a way of understanding the conflicting and intersecting aims that continue to define current practice. English studies are multiply determined—arising out of reform movements in the late eighteenth and early nineteenth centuries, a growing secularization of education and industrialization, and the growing power of and faith in science; tied to a rising middle class and the countermove to contain reform, science, secularization, industrialization, and the middle class; associated with nationalism and the desire to establish and disseminate a national language at home and abroad; and springing from a desire to normalize discourse, to further construct and institutionalize a literary heritage in part as a way to establish what would count as correct usage and therefore what would count as socially acceptable language behavior. The deceptively simple matter of teaching the student his and increasingly her own language was from the start bound up with major, deeply divisive cultural movements (cf. Court, *Institutionalizing English*).

Examinations were of course not the sole shaper of English studies, but they played a key role in popularizing modern subjects—English and the sciences in particular—in the schools and universities. Certainly, examinations today drive curriculum just as they drove curriculum in the nineteenth century. As Alexander Bain put it, his eleven years' tenure as an examiner for the University of London made it possible for him to put his stamp on the examinations and consequently on the curriculum. He had argued in print for curricular subjects to be selected on the basis of their vocational utility (*Practical Essays* 74–75), but he was able to effect change most clearly through his presence on the examination board. Through Bain's efforts, potential examinees read Bain's own work and that of his colleague, John Stuart Mill, for the examinations, and such changes in the examination contributed to curricular change, particularly in more firmly securing the place of utilitarianism in London University (*Autobiography* 280).

But perhaps more importantly, examinations make visible the conflicting aims that helped drive the establishment of English studies at the same time that they were the products of and contributed to a normalizing of discourse, of what counts as correct language use. Subjects such as English that were at first thought too "soft" for serious study, attracting relatively few students, were soon to become "not only respectable, but usual" thanks in part to the demand for an English—as opposed to a classical—curriculum generated by the very practical desire to do well on examinations (Montgomery 31). As one nineteenth-century apologist for the examination put it, "English literature is, above all, the subject in which Examinations have called a particular kind of study into existence" (Latham 264).

Standing behind the examination system and also helping to drive the institutionalization of English was an opposition to an established academic elite. In England, pressure to secularize education and the demand from excluded groups to be admitted to universities—most often members of nonconforming religious groups who had been excluded from Oxford and Cambridge since the 1662 Act of Uniformity—helped to unsettle religious monopoly in education, and instruction in English sometimes rode in on the coattails of such change. But the interplay of secularization and pressure from dissenters was not the simple tale of a coalition of Davids facing down an entrenched establishment Goliath. Indeed, in this case Goliath seems to have played a rather crucial role in letting the collective Davids inside in order to "contain the damage" (cf. Palmer 15 ff.; Vaughan and Archer 45–54).

Utilitarians urged that religion be removed from educational institutions, asserting "the claims of rationality against those of faith, as well as those of utility against those of tradition" (Vaughan and Archer 53). Henry Brougham, a reformist (rather than radical) follower of Jeremy Bentham and an influential member of Parliament, was a driving force in establishing the "godless" college, London University, for teaching medical, legal, economic, and engineering studies as well as the classics to the middle class. Brougham wrote extensively on the need for the dissemination of useful knowledge through universities and working men's and women's institutions. He was particularly interested in how literary study could play a role in developing popular support for political reform (Court, *Institutionalizing* 43).

In an 1825 pamphlet, *Practical Observations on Popular Edu cation,* he argues that while "people . . . must be the great agents in accomplishing the work of their own instruction . . . they must be aided in their efforts" (5). They must feel the usefulness of knowledge to their own lives in order to seek out learning. Book clubs, reading societies, parish libraries, and cheap editions of instructional works were all ways to give ordinary men and women a taste of knowledge that would be of direct utility in their lives. Brougham had in mind an education in citizenship, offering a knowledge of constitutional principles, ecclesiastical and civil, that would contribute to "the peace of the country and the stability of the government" (9), and a knowledge of the scientific principles underpinning the mechanics' trades in order to enhance economic well-being (35). Clearly opposed to the liberal and religious education dominating schools and universities, Brougham, significantly, does not suggest a particularly unusual reading diet. He certainly focuses on the material conditions necessary to reading—the importance of cheap publication, the deleterious effects of a tax on paper—"a tax on paper [is] a tax upon knowledge" (7)—but the suggested readings were to be found on many a list, liberal or otherwise, for working people and university students: "Those who have not attended to such matters, would be astonished to find how substantial a meal of information may be had by twopenny-worths. Seven numbers, for fourteen pence, comprise Franklin's Life and Essays; four for eight pence, Bacon's Essays; Cook's Voyages, in threepenny numbers, with many good engravings, may be had for seven shillings and Plutarch's Lives, for ten shillings, will soon be finished" (8).

The difference between Brougham's list and that of a religiously inclined liberal advocate for the teaching of English seems to lie in the absence of such figures as Hooker (the high churchman John Keble, for example, felt there was no better education than that to be found in Hooker) and, perhaps more importantly, in how such works are to be read and to what ends.[6]

The latter is evident in a comparison Brougham makes between the English reader and the Scots—Scotland and the United States both served for utilitarians and pragmatists as models of a successful practical curriculum and a popular education:[7]

> The circulation of cheap works of a merely amusing kind, as well as those connected with the arts, is at present very great in England; those of an aspect somewhat more forbidding, though at once moral, interesting, and most useful, is very limited; while in Scotland there

is a considerable demand for them. Habits of reading longer formed in that country, have taught the inhabitants, that nothing in reality can be more attractive than the profound wisdom of every day's application, sustained by unbounded learning, and embellished with the most brilliant fancy, which so richly furnishes every page of the Essays of Bacon. (8)

It is unclear in what sense Bacon's essays speak to everyday concerns. The point, however, for Brougham seems to be less in direct vocational applicability and more in the general sense that one reads for "pleasure and improvement" rather than as a way to learn rules of grammar. Bacon is particularly apt in this regard, as several writers note, to the extent that he is seen as a precursor of the utilitarians. His project was predicated on the notion that knowledge should better humankind's condition. Studying words for words' sake distracted men from the "usefulness of knowledge." Brougham is careful to add that an education that includes Bacon can hardly threaten "a pure and true religion"—an argument rather like that which Bacon and Galileo made before him. But Brougham adds an additional premise: only "to tyrants, indeed, and bad rulers, [will] the progress of knowledge among the mass of mankind [be] a just object of terror" (35).

Religious nonconformists shared with utilitarians an interest in useful knowledge but did not believe that utility required the abandonment of religious purpose so long as the schools and universities were open to all regardless of religious affiliation. From the seventeenth century forward, religious dissenters found in Bacon material useful for positing an alternative educational establishment. Some attempt was made to claim Hooker for nonconformist purposes as well, but for nineteenth-century reformists Hooker had become too closely aligned with high church interests, especially through the efforts of the Tractarian John Keble.[8]

Thus, it is far more likely to find Bacon used for pedagogical purposes by nonconformists and secularists, while high churchmen, often opposing popular (i.e., secular) education, made use of Hooker for pastoral rather than pedagogical purposes. In response to the charges of exclusivity leveled against the Anglican educational establishment, several Anglican factions—Tractarians, Broad Church advocates, and Christian Socialists most prominently—offered renewed justification for their educational monopoly. Thus, when University College, London was formed in the 1820s to institutionalize the educational program of the secularists and the nonconformists, promising professorial rather than tutorial instruction, a secular rather than religious education, and modern subjects (English and courses in the sciences rather than an exclusively classical curriculum), King's College, London, was formed as an Anglican (and Tory) counterresponse, a compromise in fact aimed at offering both the classics and modern subjects, including English, but with the whole "imbued with Anglicanism" (Palmer 16; Vaughan and Archer 54).

As part of the new, controversial (and financially shaky) program at University College, a professorship in English language and literature was instituted, the first of its kind independent of rhetoric or belles lettres (McMurtry 36–38). The curriculum emphasized composition—approximately 150 hours were available in the principles and practices of composition—and the more scientific and factual (philological) study of language. Rather little English literature—about seventy hours offered in the catalogue—was available and that primarily as an adjunct to studying the English language. King's College, on the other hand, offered under the first holder of the Chair in English Literature and History almost the reverse balance, approximately two lectures in literature to every one in composition (A. Bacon "English Literature," 602–04), and later further deemphasized composition by stressing the moral import of literature over its role as stylistic exemplar (Palmer 18). One can see early on the division that continues to mark English studies, between the practical, secular, and bourgeois composition and the elevated or spiritual and elitist literature, even though secular composition relied on literature to provide models or norms, and literature made its way into the curriculum in large measure as illustration for rhetorical or philological precepts. Because neither college granted degrees at first, they tended to serve as preparatory schools for boys, sixteen to eighteen years old on the average, who would go into business or on to Oxford or Cambridge for a degree. When Parliament finally granted a charter to the University of London as an examining body to make possible the granting of degrees to those attending either college, they were essentially admitting secular education—"the first crack in the Anglican university monopoly" (Vaughan and Archer 56). After University and King's Colleges came under the umbrella of the University of London, students for the first time could be examined in English language (1839) and later, English literature (1859) (Potter 141–42).

In the United States, the sense of clear opposition to a single-church monopoly did not attend the institutionalization of English. State universities had been chartered as early as 1785, as the "institutional expression for the Age of Reason and for a developing nationalism" (Rudolph 275). While no one church held a monopoly in education, it is nonetheless the case that until well after the Civil War, American colleges were controlled primarily by Protestant clergy. As in England, a central purpose of colleges was to prepare men for the church and secondarily for the law. New colleges founded in the West, as well as older, established Eastern institutions, with few exceptions began with denominational affiliation and "clung to the traditional ideal of establishing and maintaining a Christian community through education" (Kitzhaber 9–10). Through the nineteenth century, however, increasing pressure was placed on institutions of higher learning to democratize enrollment and revise teaching methods and curriculum, which (as in England) seemed to require offering a secular and scientific rather than classical education. Miami University, for example, in 1825 offered a course of study called "English Scientific" designed to attract "farm boys" from the surrounding Ohio countryside. This new "parallel" program did not at first displace the "ancient subjects" but offered an alternative curriculum of modern languages, including English, as well as applied mathematics and political economy. Initially, Miami's was something of a halfhearted effort in that it offered not a bachelor's degree but a "certificate of proficiency" for completion of the new program (Havighurst 44–45). But the demand for more practical training led to increased enrollments in land-grant colleges and universities at a rate not enjoyed by religious institutions. Kitzhaber reports that, between 1885 and 1895, enrollment in eight midwestern public universities increased by 300 percent, compared to a mere 15 percent increase in eight established denominational institutions in the same area (9). Popular education thus helped to reinforce the association of new and practical subjects with educational ventures conceived of as more democratic or progressive and secular.

But despite the progressive coloration, and despite the advocacy of new subjects by new men—men, that is, from the rising middle class, and members of groups excluded from the older, prestigious institutions of higher learning (McMurtry 4, 40, 65), the raw material for the study of English was not new. Recognized authority had already named who would comprise the charmed circle. Thus, whether one believed English to be impossible to teach, as did many who opposed the institutionalization of English; or that philological study was the only reputable approach; or that only a liberal study of one's own language would yield fruit—whatever the perspective, the corpus of English language and literature was treated, at least for rhetorical purposes, as a given. The question, then, was not whether the likes of Hooker and Bacon would be admitted within the charmed circle, but rather how they and other recognized greats should be read and by whom.

In the course of the debates on the teaching of English, such literary figures served as tokens of exchange, tokens of value; that is, Hooker and Bacon were used as if they were not merely important in themselves but were exchangeable markers representative of good literature more generally. Or, put differently, they were important to the extent that they were readily recognizable as classics. They were clearly and explicitly named as instrumentalities, not only by those who earnestly believed in the importance of teaching the vernacular to elementary-level children, university and technical institute students, governesses, and mechanics, but also by those who wanted to stem the tide of reform. Oddly, Hooker and Bacon operated in the discourse as if everyone—on both sides of the Atlantic—were talking about the same thing, as if the tokens signified uniformly. It is clear, however, when looking at how the tokens were deployed in specific cases, that they did not in fact signify uniformly.

The shifts in the signification of Hooker or Bacon or other greats evidence an overall narrowing in what literature was taken to mean. And here I mean not the sort of narrowing Palmer and others complain of, the Gradgrindery in too much of what passed as English teaching, but a narrowing in the conception of what would be taken as literature and how literature would function in the world. The shifts also evidence the very different, often incompatible, traditions out of which the discipline of English studies developed. And, more particularly, the differential use of Hooker and Bacon marks the growing secularization of education and the concomittant focus on science. Thus, while both Hooker and Bacon were invariably mentioned in the pedagogical literature and mentioned almost as a mnemonic pairing representing the beginnings of a definitively modern English prose style, students were rarely asked to do much with Hooker beyond know his name and perhaps read the first book of the *Laws* and occasionally parse a sentence or two from his work. Bacon, on the other hand, provided students with much matter upon which to work, serving for writers with very different pedagogical agendas as the most apt exemplar of style—the father of *English* science, architect for a pragmatic education, inspiration for a naked style that would communicate new learning more effectively and serve the needs of a new, muscular, industrial economy. The surface unanimity of valuing that persists as gloss or veneer above the shifting significations may itself suggest an origin for twentieth-century practice, for disinterested treatment of Hooker and Bacon and at the same time for a flexible, adaptable, but normative prose style. In the nineteenth century, Hooker and Bacon became specifically literary tokens ostensibly removed from other systems of exchange—church politics, science, governmental politics—but, in fact, realigned with those systems of exchange and circulating in a newly forming system as literary objects. As such they became common currency, at once signs of and support for a conception of a shared linguistic heritage that was in fact contested.

There was considerable cross-fertilization between the American and British educational systems. While British reformist writers turned to American models for democratizing schooling, most frequently the direction of influence is seen in terms of American educators tending to rely on the published works of English and Scots theorists and pedagogues in order to provide materials for poorly prepared American teachers (Conners 180; Berlin, "Writing Instruction in Nineteenth-Century American Colleges" 19). Much work has been done tracing a rhetorical genealogy for American composition teachers back through the Scots/Anglo triumvirate of George Campbell, Hugh Blair, and Bishop Richard Whately (cf. Berlin, Corbett, Kitzhaber). Of course, the cultural exchange was more complex than the metaphor of borrowing suggests, and it extended beyond these three figures.

The pragmatism of Brougham and Bain, for example, was particularly compatible with the interests of America's rising middle class, supporting as it did a practical education for a new, industrial class. Polemical writings and textbooks in general were adapted to the rather different circumstances to be found in nineteenth-century America, and yet similar patterns appeared. Most specifically, teaching English meant primarily teaching written composition with literature (as embodied in encyclopedic manuals recording facts about writers rather than providing whole texts) introduced to provide models for composing. Toward the end of the century, while composition remained the primary responsibility of professors of English, literature, including "imaginative literature," was more regularly studied "in its own right," which as Applebee uses the phrase meant that Yale chose its examination texts "as well for their probable attractiveness to the preparatory student as for their intrinsic importance" (32). The concept of intrinsic importance that Applebee takes for granted was itself a contested notion and hid systems of selection by which texts came to be included in the charmed circle, and it hid as well the pedagogical and ideological purposes that informed the ways such texts would be taught such that their intrinsic importance would become evident to students.[9]

Into this conversation came John Churton Collins's *Study of English Literature*, which was printed simultaneously in London and New York and was read as advocating teaching literature in its own right. It is perhaps all the more telling that such works were transplanted without much regard for political and religious differences, as a sort of inadvertent and economically motivated disinterestness that grew out of the rapid expansion in education in this country, the continued material dependence on the motherland, and the continued, though not undisputed, sense of Britain's cultural superiority.

The very practical matter of where books came from— whether imported or produced domestically, whether authored by Americans or pirated from foreign writers—determined in a significant way what teachers and students had available to them as models. The American book trade began by importing most books from England (Barnes 49). After the War of Independence, in part because relatively few books were published domestically, a whole printing and publishing industry developed around not simply importing but publishing, and publishing (as a matter of course, without payment) unprotected works by foreign authors, especially authors from England (Clark vii). There was a tremendous increase in the need for cheap materials to teach new students; and without reciprocal copyright agreements with Great Britain, it was economically advantageous for American publishers to supply the "hunger for knowledge" by pirating foreign works (Ricketson 19). Indeed, it was not until 1891 that, as James Barnes put it, "Congress finally recognized America's literary independence by authorizing reciprocal copyright agreements with foreign powers" (ix) through a series of amendments to the general copyright law of 1870 (Clark 183). With the new copyright provisions, there was an immediate and significant reduction in cheap books, at the same time that American publishers were able to pay more attention, at least theoretically, to American authors. Aubert Clark argues that 1891 also marked a shift away from American cultural dependence on English models (183–84), a shift evident in the American textbook writers' break from British rhetorical models in the latter part of the nineteenth century (Kitzhaber 87). While certainly indebted to British precursors, the American educator Fred Newton Scott, for example, has been characterized as producing a distinctly American pedagogy (Berlin, "Writing Instruction" 77).

Through much of the nineteenth century in the United States, the choice of what to have one's students read, largely determined by textbooks (Connors 181–86), was at least as much the result of need combined with economy and cultural imperialism as it was the recognition of the inherent goodness or value of the works read. If one looks at the works of British advocates of the teaching of English, which found their way across the Atlantic, one sees a similar complex of motives that went into choosing (or rejecting) works to be taught. Inherent value was an issue, but inherent value is intertwined so with other factors that it is difficult to argue with confidence that the work's qualities were the controlling factor, or even a dominant factor.

In a manner not unlike the inadvertent disinterestedness of nineteenth-century American pedagogues, British advocates such as F. D. Maurice, Alexander Bain, and John Churton Collins take up materials that are in a sense ready to hand. They do not present themselves as searching out the best that has been written, but operate as if they are simply accepting what already had been admitted by recognized authority to be the best. Or, as in the case of Bain, when they reject what recognized authority has chosen, they do so for pedagogical reasons rather than as a rejection of the canonical status of the writer. Authority is in fact a critical concern in the debates over the teaching of English, not in the simple sense of merely claiming authority to speak, but in the sense of speaking with that authority that comes from recognizing what has always been the case. Thus "recognized authority," or sometimes, more hyperbolically, "all mankind," knows Hooker and Bacon to be great; therefore—the argument goes—teaching should reflect that knowledge.

Editions of Hooker's and Bacon's works were readily available throughout the nineteenth century in popular and scholarly forms. In nineteenth-century histories of prose or discussions of great prose writers of the Elizabethan and early Stuart period, Bacon and Hooker are generally treated as equals, considered together as "master-builders of the English language" (Dowden 432), "first inventors" of English for specialized use (Disraeli 245), Bacon producing the "first great book in English prose of secular interest" and Hooker, the first of interest in religion (Church 206). But equality in assessment did not translate into equality in publication. The secular writer was simply more readily available than the religious. Only about thirty printings of Hooker's *Laws* appeared in the United States and England, representing some six different editions. Of these, John Keble's Tractarian edition, first printed in 1836 and later revised by Paget and Church, remained the standard scholarly edition until the current production of the Folger Library (1977–) (Edelen xxiv–xxvii, xxxiv; Pollard).

In contrast, in the course of the nineteenth century, some 130 printings of Bacon's essays, in English alone, appeared in England, Scotland, and the United States, representing forty different editions and including two novelty miniatures as well as several annotated texts for the special use of students at various levels of education. The several editions of both Bacon's and Hooker's works range from apparently simple reprintings with little or no apparatus to elaborately scaffolded works. In discussing the editing of Shakespeare's texts, Ronald McKerrow notes that a transition generally occurs in the history of editorial practice, "between the simple reprinting of an author regarded as contemporary and the 'editing' of one who has become out of date and somewhat difficult to understand, in order to present his texts in as sound and intelligible form as possible to a later public for whom he is no longer one of themselves" (*Shakespeare's Text* 5). Shakespeare, McKerrow observes, seems to have become an old author by the early eighteenth century.

Judging the editions of Hooker and Bacon along these lines, one might argue that Hooker had in a sense already become old by the nineteenth century. But Bacon—at least the Bacon of the *Essays,* the *Advancement of Learning,* and translated portions of the *Novum Organum*—remained contemporary until late in the nineteenth century. Early on, the lawyer Basil Montagu offered relatively unadorned and unaided his edition of Bacon's essays, a volume of *Selections* that included some of Bacon's works (alongside Taylor, Barrow, South, Latimer, Brown, Milton, and Hooker), and the 1825–1834 edition of Bacon's works (a remarkably popular edition on both sides of the Atlantic). The brief preface to the *Selections* expresses the simple hope that the works will "give immediate delight," perhaps sparking "a holy fire in some man reading them"—with relatively little guidance required from Montagu (viii). Similarly, Montagu presents Bacon's *Essays* as if they require little assistance from an editor beyond making them available. In the collected works, he suggests that this new edition will clear Bacon's name of any libels "scrawled upon [the] base" of his monument (Montagu, *Works of Bacon* viii) by those who saw in his life what Macaulay described as the "checkered spectacle of so much glory and so much shame" (Macaulay 495). But he does little more than suggest that reading Bacon's writings should be enough to clear him of such charges. That Bacon might even require such a defense suggests that he was alive enough for readers to stir up some controversy.

Later in the century, however, as the new scholarship laid claim to literature as a specialized discourse, Bacon, like Hooker, came to require "resuscitation" (cf. Rawley, *Resuscitatio*). Samuel Reynolds offered a new edition of Bacon's essays (1890) with a lengthy introduction and extensive glossarial helps. He disagreed with W. Aldis Wright, whose earlier edition of Bacon's *Essays* (1862) had set a standard for bibliographical practice influencing scholars into the twentieth century. Wright had stated that the "English reader will find few difficulties in Bacon's language or style." But Reynolds argued that, on the contrary, "almost every page . . . bristles with difficulties some of them the more likely to mislead, because even a careful reader . . . might fail to detect them for what they are" (xxi). Reynolds as master reader must thus alert the novice reader to those easily overlooked elements. He thus reconstructs Bacon as the specialist's property.

McKerrow has remarked that if it were not for the "less careful," almost "less respectful" treatment accorded to Shakespeare by early editors, "he might never have reached the position in the world's esteem which has made the later scholarship seem worth while" (*Shakespeare's Text* 4). One might argue that the less careful editions or collections in the eighteenth and early nineteenth centuries helped to contribute to the sense that recognized authority had already established the importance of Hooker and especially Bacon. From the Evangelical minister Vicesimus Knox and his *Elegant Extracts in Prose Selected for the Improvement of Young Persons* (1816), and the *Readers' Digest*–like condensed version of the Baconian corpus in *Verulamiana; or Opinions on Men, Manners, Literature, Politics, and Theology* (1803), to the scholarly reclamations of Hooker and Bacon, recognized authority makes itself felt through the material availability of the works and the continued presentation of those works as representative of a key, even originary stage in the history of English prose.

Advocates for the teaching of English could take for granted the place of Hooker and Bacon in the canon and could redeploy these figures in the service of larger cultural aims, at the same time consolidating, at least in the sense of affirming, their canonical status. In the course of the institutionalization of English, conventions were established for determining how and by whom writers such as Hooker and Bacon should be read. This ongoing process of literary canonization was fundamentally pedagogical, helping to establish a normative literacy. It was and is a process by which, in Gauri Viswanathan's terms, humanistic ideals developed in the Enlightenment would "coexist with and support education for social and political control" (3).

3

The Charmed Circle
Part 2: The Pedagogues

A vital if subtle connection exists between a discourse in which those who are to be educated are represented as morally and intellectually deficient and the attribution of moral and intellectual values to the literary works they are assigned to read.

Gauri Viswanathan, Masks of Conquest

The complex and dynamic process by which canonical literary works intersect with pedagogical practice to institutionalize a normative literacy is evident in the efforts of various advocates for the formalizing of English studies. I have focussed on four cases that span the nineteenth century and represent some of the very different motives that came together uneasily to establish English as a discipline: F. D. Maurice and early efforts to stem the tide of secularization; Alexander Bain and midcentury attempts to separate manner from matter in order to insure nondenominational access to literacy; John Churton Collins and the late-century "literature for literature's sake" movement; and, finally, Fred Newton Scott and the turn of the century development of a more distinctly American English studies curriculum. For all the real and important differences among these advocates for the teaching of English, each nonetheless makes clear the extent to which teaching the vernacular was an enculturating process intimately tied to definitions of an orderly, civilized society. No one figure (nor four isolated figures, for that matter) can explain the origin of present-day practice. Each of these figures might be thought of, instead, as a nodal point or intersection for a number of conflicting forces—some of which have already been delineated in the preceding chapter—that together produced the discipline of English.

I

John Frederick Denison Maurice is perhaps best known as a Coleridgean who adapted the Romantics' organicist critical theory to theological and social questions. His Christian socialism, or Christian social philosophy, had at its center the notion of a vital link between literature and society: language is key to an understanding of humanity. For Maurice, "social forms and institutions pre-suppose language and, thus seen, the literature of a nation is the soul of that nation." Conversely, if there is political disunity or disruption in a nation, there is also bound to be a disrupted literature (Hartley, Preface xv). Such a philosophy places style—in the classical sense of decorum—at the center of language education: to each group or class is assigned an appropriate style, an appropriate way to use language. To step outside the appropriate bounds is to risk disruption.

Maurice was educated at Cambridge and Oxford and was ordained in 1834. He became professor of English literature and history at King's College, Oxford, in 1840, the second person to hold the chair, giving it up in 1853 when he refused to subscribe to the notion of eternal damnation. In 1848, he helped found Queen's College for Women, primarily for the training of governesses. Publishing mostly religious materials, Maurice also entered the lists as a champion of education for men and women from the working and middle classes. Though hardly a reformist himself, he argued, along with the reformist Henry Brougham, that such education was necessary to social stability.

Maurice's teaching of English is perhaps best exemplified by the humble set books, the prescribed texts forming the reading for a particular course of study. If there is one continuous thread through all the controversy over the teaching of English, it is that advocates rarely believed any work, by however eminent and revered an author, was worth a student's reading in toto, and certainly not in the raw. The teaching of English was almost universally thought to require the selection and packaging of works in forms convenient for teaching. Publishers understandably recognized the value of learning the titles to be set or assigned in a given year in order to have available the necessary volumes for this new market. In the year 1859, the first set books specified were Bacon's *Essays* and *King Lear* for a pass; more Shakespeare, Milton's *Lycidas* and *Areopagitica*, Bacon's *Advancement of Learning*, and Clarendon's *History of the Great Rebellion* for honors (Potter 151–52). These early editions offered relatively little in the way of commentary or teaching apparatus. The aim was to provide a cheap edition of the assigned works. But these relatively simple editions soon developed into the kinds of texts Collins's School and College series and other publishers supplied (see chapter 2), providing more apparatus, more shaping of the student's reading, with American textbooks offering in general even more apparatus, more helps for the teacher and the student.

Maurice's immediate concern in making available cheap copies of specific books was to provide his students with common material for "construing," a procedure borrowed from instruction in Latin and Greek for analyzing the grammatical construction of sentences in order to derive (etymologically, to construct) meaning. Selections were made in part so as not to "scandalise" students or other teachers (Potter 146–47). Thus Bacon's *Essays*, already widely available in both popular and expensive editions, was deemed appropriate (safe) for student consumption. Bishop Whately, after all, had recently demonstrated the value of the *Essays* for moral and religious enlightenment (rather than for the more secular purposes to which Brougham and other reformers might put them) in his large and very popular annotated edition (cf. British and American editions). Thus the choice of Bacon's *Essays* was neither innovative nor daring. But it is such conservative choices in the midst of innovation that characterize the processes by which a discipline comes newborn into the world already with the patina of age and by which the objects of study appear to have always been there.

For Maurice, as a classically educated scholar, the set book was a selection from a rich and varied corpus. Bacon's essays were understood by him not only in relation to others of Bacon's works but also in relation to works from the Latin and Greek. But in extracting the essays out of this learned context, Maurice realigns them for new use. In a series of lectures published the year before he joined King's, Maurice gives a clear indication of what was at stake in such a realignment. He addresses the question whether the church or the state has the power to educate the nation. This was a question of moment in the midst of the liberal and Whig reforms effected during the first third of the century, when exclusive Anglican control over much of English education was being challenged by Parliament. In the fifth lecture, Maurice discusses the question in terms of English teaching.

His primary focus is on educating the middle class, who were, not incidentally, those most likely to benefit from the proposed reforms. The middle class, as Maurice sees it, "has or ought to have a peculiarly national character" (*Course of Lectures* 206). They are the segment of the population that makes England peculiarly English. While "catholic cultivation"—training, that is, in Latin and Greek—is desirable for some individuals, for the "sake of the nation" such cultivation is deemed insufficient for preserving the peculiarly English character of the middle class. Thanks to this middling group, Maurice reasons, the English in the sixteenth and seventeenth centuries came to recognize that they "were something within [them]selves, not using a common Christendom [not speaking Latin], but speaking a homely native tongue." What is required, then, is "to give the middle class of this day a thorough, hearty understanding of that language which their fathers did so much to secure for us." Again picking up the horticultural metaphor, which suggests something of the noblesse oblige characteristic of his writing, Maurice outlines the "intellectual cultivation" that will best call forth the "humanity" of the middle class (*Course of Lectures* 207).

In packaging the great works of literature, however, Maurice makes some instructive distinctions. He distinguishes between what is appropriate for scholars (the "we") and what is appropriate for the middle class (the "they"). Scholars may understand how "the principles of language govern the usage of the English language" because they have studied Latin and Greek, but such knowledge is not "needful" for the middle class. Scholars are chosen for their task: they are "marked by Providence for the business of keeping up an intercourse with men of all countries" and therefore require the "catholic languages." But men whose business it is (who have also been ordained by Providence) to "work on their own soil, with the men of their own soil" can speak and write for their own purposes well enough in English without recourse to "scholarship" (*Course of Lectures* 208). They require only the "study of their own tongue in its vigour and purity" (207), "sound instruction in English" without extraneous matter, "providing only the person who gave it had himself been bred a scholar" (209). The middle class is thus deemed capable of learning to use the mother tongue with "vigor," as long as someone who is ordained to know more can serve as Providence-provided gatekeeper. Set books, the selecting of inoffensive reading, the training in "construal," are all forms of gatekeeping. But perhaps most important, Maurice places divine authority behind the authority that does the choosing, behind those who say what a book means, who set the books, who pick (or in Maurice's term, "recognize") the members of the charmed circle.

Part of the gatekeeping function is to define what is characteristically English; that is, what is "vigorous" and "hearty" and, significantly, "masculine" expression. In an address to the committee of Queen's College, later published as a pamphlet, *Queen's College, London: Its Objects and Method* (1848), Maurice offers a rather interesting angle on what "masculine expression" or "masculine style" means. In considering the education of governesses—actually, the education of girls as young as twelve who had the potential to become the educators of children from wealthy families—Maurice urges that the "master key to that knowledge [necessary for teaching] is assuredly English Literature." And he adds, "by that I mean the books of really great Englishmen" (*Queen's College* 22).

Significantly, however, it is not to develop a style in writing that the governesses should be exposed to the greatest men of letters. Rather, the young women should be helped "to understand what they read, and [to have awakened] in them thoughts which they shall wish to express in the most suitable and reasonable language" (*Queen's College* 23). They are to observe, in other words, what the Renaissance would have understood as the rules of decorum—the harmony or resonance between the inner and the outer, between the letter and the spirit, the writer and the audience or purpose (Kranidas 101), what Thomas More would have called the propriety or decency to act that part which has fallen to one's share. Part of what motivates Maurice's concern here, however, is also a Romantic understanding of decorum, of an organic style, a style that grows out of having something to say and saying it in a way appropriate to the circumstances of each particular writer: "The teaching men, or women, or children, to write after the manner of Addison, or Johnson, or Burke, or to separate the style of these men from the business they were about, must, it seems to me, encourage the growth of a wretchedly artificial feeling" (Maurice, *Queen's College* 23).

But understanding what is suitable, producing a prose appropriate to one's station, purpose, and audience, however ancient a rhetorical principle, is clearly a highly charged cultural concept. If the characteristically English expression or style is masculine, as Maurice and others argue it to be, then, given Maurice's essentialism, such expression would be unnatural for women. From the start, then, even though women are considered by Maurice to be "naturally" the teachers "of some person or other, of children, sisters, the poor" (*Queen's College* 8), and even though he is acknowledging their educability (in the face of continued arguments to the contrary) and their ability to develop a "real grounded knowledge of that which is taught" (8) and a need for their acquiring something more substantial, something of greater "utility" than what has traditionally been thought of as ladies' "accomplishments" (12), he has nonetheless defined the normative style of expression in such a way that women cannot by definition be producers of it. Not only do they not read any great women of letters (if there are any such in his view) according to his schema, but they are barred from producing the style deemed characteristically English. Presumably, they can be transmitters of what is naturally English—as if they somehow carried an X chromosome for style that they could pass on but that did not affect their own genetic makeup.

One thus needs to read the development of English and of a normative style not only as clearly class-demarcated but also gender-
demarcated in ways that continue to trouble English studies.

Maurice defines the canon, for purposes of educating the
middle class, as the old English chronicles, "our principle poets,
especially the earlier ones, because these tend so much to illustrate the growth of our language," and any other native writings
that "answer most nearly in spirit and clearness to those which
the master of a Latin and Greek school would put into the hands
of his scholars" (*Course of Lectures* 212). Some sense of what this
latter might include is offered in advice concerning practice in
composition from Thomas Arnold, a broad churchman and eminent headmaster of Rugby: "In translating Homer hardly any
words should be employed except Saxon and the oldest and sim-
plest of those which are of French origin. . . . In translating the
tragedians, the words should be principally Saxon, but mixed
with many of French and foreign origin, like the language of
Shakespeare and the other dramatists of the reign of Elizabeth
and James I. . . . So, also, Thucydides in that of Bacon or Hooker"
(Fitch 45). Arnold's principle of selection is based on a comparison of the stages in the development of English with the stages in
the development of Greek, but the schema is clearly more than a
matter of chronology. The English authors are presumed to "answer in spirit and clearness" the works by Greek authors. It is
such a notion with which Maurice is dealing.

What is evident here is how much apparatus is apparently necessary to shore up the selection process: in the case of Arnold, an
elaborate—and, one might say, arbitrary—analogy between the
style of ancient, already authorized literature and the style of vernacular literature; in the case of Maurice, a specialized, fitted—
and limiting—correspondence between a class of people and some
body of literature deemed appropriate to that class. The need is
clear to find some standard outside the text by which to judge its
worth. The text apparently cannot speak its value independently.
And behind the standard stands some authority, whether all
mankind, recognized authority or, in Maurice's case, "Divine Authority," to certify that the standard is correctly applied.

For Maurice, the process of selection is intended to help bring forth the "humanity" of the middle class, something they presumably cannot cultivate on their own without the intervention, the gatekeeping, of men such as Maurice. And what bringing forth humanity means becomes clear toward the close of his lecture. One of the advantages of teaching English to the middle class via "good English authors" is that it should help "cultivate the faculty of expression," which is a necessary part of a man's freedom (Maurice, *Course of Lectures* 215). But that freedom, like all good English gardens, is tended rather than free-ranging.

Maurice would like the middle class to recognize that "human culture" would make them "better and worthier tradesmen," not because they will have acquired a knack or skill but because they will have become better men. The scheme for education Maurice has in mind would counteract what he disapprovingly calls the "trade spirit" (*Course of Lectures* 217), presumably a reference to the vocationalism of secular education, by teaching them the "English habit of reserve" (215). The well-cultivated member of the middle class, then, "will have learned nothing to make him proud of himself, but will have learned to understand himself; nothing to make him despise the place in society which he is appointed to fill, but much to make him know that he has a dignity which the highest place in society could not give him" (*Course of Lectures* 219–20).

Having learned the style appropriate to his social station, this cultivated member will thus be content with his place and will be less vulnerable to "political agitators" who would point out inequities between those who walk on foot and those who ride in carriages. Because members of the middle class would now know "what words signify" they would be resistant to "large sounding phrases" that might otherwise terrify or amaze. Instead, this newly cultivated group would become "calm, solemn, patient, [and] earnest [in] spirit," understanding that men are sent into the world for a purpose and learning to be content to do what they have been assigned, "and be still" (*Course of Lectures* 219–20). Thus the rhetorical concept of decorum reveals itself most clearly as a principle of class stability and control.

Reading Bacon's *Essays* or Milton's *Aereopagitica* under the tutelage of a scholar, Maurice argues, will connect with man's "*political* feelings" such that he will be delivered from the "bondage" of what is "material and worldly." Literature thus allows the reader to transcend the immediate historical moment—not as mere escape, but in coming to a better sense of himself and of the world. This line of reasoning leads Maurice to the conclusion that the study of English is entirely antithetical to secular studies. English is an instrument "given to us for the very purpose of destroying secularity" because the study of English authors grounds teaching not on the material but on the spiritual being of the students who are under the scholar's care (*Course of Lectures* 220–21). Maurice thus returns to the question with which he began: whether the church or the state has the power to educate the nation. English, a subject already laid claim to by those excluded from church-governed educational institutions, is retrieved for religious purposes as an instrument not of a secular but of a spiritual education. In thus reclaiming the subject area, he also reclaims the selected works chosen to make up that subject. Bacon's *Essays*, Shakespeare's *Lear*, or Clarendon's *History of the Great Rebellion* are ostensibly removed from any connections that they might be made to have with the worldly and material—in this case, that is, removed from any part they might play in secular reform—and recreated as spiritual instruments— an oxymoron revelatory of the materiality of Maurice's political agenda. In Maurice's hands, Bacon's *Essays* or Shakespeare's *Lear* become instrumentalities of a supposed new order, tools for reinforcing a class-governed spirituality, a contented, decorous class order.

Clearly, Maurice could not insure that Bacon's *Essays* or any other selected work would teach the middle class to be content. In fact, to the extent that he contributed to the expansion of English education to include some of those previously excluded from the academy, he may well have opened up avenues of change, enabling some of his students, who could not be content, to alter their appointed positions in life. Teaching students to construe the spiritual rather than the material text could not insure that construal might not become either a tool in the service of other than spiritual ends or another kind of spiritual end. But the major thrust of his work was to control and limit what was appropriate discourse—what should be read and what was appropriate language to be used—in order to control and limit the aspirations of a class.

By himself he could do relatively little. But Maurice is important as a representative of a more general effort to harness literature or, perhaps more accurately, to keep literature harnessed in the service of a particular religious and political establishment. Maurice helped to form one approach to teaching English through his emphasis on disseminating the spiritual meaning of a text, and he reinforced the received notion of what texts would best serve spiritual ends through the practice of setting or assigning texts. Thus Bacon's *Essays* were more firmly established as safe texts to be construed in order to cultivate a particular kind of class-marked literacy for the English middle classes.

II

The sort of spiritual approach to the teaching of English represented by Maurice and others was anathema to Alexander Bain, who saw it not only as inefficient pedagogically, but exclusive—barring people like Bain himself from access to higher education. Even though in a fundamental way Bain shared with Maurice a clear sense of what distinguishes the "we" from the "they," he nonetheless advocated a reformist secularized curriculum designed to increase educational access. His curricular innovations were predicated on an attempt to keep literacy instruction as content-neutral as possible. To the extent that one could keep the content neutral, one could make a disinterested, formalist education available to anyone, regardless of religious or class affiliation.

William James remarked that Bain and Herbert Spencer were the two philosophers with the "widest influence in England and America" after the death of John Stuart Mill (Potter 117, n.).[1] Bain worked with both James Mill and John Stuart Mill, contributed to Chamber's Information for the People series—a publication associated with utilitarian and reformist writers—and was himself the product of a Mechanics Institution. Bain characterized himself as having "contract[ed] Reform sympathies" while apprenticed as a weaver at the age of thirteen (*Autobiography* 15). He participated in Mechanics' Mutual Instruction classes, continuing to do so as a form of self-education even after he was accepted to Marischal College. He broke from the state church early on and continued to argue for an education free from ties to any particular religious institution, even though such views kept him from an appointment at a Scottish university until he was finally appointed in 1860, at the age of forty-two, professor of logic at the University of Aberdeen. Bain was in most respects the antithesis of Maurice: he was quite frankly the product of educational reform and a participant in and advocate for continued reform. For him, the teaching of style—central to composition teaching as he saw it—should have practical (rather than primarily spiritual) consequences. One's spiritual life ought to be one's own business.

To the twentieth-century reader, Bain's program for the teaching of English would no doubt seem familiar, suggestive of the extent to which his work has become a part of the discipline he helped pioneer (Great Britain 243; Gage xii). As professor of logic at the University of Aberdeen, Bain's duties included teaching English composition. His "scheme" was to make English style the primary subject (*On Teaching* 48), a practice that dominated the field of composition well into the twentieth century. But Bain distinguishes his own method from what he characterizes as more traditional instruction in rhetoric, based as it was on the statement and illustration of rules of style, by proposing to join to an "outline of Rhetoric" the criticism of "authors, or passages from authors, with a view to the exhibition of rhetorical merits and defects as they turn up casually" (*On Teaching* 49). As Arthur Applebee has pointed out, such practice was common among the Scots rhetoricians, for whom the terms *rhetoric, analysis,* and *criticism* were used more or less interchangeably to designate a course of study in which "a literary text would be critically examined to insure that it conformed with the prescriptive rules of grammar and rhetoric, all in the ultimate service of the student's own speaking and writing skills" (9).

In arguing against the mere recitation of rules, Bain was positioning himself within the Scots tradition developed out of the work of such eighteenth-century lecturers as John Stevenson and Adam Smith, popularized and brought into the nineteenth century with Hugh Blair. Bain formalized the procedure by compiling and publishing extract books of English prose and poetry for the use of his students akin to Maurice's set books (Great Britain 244), basing his lectures on selected extracts (see, for example, *On Teaching*). In addition, in the final weeks of his course, Bain would offer a "summary of the English authors," giving "dates of the authors, the list of their works, and the recognised specialities of their style" (*Autobiography* 273), much as examination manuals would do. To those who had known only instruction in the classics, Bain "opened up a new world," introducing his students to the "mysteries of style," sending them off to read and discuss English authors (Potter 115).

For Bain, however, such lectures in literature were strictly subordinate to instruction in the "graces of composition" (*Education* 354–55). Bain devotes a chapter in one of his several manuals on the teaching of English to "How Not to Do It," specifically how not to teach English using Bacon's *Essays*. He acknowledges that the *Essays* are among English classics of the first rank, but they are not "fitted to be a text-book" (*On Teaching* 38). Much of the emphasis in his various writings centers on what is "practical," what is efficient. If the English language were to be treated merely as "learned lore," then, Bain argues, "its ancient history, its derivation, and its stages of its growth," would all be "worthy of being studied." But English is "an instrument of everyday life" and "practical needs are not to be slurred over" (*On Teaching* 96). This emphasis leads Bain to mention Hooker only in passing as a great prose writer "of his day," a figure of historical interest for students of English but of no immediate practical importance. Bacon, however, requires more attention, not simply because he is a greater writer—Bain yokes the two together—but because he has been employed already so frequently as an instrument of education. Bain ultimately rejects Bacon as an instrument for the most *efficient* teaching of English (in favor of Macaulay, who "absorbed" Bacon), but his reasons for doing so are instructive not only for what they reveal about the treatment of Bacon but also for what they reveal about one ancestral strain of present-day English departments, which continues to play a prominent role in defining the separate but interdependent domains of literature and composition and defining particularly the content of composition instruction.

Dedicated to promoting a modern, scientific curriculum, Bain argues that teaching—"scientific teaching"—ought to be governed by "the great principle of Division of Labour," that is, "the separation of the language from the matter" (*Education* 357). A portion of Bacon or Macaulay or any writer "may be a knowledge lesson, or it may be a language lesson," and, according to Bain, in "present practice" it is "apt to be both." But if the teaching of English is to be "scientific," the English teacher "should have nothing to do with the matter, except in relation to the manner." Bain has not cast much light, in conceptual terms, on the rhetorician's oft-repeated form/content opposition, threatened as it is here by the potentially self-cancelling "except." But he does go on to indicate the extent to which such a concept marks off disciplinary territory. Bain argues that the English teacher

> may read with his pupils Burke on the French Revolution, but he should not trouble them with the political thoughts, but only with the conduct and method of the exposition—with the sentences, the paragraphs, the illustrations, the figures, the qualities, the diction. . . . It is his business to indicate important peculiarities in the expression and in the handling—what to imitate and what to avoid in the one or in the other. When he has got out everything of this kind that the work can yield, he has done enough. (*Education* 357–58)

In his manual, *English Composition and Rhetoric*, derived from his teaching first-year students at the University of Aberdeen, Bain gives some fuller sense of what work students and teachers ought to be engaged in. In the preface, he reiterates his belief that the "matter" of writing is not the business of the English class. Practice in writing ought to be the prime consideration of the English teacher. But because "writing Themes involves the burden of finding matter as well as language," such composing "belongs rather to classes in scientific or other departments, than to a class in English composition." The English teacher thus must engage the student in writing exercises in which the matter is supplied and the "pupil disciplined in giving it expression." Bain suggests the best method is "to prescribe passages containing good matter, but in some respects imperfectly worded, to be amended according to the laws and proprieties of style." Or, students might be asked to convert poetry into prose, abridge or summarize, or fill up and expand brief sketches (5–6).

To put Bain's plan in perspective, it should be noted that not all writing instruction attempted to separate matter from manner in quite this way. William Collins and Sons' *Composition Exercise Books,* for example, geared to the school rather than university student, present as the first priority the students writing "only what they know." Writing instruction should thus encourage students to gather information, talk about their subject with teachers and friends, and in general think about the subject before attempting to write. The difference, however, is that the "matter" is rather general. Younger children are asked to describe familiar objects (mosquitoes, clouds) or to compose imaginary sketches (a trip to the moon, though such topics should not be "exercised too often"); older students, after practicing the skill of restating ideas in passages read orally by the teacher (an activity tested on examinations as well) or reproducing the style and substance of a work studied, move on to essays in which they consider "ambition," "honor," "the ideal and the real," "no and yes" (there is no indication of what this topic might yield), "make hay while the sun shines," or "has civilization been more effectively promoted by war, commerce, or missionary enterprise?" (see the Appendix).

Bain could expect that most of his first-year students not only had the fundamentals of grammar but had had some experience with the sort of writing that such exercise books suggest (*Autobiography* 272). When he talks of separating matter from manner, then, he is presuming prior writing experience as well as university practice that includes writing in all subjects. Matter is not banned from the writing universe, but it is banned from the English classroom. Bain assumes that his students will be reading and writing about the sorts of texts he himself had read and written about as a student, from Newton's *Principia* to Spenser's *Faerie Queen*. Because these are works deserving of serious attention, and because teaching for him is primarily a matter of transmission, Bain sees the only sensible path for the composition teacher to be one of separating content from form.

There are only so many hours in the day, and if one needs to lecture on figures of speech, arrangement, the qualities of style, the sentence, the paragraph, modes of exposition and persuasion, as well as poetry, there is little time left over to deal satisfactorily and seriously with what is being said. Students thus are asked to read an extract from Macaulay's *History*, "an expository and moralizing episode," not explicitly to learn about his thoughts on revolution but to notice (because Bain has pointed it out) how Macaulay makes use of "obverse statement, iteration, and balanced structure," or how he might have (but did not) collapse two sentences into one, or to admire how one of his sentences "passes the limits of poetic pathos, to answer an oratorical purpose" (*Autobiography* 333–34). Having been tutored in all that would contribute to simplicity, clearness, and strength in composition, students are expected to exercise this knowledge in the production of their own writing not simply in the English class but in what we would now call the content areas.

In thus separating matter from manner (and in maintaining a transmission model for the dissemination of a particular kind of literate knowledge), Bain carves out what he understands to be a new field. "English" will not be "history, mythology, geography, natural history, manners [or] customs." "English" will be defined "scientifically" such that division of labor will "exclude from English teaching . . . all occasions for calling forth patriotic and moral sentiment" (*Education* 358). Bain has in mind as a negative example the sort of teaching evident in Maurice when he separates "scientific" teaching from such efforts that so clearly foreground nationalism and morality. A more formalist approach promises a less discriminatory pedagogy. Patriotism and morality, as the son of a Scots weaver would know, exclude those who do not share in the official notion of either nation or church. Nowhere does Bain say, however, that what is taught in the composition class is the whole of literate behavior. Formalism has its own acknowledged limitations, but for Bain those limitations are preferable to the ideological restraints of the traditional curriculum.

Bain's pedagogy was not confined to the Aberdeen context, however, but was broadcast to sprout up in other settings where the limited literacy of manner over matter was *the* literacy. If a given discipline creates the object of its study, then literature, as defined by the teaching of English, was created as a pure language object, which regardless of content (or politics) could serve as exemplar of style, as model for composition. Works are to be harvested for what they can be made to yield by way of instruction in the composition of "Simple, Clear, Impressive English" (*On Teaching* 49), a phrase that, needless to say, begs the question, as a logician should know, but which does suggest the extent to which the issue is not logic but territory. To be viable, the new subject must be distinguishable from other, already established subjects. English is thus defined by negation, by saying what it is not.

If literature becomes a collection of models for instruction in composition, the question then arises, what examples should be chosen for teaching to be most effective? Bain poses the question in terms of the use that should be made of "our classical English writers" (*On Teaching* 15). Only habit, he suggests, can explain why such venerated texts as Bacon's *Essays* are "usually prescribed" for the teaching of English (*On Teaching* 38). He mentions with disapproval that the India Civil Service exam of 1882 prescribed reading all thirty essays, and that such exams tended to dictate what was taught in training colleges and schools (*On Teaching* 40; see also Great Britain 294). Bain was not altogether opposed to reading Bacon. His own reading included Bacon's *Novum Organum*, a "wonderful . . . book" whose "freshness of thought and language" captured his interest to such an extent that he had thought about developing "an art of discovery" or methodology like that found in Bacon's work (*Autobiography* 47, 105). But, while Bain admires Bacon's language and thought and reports frequently on his similar admiration of other writers, he does not take his experience as a largely self-tutored learner to be a model for pedagogy. Faced with teaching a course to first-year students, with little preparation other than an article he had written on language for Chambers's Papers for the People series, he looked for a practical way to teach composition. Rather than get bogged down in the matter—matter Bain was certainly interested in—he focusses on those writers who more cleanly exhibit the linguistic features he wants to teach.

Bacon's continued presence on reading lists was already assured through the efforts of men such as Maurice and the work of others such as Robert Lowe, the author of the Revised Codes for government-run educational institutions. In 1858, the Newcastle Commission was appointed to "inquire into the present state of popular education," prescribing through various codes what ought to be taught in public schools at all levels. Training colleges were expected to assign certain specified books, from Chaucer to Milton, to be paraphrased and analysed in terms of both style and subject matter. Among the books to be assigned was Bacon's *Essays* (Great Britain 43–44, 54). But neither habit nor governmental prescription can excuse the fact, as Bain sees it, that teaching Bacon's *Essays* to the uninitiated student constitutes a violation of the principles of scientific teaching. Great as the essays are granted to be, Bain is concerned that teaching Bacon's essays involves exercising pupils "at once on the thoughts and the style," which is a clear violation of the principle of division of labor. But, he contends, even if one were to set aside such a criticism, the essays do not lend themselves to the efficient teaching of either matter or style. The essays are deemed too various in theme, "so miscellaneous as to admit neither of classification nor of orderly sequence"; no topic is discussed in full and many are treated with incoherence, in that various matters are mixed within a single essay; and some topics, such as "Marriage and Single Life," are simply inappropriate for youths. Bain has the good grace to acknowledge that Bacon's essays "profess to be" simply "hints, suggestions, starting-points for thoughts." But he sees little teaching value in having students read the essays in that light, even when led by a "skillful teacher" (*On Teaching* 38–40). Bain's principles of scientific teaching, involving as they do as limited a notion of the student's capacity as Maurice's, require a prescriptivist sense of what constitutes the best manner for treating a topic and prevent him, therefore, from seeing Bacon's essays as teachable.

A "clear principle of good teaching," Bain asserts, is that a "subject should be methodically laid out, and brought consecutively before the minds of the pupils." A textbook should be "full and complete" rather than "scrappy and suggestive." And finally and perhaps most importantly from a prescriptivist perspective, the text should be sufficient in itself rather than subject to the discretionary use of teachers or examiners. Thus, Bain concludes, even if one were to violate the principle of division of labor and teach "thoughts" in an English class, Bacon's essays simply could not serve as an efficient instrument (*On Teaching* 46).

But this still leaves open the question of style. If the proper object of study in English is style, the question arises whether Bacon might not serve as proper material for student use. For Bain, to acquire style is to extend "our resources of diction and expression in all its particulars":

> Being a matter of endless minute details, we may feel ourselves at a loss to compass it by the intensive study of a narrow and select example. . . . We should, however, carry along with us, the maxim exemplified under oratory, of separating our study, as far as may be, the style from the matter. We begin by choosing a treatise of some great master. We may then operate either (1) by simple reading and re-reading, or (2) by committing portions to memory verbatim, or (3), best of all, by making some changes according to an already acquired ideal of good composition. (*Practical Essays* 247)

This last procedure involves laying a writer's "merits . . . side by side with the corresponding demerits" (*On Teaching* 46). Along with such a "course of book-reading" the student should also attempt "original composition," because the aim of any course in English should be to develop the student as "a self-thinker, and a self-originator" (*Practical Essays* 254).

Independence of thought, however, must rest on a standard of correctness, propriety, and felicity. And such independence must be preceded by training in the scientifically parcelled parts of language use before the student has to face the messy whole. According to

Bain's system, one could evaluate Bacon's style against a standard of correctness, propriety, and felicity. But Bacon simply does not measure up consistently enough for pedagogical purposes. Bain is able to extract examples from various essays to illustrate the use and abuse of similes, the employment of balanced sentence structure, and the like. But in general he finds that Bacon does not serve as a "model for imitation, or a source of expression to the student of our own day" (*On Teaching* 41–42). Bacon is simply not modern enough. Bain can appreciate the fact that Bacon (and Hooker) "were in their day great writers of prose," but they are "for our purpose" surpassed by modern writers who have produced prose "at its very best" (*Education* 355). The concept of what is best derives from Bain's belief in a progressive history of English literature, a belief, more particularly, that "English prose style has improved, and is improving" (*Education* 355). It is an idea that he shares with Herbert Spencer, and it is an idea that has been taken up most recently by E. D. Hirsch.

In Bain's formulation of the theory, authors are regarded as a "connected series, each having more or less relation to the preceding" (*Education* 354). Two consequences follow from this evolutionary concept of literature: one having to do with "interest" and the other to do with "style." And both consequences argue against the then-current use of Bacon. As to "interest," Bain reasons thus:

> When an author is at once great and popular, when he is widely read by the nation, and closely studied by succeeding men of letters, his influence becomes detached from his own writings, it flows through so many channels as to be felt without reading him. . . . The original is, to a great degree, though not entirely, superseded by the reproduction of the best passages in our most familiar reading. I do not say that it is superfluous to go back to a complete text, but I do say that the impress of the author's genius is not dependent on that exclusive source. (*On Teaching* 15)

Given the accretive nature of "interest," it is thus reasonable to assume that "the greatest amount of unexhausted interest should attach to the more recent classics—the writings of those that have studied the greatest works of the past." And, in terms of style, it is thus reasonable to assume that the "best" writers are the most recent because they "have reproduced many of [the] effects" of earlier works, "as well as adding new strokes of genius." Bain acknowledges Bacon's "transcendent genius," but he argues that to use "Bacon's original," by which he means, to use all of the essays, as a textbook would be to cancel the centuries that have intervened between Bacon's day and the present (*On Teaching* 16).

For Victorian antiquarians, Anglo-Saxon scholars, and philologists—the sort of men who helped form the Early English Text Society (1865), helped produce the Oxford *New English Dictio nary*, and occupied newly established chairs in English—Bain's boldness in preferring the modern to the ancient was no doubt shocking. For the more general reading public, who continued to buy the numerous inexpensive editions of the essays, such a setting aside of Bacon made little apparent difference. But Bain was not addressing either scholars or established readers. His audience was composed primarily of teachers, some of whom were lecturers in universities and colleges. The larger market for his practical advice on choosing and teaching literature consisted of the often ill-equipped instructors, in England and the United States, who were attempting to meet the demand for English in state colleges, university extension programs, training colleges, women's institutions, and such organizations as the Ladies' Education Association and the Civil Service Commission (McMurtry 11; Great Britain 44 ff.).

From midcentury onward, a popular, primarily middle-class, and increasingly female market had developed for lectures on English language and literature. While part of the interest in such lectures was for their entertainment value, much of the impetus came from a desire for what would be useful, for what would better the individual in some way. Or, in the language of Lord Brougham, first president of the Society for the Diffusion of Useful Knowledge, lectures in English, to the extent that they spread useful knowledge, were expected to "exercise and to unfold the faculties of the mind, and to lay up a store of learning, at once the solace of the vacant moments, and the helpmate of the working hours in after years" (Great Britain 46).

Bain speaks of what is most "needful" for teaching, a term he shares with Maurice but uses to signify a different sense of need, a pragmatic rather than spiritual matter. Bain is not concerned with what mature adults should read for their own edification. He points out that while a "canto of *Childe Harold* has not the genius of *Macbeth*, or the second book of *Paradise Lost*," it nonetheless "has more freshness of interest" (*On Teaching* 16). But Bain is not an exclusive advocate of the moderns. He argues that while the "best English teaching would say little about [Chaucer, Shakespeare, Milton, and Pope], [it] would, nevertheless, give the pupils the aptitude and the zest for reading them when they have left school." Because, he adds, "not one of these writers is child's play. None of them can be read with any tolerable appreciation before eighteen or twenty and the full enjoyment of them is much later" (*Education* 357). Bain thus follows the common practice of eighteenth- and nineteenth-century Scots rhetoricians who, while acknowledging the "greats" of English literature, tended to discuss more thoroughly authors who were contemporaries or near contemporaries (Applebee 9).

Such differential treatment of authors, while clearly assuring a market for contemporary writers, also helped create a two-tiered canon based on a notion of maturation—authors, on the one hand, appropriate for the new students filling training colleges, institutions of popular education, and the like, and, on the other hand, authors reserved for mature readers. Maturation here does not denote simply age, however. It was not at all unusual for pedagogical books to be designed for both children and adults who were not yet deemed educationally developed. The uneducated adult (like the "savage") was thus viewed mentally as a child. Following what is now familiar educational practice, Bain parcels out knowledge in such portions and at such a pace considered appropriate or manageable for some class of learner, all the while withholding something of the real stuff.

In a sense, Bain's practice illustrates the Foucauldian notion of the simultaneous enabling/disabling action of acts of power. Bain distinguishes between what is appropriate for the classroom and what is to be reserved for what he calls "self-culture." And in so doing he works to enable his students more readily to move from "prose at its very best"—prose that is well written according to rhetorical prescription—to prose such as Bacon's essays, which are "less perfect" but are nonetheless "great," "brilliant," "transcendent," "classic." In the process he does introduce his students to works otherwise excluded from traditional classical education, valuing the contemporary, the current (albeit always a selection from the current) to the extent that it is useful (teachable). But by postponing— for most students, indefinitely—the greats, who become more and more the exclusive domain of scholars and the educated elite, Bain also helps to perpetuate the sort of class- (and gender-) marked dichotomy apparent in the practice of Maurice. The question posed by Renée Balibar in her studies of the production of literature for school use—what literature becomes when literacy no longer marks the difference between classes—is answered in Bain's practice. Distinctions are made or reinforced between literate groups in part in terms of the particular works deemed readable by each group and the sort of style considered appropriate. The rising middle class, men of business, civil servants, and the like, are best trained up in contemporary prose in order to carry out the business of the world. Normative prose is thus a contemporary culmination of the best that had been written in English, a functional prose adapted to the world of work. But held in reserve are the so-called greats, deemed less immediately useful in preparing men and women for daily commerce but clearly useful in demarcating the educated elite.

III

Both Maurice and Bain were concerned with what and how to teach a new educational clientele. John Churton Collins, as a University extension lecturer, was also engaged in the teaching of the new student, but he is better known for championing university training for the new teachers required to accommodate this burgeoning student population. The Board of Education report on the teaching of English in England, published in 1921, pays tribute to Collins as a man who labored in the cause of higher education "with scanty reward and no official academic recognition" (Great Britain 267). The board remembers him fondly as an unrequited hero because he represents for them what in 1921 they believed to be the proper direction for English education, that is, for a humane, liberal teaching of "English letters in their wider aspects and relations," defined along the "broad lines of classical culture" (267). While Collins did in fact manage to engage contemporaries in his cause, he also succeeded in alienating others who found him intemperate in his denunciation of the scientific or philological turn in English studies embodied in Oxford's newly established Merton Professorship of English Language and Literature (est. 1885).

Collins had put himself forward to be considered for the new professorship, but he, along with other prominent men of letters—Edmund Gosse, Edward Dowden, George Saintsbury, A. C. Bradley—was passed over and a philologist from the University of Göttingen was selected instead. Like Cambridge before it, Oxford offered a course of study in the embryonic stage of English literature rather than what Collins believed to be a course more appropriate for the preparation of teachers. Hoping to bring pressure to bear on the university, Collins instigated a debate in the popular press. Trained in the classics at Balliol College, he argued that English literature ought to be taught as the classics had been traditionally taught. But while he waged this battle to establish English studies as a continuation of a classical education, he was making his living coaching students for the civil service examinations and later serving as a university extension lecturer in English. Although he was thus engaged with the new students who would not have had, for the most part, a classical education and for whom pragmatic considerations were presumed to be uppermost, he nonetheless saw them as desiring the sort of education still available to the few.

As did Bain, Collins argues for a certain use of canonical texts in order to stake out territory. But Collins aligns himself with the ancient subjects and the reputable classics against the increasingly powerful upstart philology in order to define what the new discipline of English literature ought to be. And in the process, as was the case with Maurice and Bain, he recasts the received texts.

THE CHARMED CIRCLE, PART 2   115

Collins's starting premise is that the increased demand for the teaching of English coming from "all quarters" and "all classes" is the sign of a "great revolution in advanced education." Changes in the material conditions under which men and women live necessitate a change in systems of instruction. That change Collins describes as a return, a renewal. He senses a growing feeling among men and women that poetry, history, art, and philosophy ought to have the same "influential relation to the lives of English citizens as they [had] to the lives of the citizens in Athens and Rome." While such movements as the University Extension Scheme and the National Home Reading Union were attempts in that direction, they were liable to anarchy without guidance from some common center: "If culture of this kind is to be disseminated, it can be disseminated only by missionaries from a common centre, and that not casually, by one here and one there, but systematically, and as the reflective result of system" (Collins 2). But the universities, the logical choice for providing orderly and uniform instruction of teachers (or, as he calls them, revealingly, "missionaries"), are themselves divided. "Absolutely irresponsible, and absolutely autocratic" (1–3), Collins charges, Oxford and Cambridge have failed to alter their curricula so as to bring themselves "into direct contact with the life of our time" (viii).

Collins sets himself the task of pointing out to the Universities their "new duties and new responsibilities." In the past, Oxford and Cambridge exercised their influence over a relatively small sphere, but now, he urges, their influence is virtually "co-extensive with the kingdom." Given this sort of power, they must understand how best to wield it. Where once they helped shape popular education in religious terms, they must now help shape it in ethical, political and artistic terms. And no better "instrument" is at hand than "Literature," if—and here Collins puts the bunny in the hat—"if Literature include what it ought to include" (4). Like Philip Larkin's church, which no longer houses God but whose walls and windows remain to mark a place to house the powerful ("Church Going"), literature that is no longer a space for the religious may nonetheless enclose (signify) other powerful components of culture. The critical factors, however, are that the edifice must in some sense have already been sanctified, and that there must be curators (or curates) who understand how to interpret the structure aright.

Thus, while Collins offers a stirring litany of all that literature might effect for popular culture, he clearly predicates that effectiveness on a particular notion of what constitutes literature and a particular (liberal) approach to exegesis. As an instrument of political education, literature warns, admonishes, guides. As an instrument of moral and aesthetic education, it refines "taste," "tone," "sentiment," "opinion," and "character." But it can do so only if its boundaries are enlarged so that it includes political and philosophical treatises as well as what is "ordinarily included in *Belles Lettres*" (Collins 4–5).

In an outline for an ideal school of literature, Collins gives some idea of what literature broadly conceived might include. It is an outline that looks like the prototype for any number of twentieth-century anthologies of literature. That Collins offers no justification for his choices suggests that, while new as a curriculum, the outline was not new as a picture of the accepted view of at least a portion of the charmed circle. Collins's curriculum is divided into four categories: poetry, rhetoric, criticism, and general histories of literature. Under rhetoric, Collins includes oratory, historical composition, and miscellaneous prose—the last including, in addition to Platonic dialogues and the letters of Cicero and Pliny the Younger, several leading English writers from each century from the fourteenth to the nineteenth. Hooker is yoked to Sidney and Lyly as representing the later sixteenth century; Bacon is joined to Hobbes, Milton, and Sir Thomas Browne for the first half of the seventeenth (Collins 144–45).

That Collins must urge the inclusion of such works of prose suggests that some narrowing of the conception of literature had occurred in the passage from Maurice early in the century to Collins late in the century. Collins quotes the cardinal archbishop of Westminster approvingly for his broad definition of literature as including all the "intellectual product of cultivated nations" (100). And he urges that treatises such as Bacon's *Advancement of Learning* are as "purely art" as any great poem and as worthy of being studied as a work of art (40, 133, n.). But the form this urging takes—having to state that Bacon's prose is as much "art" as Keats's poetry—suggests the extent to which aesthetic criteria have already reduced the domain of literature.

But the primary enemy is not those who exclude prose from the field, but the philologists who, in Collins's caricature of them, are narrowly and exclusively interested in Mœso-Gothic, Icelandic, and Anglo-Saxon. With his opponent thus narrowly defined, Collins does not need to claim the Cardinal Archbishop's breadth to appear more inclusive in his aims than they. As in the case of Bain, it is clear that much of the defining of what constitutes literature operates not in some pure ether of theory but in the muck of territorial dispute. Noble goals are thus forged out of rather common human concerns. Collins wants to supplant the philological monopoly with a coalition formed of the "fading Greek" with the "master Classics" in English: "to encourage and prescribe such a study of Spenser and Shakespeare, of Milton and Wordsworth, of Bacon and Burke, as would attain the ends" that education "is calculated to attain" (149). Such a study would require, however, that literature be rescued from "its degrading vassalage to Philology" and given the same place of importance it held in ancient times.

True "classics"—both ancient and modern—are to be rescued from mere "verbal criticism" (rhetoricians such as Bain are thus indicted along with the philologists), and their true significance revealed through the sort of interpretation modeled by Lessing and Coleridge (Collins 61–62). Thus, in a move bearing some affinity to that of Maurice, though now in a secular rather than a religious cause, Collins argues that reading Bacon or Hooker or other classical authors requires placing greater emphasis on the "spirit" than on the "letter." This spirit is not Maurice's divine spirit but, more vaguely, the spirit of genius and/or the spirit of an age. In exegesis, one must not "dwell solely on what is accidental"—presumably what "verbal critics" do in concentrating on etymology, problems of interpolation and emendation, and the like. Instead, one must penetrate to "the essence which is the life" of a work (Collins 62). Employing the familiar metaphor of dissection, Collins argues that the scalpel wielded by the verbal scholar reveals only the "mechanism" of the body Literature; but a liberal, classical reading can "yield up the secret to [a work's] life" (62).

Collins thus argues that the function of the teacher of English (and of those who train teachers) is to interpret "power and beauty as they reveal themselves in language, not simply by resolving them into their constituent elements but by considering them in their relation to principles." In its privileging of principles, this is language reminiscent of Bain's. But Collins emphasizes that such an interpretative strategy involves more than noting what is "excellent" or "vicious" in form and style. The emphasis shifts from seeing literature as a vehicle for lessons religious or rhetorical to seeing literature as a means for communing with "the nobler manifestations of human energy, with the great deeds of history," with the "aristocrats of our race" (Collins 66). Style is thus important as a manifestation of the individual author's genius and the student is left to admire that genius (identified for him by the instructor) and to cultivate his own pale reflection of genius.

Collins reads Lessing and Coleridge as authorizing the view that literature consists of not everything that has been written but only those works that are the product of genius working on life to produce nourishment for the whole of the individual who partakes. The romantic conception thus leads him to suggest that the "principles" in terms of which literary works are to be interpreted have to do with the relative success of "genius" under a given set of circumstances. The teacher might confine himself to "reverent exposition" of the "luminaries"—Chaucer, Spenser, Shakespeare, Milton, Wordsworth—but in dealing with "lesser lights" he will "have to show how, in various degrees, defects of temper, the accidents of life, historical and social surroundings, and the like have obscured or distorted that vision which penetrates through the local and particular to the essential and universal" (Collins 52–53). The grand conception of an "instrument of culture" that will cultivate taste, educate the emotions, enlarge the mind, and stimulate and refine the whole man (65) is thus finally reduced, through Collins's version of the romantic conception of genius, to biography or psychology.

With each of the advocates of the teaching of English, a similar process is evident, a simultaneous opening out and closing, controlling, or confining. Collins urges that the universities make available to men and women from all classes a classical education—now broadened to encompass classics ancient and modern—via rigorously trained teachers. He urges that the universities make available good copies of Bacon, Hooker, Shakespeare, and Wordsworth through their publishing facilities so that the best of scholarship can be more widely disseminated (50–51). He believes that students can learn and appreciate a full range of culture. And his sense of the culture that literature will be an instrument for is clearly liberal. Culture both as the "process of intellectual, spiritual and aesthetic development" and as the products of the process—culture, that is, in the Arnoldian sense (Williams, *Keywords* 90–91)—appears in a generous and benign sense.

But there is the other side, and that side is made evident in Collins's yoking of the two phrases, "instruments of culture" and "instrument of discipline." Literature in being an instrument of culture is also an instrument of discipline, as is most evident in the examination system, and as such it is a fundamental part of the liberal agenda. It must be granted that *discipline* has a special sense in the debate over English education. Opponents of the teaching of English argued that, unlike the classics, English was not rigorous enough a field of study to fully discipline (educate or train) the faculties of the mind. Philology had served as a scientific rebuttal to that argument. Philology, in treating old and difficult texts in languages such as Celtic and Anglo-Saxon, established that it could supply as rigorous a discipline as did the study of Greek and Latin. The study of English literature past the embryo stage, however, still had to prove that it was more than "dilettantism." Collins thus must steer his course between the Scylla of "pedantry" on the one hand in the form of "verbal criticism" and the Charybdis of "Dilettantism" on the other hand in the form of vaporous appreciators (Collins 57). Thus he must argue that literature—broadly conceived—can discipline as well as Greek, Latin, or Mœso-Gothic. But discipline is part of the liberal project in a larger sense as well.

That Collins should have thought Matthew Arnold an acceptable substitute for himself to fill the Oxford chair in English literature is revealing. Collins shares with Arnold the larger sense of the disciplinary scope of culture. Collins calls teachers "missionaries," a metaphor that would suggest that the cultured must be sent to convert their unlettered countrymen (*Study* 2). But in some sense that metaphor is misleading. Throughout Collins's "plea" he registers the fear (expressed, as well, in Arnold) that the cultured are besieged—if not by "trade spirit," as Maurice would put it, then by a society that puts greater value on "technical and positive information" than on the cultivation of taste (26–27). Or, in the words of the Board of Education report, "We have a traditional culture, which comes down to us from the time of the Renaissance, and our literature, which is rich, draws its life-blood therefrom. But the enormous changes in the social life and industrial occupations of the vast majority of our people, changes begun in the sixteenth century and greatly accentuated by the so-called Industrial Revolution, have created a gulf between the world of poetry and the world of everyday life from which we receive our 'habitual impressions' " (Great Britain 258).

The traditional culture is threatened by those children of the Industrial Revolution who have not been acculturated. Something of this historical positioning, as we have seen, is evident in Leavis (see this book's introduction and chapter 4). There is no recognition, of course, that perhaps the culture has changed or that there might be multiple cultures. Nor is there the sense that guardians of tradition might stand as much in the way of closing the gulf between literature and the everyday world as might those valuing "technical and positive information," that perhaps the gulf in some sense defines literature as that which helps to mark the "us" in contradistinction to the "them." Rather, according to Collins, it ought to be the mission of newly formed English departments to train the teachers who will in turn discipline men and women from all quarters and all classes in an attempt to shore up the besieged traditional culture.

IV

Like Collins, Fred Newton Scott was concerned not only with the teaching of English but with preparing teachers to teach. And, like Collins, he was committed to a broad conception of English studies. He was also, like Bain, particularly interested in a "functional view" of rhetoric, that is, with the social importance of writing well (Kitzhaber 71–73). Scott coauthored a number of textbooks for high school and college in rhetoric, speech, and literary criticism; taught courses in journalism as well as in rhetoric and literature; served as president of the Modern Language Association and the National Council of Teachers of English; and published articles and pamphlets on composition, American English, teacher training, and style. Through much of his teaching and writing, he attempted to offer an alternative to the dominance of Harvard in determining what English studies in the American context should be.

Albert Kitzhaber sees Scott as an original thinker when compared to such other rhetoricians as Adams Sherman Hill, John Genung, and Barrett Wendell, who were fundamentally redactors of British writers. Scott, in contrast, according to Kitzhaber, "made a genuine effort to formulate a comprehensive system of rhetorical theory drawing on new developments in such related disciplines as experimental psychology, linguistics, and sociology" (69). James Berlin sees in Scott's blend of Emersonianism and American pragmatism an attempt to articulate "a new pedagogical paradigm, one that was distinctively American in its conception, addressing the problems peculiar to communicating in a democratic society" (Berlin 77). Both Kitzhaber and Berlin acknowledge that, however, despite some brief success in the 1890s, Scott was not able to counter the dominance of the narrowed approach to composition and rhetoric characteristic of the Harvard model (Kitzhaber 70; Berlin 77). Berlin, following Donald Stewart's lead, attempts to reclaim Scott for the present, to recreate him as progenitor for current alternative approaches to the teaching of writing. But such genealogical work is risky at best.

With each of the figures discussed here—Collins, Bain, Maurice, and Scott—there are familiar elements, parts of each writer's respective corpus that can be and have been made to speak to current concerns. But they do so most readily when some of the complexity—or, perhaps more accurately, the rather human inconsistency—of their positions is simplified. Scott, a University of Michigan professor, did position himself in opposition to what he understood to be the limitations of traditional (Eastern, Anglophilic) writing pedagogy. And he did so in the name of a more truly American (midwestern) English. But in reading his efforts as "modern and liberal" (Stewart 14) one needs, at the same time, to read them as responsive to the "social demands of a great industrial state" (qtd. in Stewart 17), as nationalistic, and as limiting in their emphasis on a natural order, a native tradition, and an unexamined notion of sincere and simple American English. Whether one likes it or not, Collins, Bain, Maurice, Scott, and a host of other primarily white male teachers of English shaped the discipline we live with today, but they did so not in any simple or innocent way. If one were allowed to choose one's parent, not one of these figures would be adequate to the present. The best they can do for us is to serve as cautionary tales, as partial historical explanation for contradictory institutional structures and practices.

By the time that Scott was teaching rhetoric at the University of Michigan, literature in its own right had gained enough strength (thanks in part to the dissemination of works such as Collins's *The Study of English Literature*) to loose itself from its "vassalage" to rhetoric. Throughout his career, however, Scott argued for the importance of seeing composition, rhetoric, and literary study as intertwined. Style provided an important link. For a number of years, he taught the course, "The Principles of Style" as part of his responsibilities in rhetoric and criticism and published a small pamphlet with the same title in 1890.

In general, Scott was interested in restoring rhetoric to its former central role in learning as a "broad humanistic discipline." Thus, the study of style was not simply the learning of rules of composition but involved, in its higher form, the exercise of imagination and feeling. As Kitzhaber puts it, "Scott not only was convinced that literary effects, no matter how subtle, are capable of being studied and explained, but he believed that it is the particular office of rhetoric to make this study" (93–94). In reading literature, the student would come to understand style in Emersonian terms as the expression of personality—the greater the personality, the greater the style. And in writing the student would learn that to write well he would need to write in such a way as to express his personality, just as a healthy organism radiates good health. Central to Scott's notion of style is his understanding of the organic relationship between the whole and its parts, an organicism that derives as much from Herbert Spencer, however, as it does from Emerson, both of whom Scott cites.

In 1892, Fred Newton Scott published his edition of Herbert Spencer's *The Philosophy of Style* for the use of rhetoric teachers. He introduced the essay with a biographical sketch of the still-living Spencer and an introduction placing the essay in relation to Spencerian philosophy as a whole. Scott is particularly concerned with retrieving Spencer's thoughts on style from a too-limited reading of Spencer's principle of economy:

> As commonly conceived from a reading of the essay, the principle of economy is in brief as follows: Thought cannot be conveyed from one individual to another save through an apparatus of symbols, to apprehend which requires some mental effort. Whatever energy, therefore, can be saved in interpreting the symbols, goes to the apprehension of the thought. The effectiveness of language as a bearer of thought is thus measured by the ease with which it gives up its contained idea. . . . In other words, the cheaper the cost of transmission, the larger the bulk of freight. (Scott, Introduction xviii–xix)

This principle is quite simple and "readily applicable to all forms of expression." But upon further reflection, Scott suggests, one can see that the principle, if taken in the abstract—"without proper reference to social conditions"—can in fact be misleading. There are, after all, two kinds of economy: simple accumulation without purpose by isolated individuals, and wise expenditure and investment. One cannot tell in the abstract whether the first is miserliness or dead loss: "So long as the individual is isolated, no standard can be applied. . . . Considering men as separate individuals whose relation one to another is of an accidental character, one cannot say whether the language they use is economical or otherwise" (Introduction xix).

In order to reclaim Spencer's treatise on style from this too-limited notion of economy, Scott invokes or, perhaps more accurately, reconstructs a Spencerian organicism: "The function of the parts, that is, figures, sentences, paragraphs, and composition generally, is inexplicable, or misapprehended, until they are given their proper place in the operation of the whole. . . . The content of any adequate theory of style must embrace all manner of expression in which there is adjustment of utterance to comprehension" (Introduction xviii). Scott finds this organicism in Spencer's writing on evolution, especially in his prospectus for a proposed "Principles of Sociology."

Emphasizing first the principle that the evolution of man and of society are both determined by "the action of circumstances," Scott then turns to Spencer's plan for the treatise on sociology in which Spencer includes, along with sections on "lingual," "intellectual," and "moral progress," a section on "aesthetic progress." Under this heading, he suggests such topics as "the origin and function of music" and "the philosophy of style." Scott understands such a classification system to signify, among other things, the extent to which style operates as a psychological phenomenon determined by social conditions. Spencer, admittedly, does not do much with this idea in the version of "The Philosophy of Style" published in the *Westminster Review* that Scott is reissuing in 1892. But Scott argues that Spencer's concept of style is retrievable only if read in such terms. This more complex principle of economy, that speaks more fruitfully to the issue of style, Scott derives from Spencer's notion of organicism in an essay on ethics: "Conduct is a whole, and, in a sense, it is an organic whole—an aggregate of inter-dependent actions performed by an organism. That division or aspect of conduct with which ethics deals is a part of this organic whole—a part having its components inextricably bound up with the rest" (Spencer qtd. in Scott, Introduction xvii).

Scott then works by analogy to extend Spencer's thinking: "Just as without the conception of an ethical organism, we have no standard for the ethical evaluation of conduct, so without the conception of an aesthetic or literary organism, we have no standard for the evaluation of art or literature . . . as the content of ethics embraces all conduct in which there is adjustment of acts to ends, so the content of any adequate theory of style must embrace all manner of expression in which there is adjustment of utterance to comprehension" (Introduction xviii). Economy of style, then, cannot be an absolute standard but must involve the judgment of how well utterance adjusts to the demands of comprehension in a given social context, and not as a matter of individual atom contacting individual atom: "Whether any given expression is an example of economy or of waste must be determined by inquiring what service it performs in maintaining the integrity of the organism, that is, in furthering the intellectual life of the whole community" (Scott, Introduction xx).

What appears to be the radical relativism of Scott's reading here (akin to the radical relativism of Darwin's theory of evolution, which posits no *telos*), is a potentiality only, titillating perhaps to late twentieth-century readers but not actualized in Scott's textbooks or in his articles. In the 1902 textbook, *Composition-Literature,* Scott and his coauthor, Joseph Denney, offer a reader-rhetoric for the more advanced classes in the secondary schools. There is little evidence of a socially embedded rhetoric here, even though there is the now long familiar injunction to imagine an audience for one's writing. The text is remarkably like both the earlier Collins Composition Books (see the Appendix) and Hall's later *Contemporary Essay* (see the introduction) in its emphasis on the individual writing out of his or her experience.

The textbook includes sections on "saying what you think," "how compositions grow" (rather like a description of the now familiar writing process), "structural elements of the composition," "figures of speech," and "forms of prose" (or modes of discourse). Under "saying what you think," the authors counsel that the writer "must be deeply and sincerely interested in his subject"; he should see things with his own eyes, think with his own mind, and have his "own sincere feelings." Then "the words will have an honest ring" (Scott, *Composition-Literature* 9). To get to this level of sincerity, students are instructed to read the most "successful men-of-letters" to see what they have to say about their own methods of writing as well as to see how they have practiced the craft.

The men of letters anthologized in the volume include a mix of mostly nineteenth-century British and American writers. Among the selections, however, is Bacon's oft-anthologized essay, "Of Studies." After the reading, the student is invited to make notes for an essay on a subject selected from a list including "a quiet street," "the danger of success," "the habits of squirrels," and the "ideal spot for a home." The student is to think of a person to whom to write, taking into account the person's age, "habits of thought," and "way of looking at things." In making notes, the student should try to think how best to interest this imagined other. What such an exercise has to do with Bacon's essay can only be inferred. Presumably, the essay on an ordinary subject—"of studies"—serves as model, but the relationship between such a model and the injunction to write only what one is most deeply and sincerely interested in is unclear. The editors do not show what "in" Bacon's writing is deeply interested and sincere. Nor do they show what other qualities of style the student should emulate. (Those readers of Bacon who see in his writing a Machiavellian calculation might find his redeployment as exemplar of sincerity particularly ironic.)

Bacon's essay "Of Despatch in Business" is later cited as providing further guidance in writing. "What Bacon said in his essay Of Despatch in Busines [sic] is true of planning a composition. 'Above all things,' said Bacon, 'Order and Distribution and Singling out of Parts is the life of Despatch; So as the Distribution is not too subtile. For he that doth not divide well will never enter well into Business; and he that divideth too much will never come out of it clearly.' As Bacon indicates, the plan should be simple and natural, and the divisions of the subject clear and well marked" (Scott, *Composition-Literature* 52). Following their own precepts, the editors look to Bacon to model through his writing but also to provide method. But again, just as what exactly Bacon is modeling is not made clear, so too how the editors get from Bacon's advice about dividing to a prescription to develop a simple and natural plan is not at all certain. Later, the editors will indicate that "natural" order has something to do with cause and effect, contiguity, and comparison/contrast (Scott, *Composition-*

Literature 66), conventional modes that are natural and simple only to the extent that their conventional familiarity makes them appear so. But the conventionalized character of the natural is not—and indeed cannot be—made explicit. Indeed, Scott here and elsewhere takes for granted the naturalness of language use, associating it with racial and national identity. He does not understand such identities as themselves constructions, great stabilizing abstractions that serve tautologically as defining points of reference for the teaching of English. The natural language derives from a notion of a people, race, or nation, categories that are themselves defined in terms of the natural language.

In discussing the training of teachers, Scott and his coauthors George Carpenter and Franklin Baker caution against viewing grammar instruction as "a study merely of abstract rules and formulas" and instead urge that teachers see it as the "underlying subject . . . virtually the same as that which underlies composition and literature, namely the expressive and communicative activities of the English-speaking race." In teaching grammar, then, the "chief duty is to awaken the minds of . . . students to the meaning of their own familiar modes of expression" (317). While it is familiar enough advice now to start with the students' "own" language, to tie discussion of grammar and usage to the students' living language, to help the student establish "ownership" of her language, it is important to resist too readily making Scott and his colleagues our pedagogical contemporaries, or perhaps put differently, it is important to defamiliarize Scott's advice long enough to critically read his (and our) practice.

The order or sequence of Scott's and his colleagues' advice suggests that grammar does not derive in any simple way from students' language. Grammar is not based on an empirical sampling of English speakers to determine the varieties of use but is based on an ideal. The nature of this ideal is perhaps most apparent in Scott's 1916 address to the National Council of Teachers of English on "The Standard of American Speech." He asks whether teachers should maintain some standard of American speech: "The idea of a fixed standard to be settled arbitrarily once and for all by some authority or set of authorities may be abandoned summarily. It is untenable, both in theory and practice. . . . It is of the essence of language to change" (7). But to oppose an arbitrary standard does not mean that teachers should abandon the possibility of a standard altogether. Instead of a single dialect (something Scott sees as elitist), Scott suggests instead a conception of a national style, taking his inspiration from Walt Whitman's *American Primer:*

> The subtle charm of beautiful pronunciation is not in dictionaries, grammars, marks of accent, formulas of a language, or in any laws or rules. The charm of the beautiful pronunciation of all words, of all tongues, is in perfect flexible vocal organs and in a developed harmonious soul. All words spoken from these have deeper, sweeter sounds, new meanings, impossible on any less terms. Such meanings, such sounds, continually wait in every word that exists—in these words—perhaps slumbering through years, closed from all tympans of temples, lips, brains, until that comes which has the quality patiently waiting in the words. (Whitman qtd. in Scott, "Standard" 9)

If we accept Whitman's doctrine, Scott exhorts, then we must understand that a great national language derives not from a prescriptivist grammar but from "the simple, homely expression of sincere feeling and sturdy thinking":

> Live nobly, think good thoughts, have right feelings, be genuine, do not scream or strain or make pretense, cultivate a harmonious soul—follow these injunctions, and you are laying the foundation of a standard American speech. Whence the speech comes does not matter. It may be the language of Potash or Perlmutter. It may be composed of all the dialects spoken in Chicago or in San Francisco. It may be the speech of Boston, of Texas, or of Montana. No matter. If it is the voice of high wisdom, of moderation, of human nature at its best, the words will take on that power and charm which is the test of a great national speech. ("Standard" 9)

Such an appeal to American pluralism has earned Scott the respect of such historians and teachers as Kitzhaber, Stewart, and Berlin. But it is well to consider what constitutes the Other in this hymn to a beautiful American language. What is the ugly that defines the beautiful?

If American speech at its best is "kindly, natural, unaffected," the linguistic Other is embodied for Scott in the Billy Sundays of the world, with their rant, pretense, vulgarity, sensationalism, and "orgiastic appeal." Beautiful American language is thus defined by its opposite, the "language of degeneracy," the language of the "abnormal" ("Standard" 9). But such degeneracy is not confined to hucksters and Bible-thumping preachers. In an essay, "English Composition as a Mode of Behavior," Scott looks at more ordinary forms of "degeneracy" by considering the sources of "error" in student writing. There are three such sources: the influence of spoken foreign languages (the melting pot that Scott extolls in his rhapsodic Whitmanesque description of American speech is at the same time a source of error); the breakup of "what may be called the family tradition" (that "bulwark against the forces which naturally tend to degrade and brutalize the vernacular"); and a clash between "the instinctive, inherited impulse to communication, and . . . the scholastic system of abstract symbolism . . . we now use in school" (465). It is this last that both Stewart and Berlin are drawn to as a sign of Scott's emphasis on the student's allegedly natural capacity to communicate, which is too often thwarted by traditional pedagogy. Unfortunately, the concept of the natural is not so easily separated from either Scott's xenophobia or his distaste for popular forms of communication that threaten the so-called family tradition. To be natural in Scott's discourse is to be highly cultivated, restrained (repressing desire, repressing sensuality in un-Whitmanlike fashion, one might say), and domesticated.

"Error" derived from "translation English" will eventually disappear, Scott predicts, but the more pernicious influences of newspapers, the telephone, the automobile, and the movie (the latter threatening to "corrupt even the speech of Great Britain") are far more difficult to combat. When families maintained more exclusive control over their young—with daily reading of the Scriptures, "earnest admonition . . . couched frequently in conventional but nevertheless elevated language," and the exclusion of "lighter forms of literature"—they were able to maintain "a certain tone and choiceness and gravity of speech that are the essential characters of a national idiom." But the family has been invaded by cheap reading matter—

"some of it good, some of it neutral, some of it . . . of the silliest possible character." Newspapers bring much that is vital to modern civilization, but they also bring "smartness, slang, sensation, flippancy, and insincerity—qualities that are like poison to the body of our national speech." The telephone brings with it the "curt unmannerly summons"; the automobile transports people from their former relative isolation to the "heart of the many-languaged metropolis." Each of these modern innovations plays a part in the "life and progress of the Republic," but "their reactions upon the mother-tongue are, to say the least, disconcerting." "They operate to confuse the standards of usage, to syncopate the natural rhythms of the language, and to unfit the common speech for the expression of noble feeling and sustained thought. It is the business of the teacher to watch them and wherever their influence is baleful to seek to counteract it" ("English Composition" 465–66).

Only after warning against the evils of modernity does Scott turn to the students' "instinctive, inherited impulse to communication." That "natural" impulse, then, has to be seen as a capacity requiring careful cultivation and protection against the jazzy syncopation of contemporary life. In fact, Scott does not say that students should not learn the "scholastic system of abstract symbolism . . . that we now . . . regard as indispensable as a medium of culture" ("English Composition" 467). He grants that such a system is "indispensable in education of any sort . . . the mode by which culture has always been and always will be acquired and imparted." Scott's complaint is not with what in current parlance we would call academic discourse but with the way it has been taught. Put most simply, Scott argues that one cannot assume that the student is an empty vessel ready to be filled with proper academic language. To cultivate their linguistic capacities requires "finding in the [student's] impulse to untrammeled communication, in spite of its seeming waywardness, the vague beginnings of a sense for unity, for symmetry, for restraint, for proportion" and adding to this "symbolic apparatus the ideas of sociability and quick communication." How precisely to do this Scott in this article does not presume to say ("English Composition" 468–69).[2] He finds it difficult, as have English teachers before and after him, to imagine how to cultivate what is conceptualized as "natural" (what is already inherently there in the student), how to civilize, order, and control what might otherwise degenerate into "error," defined as deviance from a domestic, native, noble standard. Natural is defined in terms of the nation and a people; however, that nation and that people do not just naturally use the language that is definitively theirs but must be taught how and must be protected from foreign and corrupting influences.

V

The American pedagogue Scott, like the British advocates of the teaching of English—Collins, Bain, and Maurice—wanted to teach English to a "new" population. Scott wanted to shape a new discipline, but in choosing what and how to teach and in defending the new discipline while attempting to alter the academic study of the vernacular, he nonetheless reinscribed what can only be read as antidemocratic dichotomies. Whitman's comprehensive embrace of Everyman is romantically invoked, only to be taken away again, as normative style is defined in opposition to the living American language that is sometimes intemperate, brash, jazzy, polyglot. The teaching of the native tongue to the natives, for all four advocates, requires ordering and controlling what otherwise might be anarchic. Normative style—whether in service of state, church, or secular education, literature for its own sake, or American English—is constructed to resist such anarchy.

All four advocates relied on academic traditions, which had in fact precluded the very students they hoped to train. The works of Hooker or Bacon would not be in themselves counter to the teaching of any population. But in the course of attempting to justify the new discipline, advocates relied on traditional and class-marked conceptions of culture such that Hooker and Bacon (especially Bacon) were deployed simultaneously as instruments not only of change but for consolidating a culture perceived to be under seige. The apparently generous desire to open up the avenues to culture is inevitably joined to the perceived need to discipline in order to shore up that culture. The desire to preserve the past and make that past available to the present and future becomes intertwined with the effort to control "for their own good" the acculturation of groups of people who desire to be educated. And that effort is intertwined with the desire to protect the often idealistically conceptualized traditional culture. The commitment to find the best, the most scientific ways to educate people is intertwined with an effort to define a new area of study, to mark off territory. And that effort to mark off territory is intertwined with the process of admitting works into the canonical circle. The institutionalization of English study is thus marked by the tension between change and preservation, between enabling "new" students and controlling those students, between creating a new discipline and justifying that new discipline in terms of its adherence to traditional processes of learning and traditional values.

This history of tensions provides what might be called a genealogical record of interests for the study of English, a record of interests that have shaped the discipline and shaped what and how we teach. It is evident in the readability movement—the desire to teach new clientele a more "appropriate" style justified in part through a reconstruction of the past in the form of a canonical figure such as Bacon. It is evident in E. D. Hirsch's justifying, through the use of a history of prose style, a "new" pedagogy in answer to a "new" literacy crisis. Literature is conceived in the nineteenth century as an instrument of culture and continues to operate as such. But to the extent that culture is the province of a defining authority rather than the ongoing construction and reconstruction of an entire collectivity, the liberal spirit that would have all women and men from all quarters and classes to partake of culture inevitably is compromised.

4

"Eliot's 'Axe to Grind'"
Locating Origins

Doesn't plainness of style, and the epistemological naiveté
it suggests thus function as a guarantee of profound identity, . . . across a gulf which we call history but which by the
very nature of this very claim to intelligibility is nothing
more than the deployment of sameness along a chronological
axis? . . . Plain style works as a mask, or at best a detour.

Francis Barker, "The Tremulous Private Body"

I must looke as nature, speake as custome, and think as
gods good spirit hath taught me, judg you howsoever either
of my mind, or of my stile, or if you will of my looke also.

Richard Hooker in answer to A Christian Letter

Here . . . is the first distemper of learning, when men study
words and not matter; whereof, though I have represented
an example of late times, yet it hath been and will be *secun-
dum majus et minus* in all time. . . . It seems to me that
Pygmalion's frenzy is a good emblem or portraiture of this
vanity: for words are but the images of matter; and except
they have life of reason and invention, to fall in love with
them is all one as to fall in love with a picture.

Francis Bacon, The Advancement of Learning, Book 1

In a lecture delivered at Cambridge in 1967, entitled "Eliot's 'Axe
to Grind,' " F. R. Leavis attempts to make sense of Eliot's famous
phrase, "the dissociation of sensibility." He offers a rather tidy assertion by way of beginning. "About the causes of the process of
'dissociation' Eliot says very little. He is aware (as who is not?)
that civilization underwent something like a total change in the
seventeenth century" (91). Some seismic, cultural, discursive shift

is supposed to have occurred sometime in the late Renaissance: F. D. Maurice locates here the origins of a peculiarly English, homely, and native tongue; P. O. Kristeller sees in this period an epistemological shift from the poetic to the prosaic; Foucault also names this as a hinge period, a shift in *episteme;* Eliot finds a "dissociation of sensibility." How one situates oneself in relation to this apparent shift marks one's stance in regard to the modern. Eliot not only names it, but attempts to look over and past it, as if over a fence, to a time before—to the Elizabethans, to the metaphysical poets, to Hooker, Lancelot Andrewes, to Bacon—to writers who represent values that might be reclaimed and redeployed in order to reform the modern. In the case of Hooker and Bacon as fathers of the modern philosophic prose style, however, so much of what counts as "Hooker" or "Bacon" is determined materially and ideologically by the supposed seismic shift that, in attempting to reclaim them, Eliot (and I take him as representative) reinscribes the "dissociation" he appears to want to resist. He accepts as definitive the dichotomizing terms made possible by the apparent shift.[1]

All eight books of Hooker's *Of the Laws of Ecclesiastical Polity,* though composed in the late sixteenth century, were not available until after the Restoration of 1660, and it is then that Hooker is "cleansed" of the "dust of controversy" and recognized not only for his "vindicat[ion of] the CHURCH OF ENGLAND, As truly *Christian* and duly *Reformed*" but also for his judiciously moderate discourse (Gauden). One might make a similar case for Bacon, that it is only after the Restoration, with the establishment of the Royal Society, that Bacon is cleansed of any taint of religious radicalism and offered up as the father of a secular English science and a "Methodically, Manly, Elegant, Pertinent" speech (Archbishop Tenison, 1667, qtd. in Vickers, *Bacon* 233–34). The originary style that both men represent begins in some sense not with their biological persons but with a tradition-building that is underway within a generation of their deaths, a tradition-building that has a great deal to do with silencing dissent and establishing a more reasonable and orderly national climate in which one could get on with business.

Marilyn Butler has argued that inventing a tradition is part of an effort to maintain one's legitimacy and "someone else's lack of it." One's "mythical past" serves as a "defensive strategy in a real present" (39). The preceding discussions of the readability movement and the construction of English as a university discipline suggest something of the conflicted notions of a present that has been legitimized in part through an invention of a mythical past, a past read in terms of the beginnings of a more objective, reasoned, moderate language, a language of the people, purer, more natural, closer to truth and to things as they are, trustworthy. To return to that past, then, is to find that it is itself a present inventing a past to justify its practice, and that one could continue this infinite regress, looking at how, for example, both Hooker and Bacon construct a past (and so on). To deconstruct the originary move, however, is less my interest than to challenge the history-making that depends on it and to challenge those practices that are legitimized by it.

F. R. Leavis offers a useful (and ultimately critical) characterization of the presumed seismic shift and its relation to prose style. The prose first established and put into general use in "Dryden's hey-day" was a "prose of common currency—lucid, logical, business-like and idiomatic":

> When we ask how it was that modern prose appeared so decisively in the first decade of the Restoration, with an effect of having prevailed over-night, the answer is an account of the total movement of civilization that then, after twenty years of civil war and Commonwealth, made itself felt as the decisive start of a new age, and the sure promise of triumphant human achievement. A modern prose, the product of the conditions—something like a new civilization—represented by the new status of London, was there when the Court came back, and the Restoration gave it the endorsement of the characteristic positive ethos that so rapidly defined itself and established its dominance. (93–94)

All these positive—confident, unqualified, and *positivist*—forces of change that Leavis sees as having been at work through the century came together to begin "the triumphant advance towards the civilization, technological and Benthamite, that we live in" today (95). Nineteenth-century Benthamites such as Lord Brougham or utilitarians such as Alexander Bain would have seen such an advance as indeed the sign of progress. But coming from F. R. Leavis, "triumphant advance" has to be read ironically.

Leavis turns to the Royal Society to bring into relief what is amiss in this "triumphant advance." He wants to argue for the "concrete livingness, the immediacy of sensuous and life-charged presentation" more characteristic of the writing before the seismic shift that he believes was crushed by the "positive culture" that followed. The post-Restoration ethos, as Leavis reads it, amounted to a "blank denial of creativity—creativity as an inescapable fact of life" (97–99).

Citing Thomas Sprat's *History of the Royal Society of London* (1667), Leavis comments on the well-known passage describing the prose style sanctioned by the society: "a close, naked, natural way of speaking—positive expression, clear senses, a native easiness, bringing all things as near the mathematical plainness as they can, and preferring the language of artisans, countrymen, and merchants before that of wits and scholars." Leavis sees the passage as significant because it "testifies to the nature and strength of the new ethos" and, perhaps as importantly, because it seems to shift unawares from one set of criteria to another: from "close, naked and natural" and "native easiness," to "mathematical plainness" and then again to "the language of artisans . . . and merchants." Leavis argues that "The intellectual and methodological ideals associated with the Royal Society and the great name of Newton consort, as if belonging to the same realm, with criteria of polite manners, commonsense and social reasonableness. This is the age of Locke and the Glorious Revolution, and of Dryden, the great poet who showed what it was to be 'correct' (and what does 'correct' mean?)" (94–95). Leavis hits on something of the ideological muddle normative style presents. The assumption that "mathematical plainness"—mathematics as a constructed abstraction—can be part of a "native easiness"—something one does with ease and yet in this context is of necessity a *studied* easiness crafted to appear as if it were effortless,[2] and the assumption that this native/studied easiness is the language of artisans, countrymen, and merchants (even though the Royal Society consisted "chiefly of gentlemen" [Sprat, *History of the Royal Society, Complaint* 745]), suggests the extent to which the Royal Society's project for reforming the language of *scientia* was, as with all such claims, necessarily "tainted by the contingencies of the world in which they were made" (Street 40). Calls for linguistic reform were intertwined with a reaction against the perceived chaos of the civil wars and the Interregnum (cf. Williamson 303), along with efforts to garner institutional support from the Crown and from other patrons, jockeying among various institutions to claim what would count as knowledge, educational reform, a commodifying of knowledge, and a cultivation of nationalistic interests by asserting that the English—the native stock, calling to mind similar arguments in the nineteenth century—were fully capable of competing in the European intellectual market.

Whether or not one wants to argue for the reality of a moment before the positivist muddle, when creativity still thrived, Leavis's reading of the mixed motives of post-Restoration stylistic reform gets at the complex process through which figures such as Hooker and Bacon are constructed to serve as stylistic exemplars. It is helpful to consider the extent to which discursive domains we now take to be discrete—religion, science, literature—were only then in the process of becoming so. Educational reform is difficult to distinguish from religious controversy, which is tied to shifts in political power, changes in family structure, and realignments in the economy. To the extent that language both reflects and makes possible a way of seeing the world, stylistic reform is produced by and supportive of this matrix. But the materials made use of by reformers were not new. Seismic shifts (to stay with the geological metaphor) are made out of forces and materials that have been in place. The Elizabethan and early Stuart periods were themselves marked by a rather remarkable preoccupation with language, "by a complex array of attempts to reconceptualize, reform, and reconstitute language as an instrument in the service of the mind, the spirit, and the social order" (Bauman 1). Figures such as Hooker and Bacon were treated in the post-Restoration period not simply as relics of a dead past but as writers whose work could be put to new use. Their work was monumentalized and, at the same time, transformed into living work, matter to work on, for a new age.

Hooker's *Laws* has been read traditionally as a moderate defense of or, more precisely, a reasoned argument for a particular version of the established church under Queen Elizabeth. W. Speed Hill has argued that Hooker's lifework "was conceived as an attempt to cleanse of every ambiguity and to ground in all possible certainty [a] fundamental truth of human experience" ("Doctrine" 193). But such a view of Hooker as representing religiopolitical and stylistic moderation had to be constructed by the post-Restoration episcopate, some sixty years after the death of Elizabeth I. Only after the collapse of Elizabeth's via media—her delicately balanced church compromise—and after the noise of battle had subsided, when the Restoration church attempted to vindicate itself after the abortive puritan Rule of Saints, was Hooker's work recast as a document that in its very reasonableness could speak for a new era hungry for peace and stability.

John Gauden, Bishop of Exeter, published in 1662 for the first time the full eight books of the *Laws* (only five were published during Hooker's lifetime). In commending the whole of the *Works* to the newly restored king, Charles II, Gauden refers specifically to the fact that the last three books had been so long "concealed" that they had been kept from the public eye. It appears likely that such had been the case, but it was apparently the church hierarchy itself that had done the concealing, rather than seditious sectaries, as the seventeenth-century biographer Isaac Walton later suggested.

Gauden suggests that Hooker's newly restored work is a "great and impregnable shield" for the "still crazy Church of England," providing a "treasury and an armoury" of those "rules and proportions of true Polity." Throughout Gauden's prefatory addresses the emphasis is on the potential stabilizing and pacifying qualities of Hooker's writings. He notes that when the first four books of the *Laws* first appeared in 1593, the work had had quite the opposite effect: that is, because the opposing party could not "answer" Hooker's book, "they conspired at last to betake themselves to

Arms." Now, Gauden is conflating a series of events—from the appearance of the books in 1593 to the beginnings of civil war in the
1640s—emphasizing the unreasonableness, indeed the failure to
perceive reasonableness, that led to "our late troubles." In another
time and place, the same work that Gauden hopes will now bring
peace and reconciliation was a spur to arms. But with the king
and church restored, with those who took up arms defeated,
Hooker's work can help provide "Christian Moderation and Sea-
sonable Charity" duly executed with "Justice, and impartiality"
(Gauden, dedicatory epistle n.p.). According to Gauden's account,
it is what stands outside the text that makes the text work in a particular way; some external power defines the possibilities of the
text. In such terms, moderation is a quality that is evident "in" a
text only when opposition is silent, only when opposition capitu-
lates or is defeated.

The language that has canonically been applied to Hooker
and is particularly evident in Gauden—the language of moderation, judiciousness, impartiality—is embedded in a particular political and religious context, a context that is necessarily partial.
The context shifts a bit with Izaac Walton's edition of 1666, sponsored by the Restoration episcopate in order to "correct" some of
Gauden's errors, specifically to cast doubt on the authenticity of
the later books, which could have proved embarrassing to the
reestablished church. Gauden may have thought that the publication of the seventh book, with its "ambiguous position on apos-
tolic succession and on the divine right of bishops" (Novarr 218),
would help make the Restoration more palatable to Presbyterians
and Independents, who had the most to lose with the reestablish-
ment of the episcopacy (Houck 145–46). But, as Houck puts it,
"the time for compromise . . . had not arrived" (146). Instead,
the church leaders, in authorizing a new edition with Izaac Walton's famous life of Hooker appended, hoped not merely to vindicate the episcopal form of church government but to silence
opposition.

The Restoration not only redirected publishing efforts to
make it appear that the *true* church had been rescued along with
the hereditary Crown, but there was also an effort to wrest control

of the new learning from revolutionary Puritans and parliamentarians. While few material changes in education had been effected during the revolutionary period—the civil wars and the Commonwealth had disrupted social institutions and there was not time enough for new institutions or practices to emerge—there was nonetheless a surge of publications on educational reform. Some radical Protestants had seen during the brief interregnum the possibility of not only a new kind of government—a Rule of Saints—but a new kind of educational system that might allow men (and, for some radical reformers, women as well) to reclaim what had been lost through the Fall of Man. "Educational optimists" argued for universal schooling "in English rather than Latin, and with a pious and practical curriculum . . . to usher in a new social order" (Cressy, *Education* 10). Such reformers found in Bacon's work support for their interests, especially what they read as his "charitable learning"—a " 'duty' toward the world rather than toward the 'private and particular' " (Briggs 7). The secular utilitarianism that post-Restoration Baconians seem to epitomize for Leavis and others required that they put aside what the pre-Restoration educational reformers found so appealing in Bacon's apparent Christianity.

Throughout Sprat's *History of the Royal Society*, there is mention of the formative desires of the founding members to "converse in quiet one with another, without being engaged in the passions and madness of" the Interregnum, to arm against the "enchantments of enthusiasm," to appeal to *disinterested* men, to avoid "spiritual frenzies" (736). The founding members "pitched upon" natural philosophy, finding their inspiration in Bacon's plan for the instauration of learning, as an alternative to—a "fitter subject" than—theology. They wanted a society where they could differ "without any danger of civil war" and where the excesses of the "gloomy season" of regicide, war, and disruption could be avoided (737). The close, naked, natural style, the desire for naturalness and mathematical plainness that Leavis rightly sees as at odds with itself, is perhaps best read, then, as reaction against excess, enthusiasm, and conflict, perhaps not the death of creativity but an understandable retreat from disorder. In turning to Bacon, the Royal Society drops out the Christian zealousness read in his work by the radical Protestants and finds instead the "one great man, who had the true imagination of the whole extent of this great enterprise as it is now set on foot": a defense of experimental philosophy, directions for promoting that philosophy, and the call for a language that would do the double work of science, developing and promoting learning (Sprat, *History of the Royal Society* 879).

Such a redeployment of Hooker and Bacon in the service of moderation and mathematical control is a matter not of misreading or distortion but of taking what is a potentiality in both writers and foregrounding it, and in the process dropping out what does not fit, what is troubling or ambiguous. Both Hooker and Bacon attempted to redirect attention away from excessive interest in words and toward the matter at hand. They posed themselves as, in some sense, reluctant rhetoricians, understanding the necessity of rhetoric in a fallen world and displaying their rhetorical dexterity but wanting to get at the matter at hand, whether it be church polity or the instauration of learning. Such ironic and perhaps inevitable doubleness (one might think of George Herbert's "Jordan" poems, as well) led contemporaries and subsequent readers to persist in returning to the question of style, bracketing the matter at hand, reading it in terms of style. Hooker's and Bacon's works were not immune to the ideology of style that ahistoricizes and attempts to remove works from the dust of controversy. Indeed, both writers contributed to efforts to monumentalize their own works, to preserve them for posterity, to protect them from attack; and subsequent readers and partisans were ready to redeploy those newly monumentalized works in support of other projects, other agendas. But in the pre-Restoration period, their works were perhaps more volatile, multivalent, and polysemic than they would be again (with the exception perhaps of the recent postmodernist readings of Bacon [cf. Perez-Ramos, Whitney, Gillespie]).

Such volatility is evident in early responses to Hooker's and Bacon's works. The earliest printed response to Richard Hooker's *Of the Laws of Ecclesiastical Polity* (Books 1–5) begins and ends with a highly charged critique of Hooker's style. The anonymous *A Christian Letter,* published in 1599, employs familiar images of lapsarian trickery, placing style within a constellation of words having to do with deception. In his unpublished marginal notes to the letter, Hooker dismisses what he labels as "invectives against my stile" as having no more importance than if the anonymous writers were to have criticized his looks (Booty 71). Hooker attempts to claim for himself a style as natural as his countenance, a style that is virtually no style at all and certainly of little consequence in determining his relative orthodoxy. Hooker asks that his readers pay attention to what he has to say, rather than how; he asks that they attend to the reasonableness of his arguments.[3]

Francis Bacon's oft-quoted charge that men have for too long sought "more after words than matter" can be read as a similar kind of gesture, as a by-then familiar dismissal of undue attention paid to the dress rather than the ideas themselves. In Bacon's figured (styled) prose, what began in the "last age"—in the early Renaissance—as a reasonable concern for translating newly discovered works by ancient authors and a desire to more effectively preach to the broad range of humankind, "grew speedily to an excess . . . for men began to hunt . . . more after the choiceness of the phrase, and the round and clean composition of the sentence, and the sweet falling of the clauses, and the varying and illustration of their works with tropes and figures, than after the weight of matter, worth of subject, soundness of argument, life of invention or depth of judgment" (*Advancement* 24).

As with Hooker's readers, the contemporaries and near contemporaries of Bacon, who were traditionally trained in rhetoric, understood this charge in rhetorical—i.e., political, social, and religious rather than simply idealist—terms. Neither Bacon nor Hooker suggested that there was some possibility in this fallen world of a language of pure denotation to the extent that the pure word was God's alone. Their contemporaries understood that one could pay *more or less* attention to words as opposed to matter, and that how one measured degrees of attention, degrees of style-consciousness, was a matter of judgment, a matter of dispute. Ironically, perhaps, one might have to pay attention to style in order to argue that one's predecessor or one's opponent was paying too much attention to language and hence was distracting his audience from the more important issue at hand or was not living up to his own precepts. Two pre-Restoration texts—the attack on Hooker by the anonymous writers of *The Christian Letter* and Gilbert Wats's translation of Bacon's *De Augmentis Scientiarum*—suggest the volatility from which the post-Restoration (and most subsequent readers) turned.

I

The style of Hooker's *Laws* was read by the writers of *The Christian Letter* as both a sign of Hooker's relative proximity to Christian truth and his divergence from established and acceptable practice. Given the near identity of church and state polity, then, Hooker's style, to the extent that his work was officially endorsed by the church hierarchy, served as a troubling gauge by which to judge shifts in the religiopolitical climate. Hooker's marginal notes, which are evidence of a planned (but apparently never published) answer to the charges raised by the *Letter,* and William Covel's "authorized" response, *A Just and Temperate Defence of the Five Books of Ecclesiastical Policie,* published in 1603, after Hooker's death, both suggest the extent to which the *Laws* were viewed by Hooker and his supporters as requiring defense to be understood aright. Clearly, the two levels of defense are related: to defend the church, Hooker's work must be heard. To the extent that style is the site for a defense of the text as text, it is also then a site for the defense of the church. Thus, style operates as a kind of displacement for (a mask or detour around, to use Barker's language) the larger issue of the struggle over the control of the emerging Church of England.

That style would be an issue at all is an indication that the disputants were educated, literate men. While more men were entering the universities under the Tudors to fill the ranks of the growing government bureaucracy, education was still only available to the few. But for those few, style as a central component—sometimes the primary component—of rhetorical study was an issue of some concern. And it was an issue already ideologically laden. Because sixteenth-century English education from the schools to the universities was dominated by the study and practice of rhetoric (cf. Curtis; Lanham, *Renaissance Rhetoric;* McDiarmid; Slaton; Vickers, *Classical Rhetoric*), it is likely that the anonymous writers shared with Hooker an intimate familiarity with humanist and residual scholastic conceptions of style. An acute consciousness of style was a natural consequence of the sort of education common to both. But in the latter part of the century, particularly with a surge of publications in the 1580s and 1590s, Ramist rhetoric, challenging fundamental tenets of humanism, gained in popularity—"Ramist textbooks were a runaway printing and teaching success" (Grafton and Jardine 161)—particularly among Puritans, who desired continued and greater reform of the English church (McDiarmid 231–32). Among those who have been identified as Ramists or sympathetic to the Ramist brand of pragmatic humanism were two important Puritan figures against whom Hooker argued from the pulpit and in print, Walter Travers (whom Bacon heard preach) and Thomas Cartwright (McDiarmid 273–74). The writers of the *Letter,* identifying themselves as aligned with men such as Travers and Cartwright, also share in Ramist sympathies.

Though in some respects an amalgam of humanism and scholasticism, Ramism was perceived by English opponents and advocates alike to offer a challenge to older conceptions of the relationship between matter and manner. Roger Ascham, for example, in 1550 notices Ramus's opposition to "narrow stylistic Ciceronianism"—to one aspect, in other words, of the humanist program—and later, Gabriel Harvey, friend of Sir Philip Sidney and a reformist Protestant, in his Ramist redactions emphasizes the anti-Ciceronianism of the new rhetoric, urging his audience to "unite dialectic and knowledge with rhetoric, thought with language" (McDiarmid 232, 237, 242). John McDiarmid has characterized Ramus's anti-Ciceronianism as a "linguistic expression of . . . anti-authoritarianism" (237). And it may be that such an expression combined with a functionalist view of rhetoric contributed to the appeal of Ramist thought for Puritans.

Of course, the suspicion of style expressed by many Puritans has antecedents in non-Ramist and pre-Ramist theories and practices. And suspicion of style is hardly confined to Puritans. As R. F. Jones has noted, throughout the sixteenth and seventeenth centuries Roman Catholic and Protestant texts abound in comments to the effect that verbal ornamentation in particular and rhetoric more generally have no place when discussing matters of divine truth ("Moral Sense of Simplicity" 267–68, 271–73). But in the Elizabethan period, the most visible opponents of stylistic display were men of Puritan leanings, men in particular who saw the simplicity of Scripture to be the truest model for pulpit oratory as well as written discourse. In the latter part of the century, it is chiefly Puritans who identify themselves explicitly with Ramist positions, and (equally important for the present discussion) it is men who oppose puritan or presbyterian views, men such as Hooker, who also oppose themselves to Ramist notions of language (McDiarmid 273).

The issue here, it should be noted, is not that expressed adherence to Ramist ideas necessarily led to a different sort of writing. Walter Ong argues that "there is little evidence . . . that anything very new and distinctive resulted immediately from Ramus' . . . prescriptions regarding actual style" (283). McDiarmid supports Ong's contention, noting by way of example that "Harvey, whose thought was crucially affected by Ramus, could write in ways essentially undistinguishable from ones which a Humanistic background might have encouraged" (271). For one thing, Ramist rhetoric was not essentially "anti-rhetorical." But Ramus, who was himself a Protestant of reformist tendencies, provided a "rational method," considered to be "natural, truthful and scientific" (McDiarmid 274; Jardine, "Place" 58), that appealed to Puritans who tended to be antirhetorical and especially to those university-trained Puritans who felt the need to bring reason to bear in teaching divine truth (Perry Miller 67). One might not be able to differentiate between disputants in the Elizabethan religious controversies purely on the basis of stylistic analysis, but one could note the differences in what disputants *said* about their own or their opponents' style.

Style in this sense refers only loosely to anything empirically available in a text, to any particular formal arrangement of words, but operates rather as a more generalized term of valuing or devaluing. Thus, for the writers of *A Christian Letter*, the fact as they see it that Hooker's writing calls attention to its style is a sign that his work wears popish colors, whether or not one could distinguish Hooker's sentence structure or favorite idioms from, for example, the Presbyterian Thomas Cartwright's, or could find stylistic affinities between Hooker and some English Catholic. Raymond Houck has expressed the doubt that any stylistic analysis could be "sufficiently minute to differentiate [Hooker's] style from that of certain of his contemporaries who were trained in the same schools and writing on the same subjects" (90, n. 19). But minute stylistic analysis was not the issue for the writers of the *Letter*, any more than it was for Hooker's nineteenth-century High Church editor, John Keble. Rather, that the writers were conscious of the style of Hooker's writing as deviation augmented their sense that his defense of the church was deviation as well.

Similarly, Hooker's rhetorically clever rejoinder that his style is no more than nature, custom, and God have taught him places the anonymous writers in the position of caring more for style than matter and therefore of being far less precisian than they purport to be, whether their writing can be analyzed as having been styled popishly or no. Hooker places himself firmly within the humanist rhetorical tradition: style as the image of the individual mind, but also the image of a particular culture, the "product of a time and a society" (McDiarmid 285). His style is natural in the sense of having been learned in the normal course of being a member of a particular culture. He writes as any learned man would write, making full use of the gifts of reason bestowed upon him by God. In a sense, then, Hooker attempts to put style out of play, to dismiss style as an issue. If Hooker's style is the norm, if it is a given—God-given and society-given—then it cannot be a sign of anything other than membership in a divinely sanctioned human community.

That Hooker might like his audience to attend to the matter at hand, rather than judge him according to his style, does not of course prevent his readers from doing otherwise. Although there were those among his contemporaries who supported his project, relatively few contemporary or near-contemporary references to what the post-Restoration will call the "judicious divine" exist (Wall 112). Covel's defense of Hooker was written in direct response to the *Christian Letter* and answers that letter point by point, as was the convention for controversial writings, rather than offering what might be viewed as a more spontaneous expression of the recognition of Hooker's "virtuous" style. It is not until the 1650s, with Jeremy Taylor's praise of Hooker (Wall 112), and more fully after the Restoration with, first, Bishop Gauden's edition of the full eight books of the *Laws* in 1662, and then Izaac Walton's edition in 1665, that praise of Hooker's work, including praise for his moderation, dignity, and judiciousness of style— what has become the commonplace reading of him—becomes abundantly evident. The *Christian Letter* is important, then, not only as the first printed response but as one of the few contemporary responses available.[4]

Booty has characterized the authors of the letter as "conforming Puritans, Calvinist, antipapal, anti-Arminian, alarmed by the new teachings at Cambridge and in Hooker's *Laws*" (xxv). *Puritan* is here used to denote all those Protestants who wished to see the church further reformed, who wished to see the church rid of any remaining traces of popery. But for others within the church, further reformation threatened the peace and stability not only of the church but of the nation. Further reformation, it was feared, might lead to fragmentation, to the proliferation of separatist churches no longer under the control of the monarch and the educated clergy. Separatism raised the specter of chaos, of churches run by the rabble, of churches run by any man or woman who felt moved to preach.

Conforming members of the church attempted to run a middle course between the "twin threats," as Peter Lake calls them, of separation and popery (77). But that middle course could be variously defined. The writers of the *Letter* fear that Hooker runs too close to popery, and Hooker fears that the writers of the *Letter* run too close to schism. Each in attacking the other attempts to define the middle. Elizabeth's via media can be seen in this light not as a single course but as multiple, competing courses in negotiation. The *Laws* and the *Letter* are instances of such negotiation, of a jockeying for the power to say what the established church would be. Within this larger religious struggle, the "struggle for the middle ground," as Peter Lake has called it (77), style operates as one of several ways of labeling and positioning one's opposition.

A consensus was possible as long as men who desired a presbyterian form of church government could quietly go about the business of organizing, forming district conferences, helping to choose ministers, gathering general synods in London, and petitioning Parliament (Neale 322–23). A consensus was possible as long as men could differ on matters of faith and preachers ordained outside of the episcopal hierarchy could quietly minister to their flocks without minute adherence to articles of faith. But Archbishop Whitgift was not satisfied with tacit acceptance of the general principles of the Church of England, and he certainly could not accept the developing presbyterian organization, however quiet. Rather, Whitgift demanded complete conformity. When some two hundred ministers refused to swear complete allegiance to the established church, they were suspended. Whitgift created the Court of High Commission, an ecclesiastic court that did not follow the practices of the common law, "had no jury and forced suspects to swear that they would answer questions truthfully" (Willson 287), in order to further press for conformity. An act of 1593 imposed the death penalty upon those who refused to attend services of the established church or who worshiped in "conventicles" or clandestine and illegal assemblies (Willson 287). Thus, while a range of men might fall within the broad outline of Calvinism in the early days of Elizabeth's reign, under Whitgift, with his tighter press for strict conformity, the narrowed middle way threatened to exclude many who had believed themselves to be "unfayned favourers" of the present church (Booty 6).

While the older established clergy were clearly Calvinist, and while Whitgift, despite his suppression of dissent, was also Calvinist, there was a growing body of younger divines who had not experienced at first hand continental forms of Protestantism, who had not experienced Roman Catholicism as a state religion, and who saw greater threat to the established church coming from reformist Protestants than from Roman Catholics. Richard Hooker enters the scene, as it were, in the company of these younger divines. When he was appointed Master at the Temple (1584–1585), where he had responsibility for preaching and ministering to an influential congregation of lawyers, Hooker was already the cause of suspicion among Calvinists. The doctrinal teachings evident in his sermons seemed to many to signify that he moved too close to Roman Catholicism, and his "anti-Calvinist teaching on grace and predestination" put him at odds with accepted beliefs within the established church (Booty xxvi–xxviii) A leader of the presbyterian cause and reader in the Temple, Walter Travers publicly challenged Hooker's teaching. The matter came to the attention of Elizabeth's advisors, Burghley and Whitgift, the result being that Travers was silenced and Hooker remained as Master. This incident, so public in nature, helped to heighten fears among conforming and nonforming Calvinists that the via media might take a route that would exclude them.

When the first five books of Hooker's *Laws* appeared between 1593 and 1597, they were already in some sense preread. It would have been difficult not to have read the *Laws* in terms of the jockeying for power given the circumstances under which it was published and the uses to which it was immediately put. The first four of the eight books of the *Laws* saw print in 1593, only through the special efforts of Sir Edwin Sandys, a student and friend of Hooker and a member of Parliament (Sisson xiii, 52). Sandys was working for legislation that would reaffirm an earlier act enforcing conformity, now widened in scope to control protestant dissenters (Sisson 64)—specifically, separatist Barrowists and Brownists—as well as Catholics. But the act threatened, as one contemporary put it, to bring within its repressive compass all Puritans (Green 124). Sandys apparently wanted to use Hooker's work to support passage of this bill and managed to hurry the printing so that a presentation copy was sent to Lord Burghley with a cover letter from Hooker dated March 13, 1592, the day Sandys spoke before the Commons on the bill. The bill passed with Burghley's approval (Sisson 64; Edelen xix).[5]

Hooker characterizes the rhetorical situation he faced by contrasting his opponents' stance with his own:

> He that goeth about to perswade a multitude, that they are not so well governed as they ought to be, shall never want attentive and favourable hearers. . . . Whereas . . . if we maintaine thinges that are established, we have not onely to strive with a number of heavie prejudices deeply rooted in the heartes of men, who thinke that . . . we serve the time, and speake in favour of the present state; but also to bear such exceptions as minds so averted before hand usually take against that which they are loath should be powred into them."
> (*Laws* 1: 56)

Hooker assumes the consonance of his own position and that of the church, but also speaks as if his opposition's primary concern is to raise the multitude against proper governance. While there were those sectaries who appealed to the unlettered and barely lettered citizenry, the bulk of those against whom Hooker was arguing were hardly interested in disturbing social order (Lake 116–68).[6]

Puritan works were concerned with the threat of popery but also, and for many, most importantly, with the pastoral duties that were central to the concept of Protestantism. Certainly there were works abroad that would appeal to antiestablishment sentiments, and their number increased through the 1590s.[7] But the popularity of such works cannot be explained merely in that way. Calvinism in its several manifestations had enjoyed under Elizabeth popularity among men and women of prominence. But puritan ministers also had the opportunity and capacity to appeal more broadly to the ordinary folk. The emphasis among Puritans on ministering, on actually performing the clerical functions of one's office, particularly the emphasis on effective pulpit oratory, contributed to their influence in town and countryside. Puritan works were popular in part because they were perceived as serving an important pastoral function, perceived as meeting spiritual needs.

Hooker's work, on the other hand, was read from the start not as a pastoral document but as an official and sanctioned political tract or polemic. It had to be approved by ecclesiastical authority in order to be printed at all. It had to be recognizable to the authorities as falling within acceptable conceptions of the established church. Whatever the work might conceivably be taken to be under other circumstances, in receiving official approval the first five books of the *Laws* came to operate, at least initially, within the constellation of orthodox or official ideology.

The writers of the *Christian Letter* thus had before them not the well-established Restoration *Laws*, but the 1597 edition with the fifth book and, more importantly, with the dedication to Archbishop Whitgift. The 1593 edition may have been alarming enough, particularly if it were known to have played a part in promoting repressive legislation. But coming in the midst of more general theological controversies, increasing signs of official challenges to the old Calvinist consensus, and increasing repression of dissent, the 1597 edition, bearing the dedication to Whitgift, required a strong response. The *Christian Letter* attempts a defense against what is perceived to be the error of Hooker's position, not on the ground Hooker chooses—not, that is, in terms of law or church governance ("discipline"), but in terms of fundamentals of faith as embodied in the Thirty-Nine Articles of the Church of England. The letter attempts to serve as warning that Hooker's treatise, even though it is authorized, is nonetheless a threat to fundamental Calvinist tenets. The basic thrust of the letter is to urge readers to open their eyes to the "real" content or the "real" tendencies of Hooker's work.

The writers' concern for Hooker's style, then, has to be read in this context. The writers of the *Letter* take the position that Hooker's work does *not* represent official doctrine, even though the *Laws* was published with the necessary official approval. They express fear, however, that because of his style Hooker may somehow "hoodwinke" others into believing that he does in fact speak for the church. That the letter was anonymous and illegally printed suggests that the writer or writers believed that Hooker had some official backing, most probably assumed to be Archbishop Whitgift, and that open opposition might prove dangerous. Taking on an officially approved work publicly, bringing out into the open disagreements that Whitgift believed ought to be kept within the quiet circles of churchmen and academics, particularly when the disagreement is with someone the archbishop had supported—these were strong reasons to be afraid of making oneself known. The letter, then, aims to warn others against the innocent-seeming cast of Hooker's work and to argue that the work is not, nor ought it be viewed as, representative of the kind of religion "authorized and professed in England" (Booty 6).

Hooker had begun his preface to the *Polity* with an explanation of his reasons for undertaking such a task: "Though for no other cause, yet for this; that posteritie may know we have not loosely through silence permitted things to passe away as in a dreame, there shall be for mens information extant thus much concerning the present state of the Church of God established amongst us, and their careful endevour which would have upheld the same" (*Laws* 1:1).

The writers of the *Letter* take up Hooker's own phrases from this justificatory opening in order to warn others against his language. The *Letter* writers pick up Hooker's dream simile, recasting it in overtly biblical terms and turning a hoped for "that" into a deductive "therefore" that is both a statement and also certainly a command:

> When men dreame they are asleepe, and while men sleepe the enemie soweth tares, and tares take roote and hinder the good corne of the Church, before it be espied. Therefore *Wise men through silence permit nothing looselie to passe away as in a dreame.* Your offer then, Maist. *Hoo.* is godly and laudable, to *enforme men of the estate of the church of God established among us.* For the Teachers of righteous things, are highlie to be commended. And he that leadeth men rightlie to judge of the church of God, is to be beloved of all men. (Booty 6)

The writers of the *Letter* pick up the gauntlet: they position themselves as the "wise men" who will refuse to permit anything to do with what they see as the "foundation of Christian Religion" to pass away as in a dream. They then proceed to warn that Hooker's "goodlie promises" may be "meere formal"; they may be, in other words, merely matters of style and deceptive style at that:

"As by a faire shew of *wishing well,* our first parents were fowlie deceaved: so is there a cunning framed method, by excellencie of wordes, and intising speeches of mans wisdome, to beguile and bewitch the verie Church of God. And such as are used for this purpose come in sheepes clothing. For he translateth him self into an Angel of light, who blindeth all men with utter darknes" (Booty 60). The writers make the comparison more direct. They cast themselves as innocents who, upon first reading Hooker's work, believed that here was a "champion" to offer combat in the defense of church, state, and queen. The "sweete sounde of [his] melodious stile almost cast [them] into a dreaming sleepe" (Booty 7). But "happelie" they remembered that in his preface, there was mentioned "other cause," which alerted the writers to the danger contained in Hooker's work.

Hooker's qualified beginning, "though for no other cause, yet for this," might be passed over as meaning simply that the cause of informing posterity of the state of the church was enough reason to write. "Information extant" concerning an "established" church and those who would uphold it seems innocent enough in suggesting a nonpartisan account of a settled state of affairs. But the "wise" writers of the *Letter* understand Hooker's intention in a way that the explicitly named audience for this work—posterity— generally did not. The writers of the *Letter* understand Hooker to be projecting his work to the future as a guise to cover his present intent: "Wee . . . opened at the length our heavie eyes, and casting some more earnest and intentive sight into your manner of fight, it seemed unto us that covertlie and underhand you did bende all your skill and force against the present state of our English church: and by colour of defending the discipline and gouverne- ment thereof, to make questionable and bring in contempt the doctrine and faith it selfe" (Booty 7). The writers of the *Letter* un- derstand Hooker's work to be one more round in an ongoing fight, that what is at issue is not a simple factual account of a settled state of affairs, but the establishing of what will be taken as the actual church. Both Hooker and the writers write about the estab- lished church, but each contends for the right to say what that church is.

From his sermons and, in particular, from his public tussle with the precisian Walter Travers over what would be acceptable preaching in the Temple, the writers certainly assume that Hooker is anti-Calvinist and conformist. The sign of that knowledge is their use of the highly coded terms *discipline* and *government*, on the one hand, and *doctrine* and *faith*, on the other. Church discipline, the governing organization of the church, was a fundamental issue that divided conforming and nonconforming Calvinists, who might otherwise find themselves in agreement on issues of doctrine and faith. If a nonconforming Calvinist wanted to show his support of the English church and of the queen, he might well choose to write only about doctrine and faith and avoid the issue of discipline altogether. But if a conforming divine who was anti-Calvinist wanted to emphasize the nonconformists' disagreements with the established church, if he wanted to heighten that which separated conforming and nonconforming Calvinists, he might well choose to focus on discipline, enclosing his anti-Calvinist sentiments in a discussion of governance. The writers of the *Letter* read Hooker as having hidden his anti-Calvinist notions of doctrine and faith behind a discussion of discipline, and such a manner of writing is, as far as they are concerned, popish:

> For we saw the theme and the cause you have in hand, to be notable simples, whereof a skillful popishe Apoticarie can readilie make some fine potion or sweete smelling ointment, to bring heedlesse men into the pleasant dreame of *well-weening:* while they closelie set on fire the house of God. And may wee not trulie say, that under the shewe of inveighing against Puritanes, the chiefest pointes of popish blasphemie, are many times and in many places, by divers men not obscurelie broached, both in Sermons and in Writing, to the great griefe of manie faithful subjectes, who pray for the blessed and peaceable continuance of her most gracious Majestie, and of the estate of the Church of Jesus Christ as it is nowe established among us? (Booty 7–8)

The writers of the *Letter* entertain the possibility that perhaps Hooker did not intend to supply with raw materials some popish apothecary, that perhaps "in the heate of disputation" his hand had been drawn too far. Or, they wonder, whether perhaps they have mistaken his meaning. Given their so highly figured barrage of language leveled against Hooker, it is difficult to read their doubt as serving any function other than to present themselves as showing restraint, as struggling to be open minded, even moderate, toward one so clearly in error. They are, in fact, taking their cue, once again, from Hooker. Hooker had devoted much of his preface and the first five books of the *Laws* to showing the errors in Calvinist positions, but he had also proposed—out of Christian charity—a forum through which disagreements might be settled, allowing that those whose errors he would "rip up to the verie bottome" (*Laws* 1: 3) might end their "contentiousness" if they would submit to some "higher judgement then [their] owne" (*Laws* 1: 29).

Hooker must have known full well that any judgment he deemed higher would not be acceptable to those he opposed, even though he no doubt believed the authority to be truly higher. He proposes a solution to strife, a conference that would restore Christian peace, but his olive branch is, for the opposition, indeed a serpent. The proposed solution is a sign of that which divides the parties. Similarly, the writers of the *Letter* offer Hooker the opportunity to "make it appeare to the world, that in these pointes you are all one in judgement with the church of Englande," when he has already at great length done just that, one would think, to his own or his supporters' satisfaction at any rate (Booty 8). He argues in unpublished marginal notes to the *Letter* that he speaks as custom and thinks as God's good spirit has taught him: he can do no other. Both Hooker and the writers of the *Letter* offer resolutions that are no resolution but that hinge on the demand for the capitulation of the other party, not a call for rational debate as one might expect from a pluralist, twentieth-century conception of Hooker's tolerance, but an urging of submission as precisely the rational choice. For the writers, such submission would be marked in part by an alteration of Hooker's style.

The *Letter* writers ask that Hooker respond to their questions about doctrine (not discipline). And they ask that he leave aside his deceptive manner of writing in order to insure clear understanding: "We thought it . . . our parte . . . in all christian love to intreat you, that as you tender the good estate of Christes church among us, and of thousands converted to the gospel, you would in like publike manner (but plainly and directlie) shew unto us and all English Protestantes, your owne true meaning, and how your wordes in divers thinges doe agree with the doctrine established among us." In asking for clarification, the writers contend that they are concerned not only for themselves, not only for "many godlie and religious Christians," but concerned as well that "Atheistes, Papistes, and other hereticques, be not incouraged by your so harde and so harsh stile (beating as it were, as we verilie thinke, against the verie heart of all true christian doctrine, professed by her Majestie and the whole state of this Realme)" (Booty 8).

What is important to note here is the way in which style operates as not only a condemnation, or a means of condemnation, but also as an out, a loophole through which the writers will allow Hooker to escape condemnation if he would. Style can be sheep's clothing, deceptive apparel that hides the true appearance of false doctrine, and as such, is to be despised and condemned. Or style can be merely careless dress, the sign of excessive zeal, and as such, an error to be corrected and avoided. But style also can be very nearly the whole of the message, to the extent that style beats at the heart of true doctrine. It is very likely that the writers know that Hooker will not give them the kind of "charitable, direct, plaine, sincere, and speedie answere" they ask for (Booty 9). And it is likely that they have few doubts whether Hooker's style does beat at the heart of doctrine as they conceive it. Hooker, in his marginal notes to this passage, suggests that the question of his style is merely an occasion for the writers to "set abroad their suspitions" (Booty 8). Given the writers' apparent certainty that Hooker is in error, Hooker's reading of their criticism of his style would appear to be correct.

But style does not operate in the *Letter* simply as pretext, as mere show to cover the writers' true purpose of making public their disapproval of Hooker's stance on doctrine and faith. Rather, Hooker's style is, within the writers' discourse, that which, almost paradoxically, makes visible Hooker's deviation from what is considered common and acceptable practice. Hooker's style is read as intended to hide his error but, in fact, the very deceptiveness of his style reveals his error. The errors are made visible because the writers "opened at the length [their] eyes" and saw Hooker's "manner of fight" (Booty 7).

In a move paradigmatic of the use of style, the writers come to Hooker's text already knowing something of what to expect from his text. He is, in a sense, inevitably preread. He prays that those who value the peace and quiet of the church "in gracious humility" come to his work without "partialities." Interweaving the language of Scripture with his own language, Hooker pleads, " 'Let not the faith which ye have in our Lord Jesus Christ' be blemished 'with partialities'; regard not who it is which speaketh, but weigh only what is spoken. Think not that ye read the words of one who bendeth himself as an adversary against the truth which ye have already embraced; but the words of one who desireth even to embrace together with you the self-same truth, if it be truth" (*Laws* 1: 2–3).

This passage could be read—and has been read—as exemplary of Hooker's moderation, his reasonable style. But such a reading is not possible for readers who already know that Hooker does not share in the "self-same truth"; that Hooker's impartiality hinges on that final "if": the writers already know that their truth, as far as Hooker is concerned, is no truth. The writers of the *Letter* already know then that Hooker's moderation is a falsehood, that impartiality means giving up what one already believes and succumbing to the truth for which Hooker argues. Hooker's style, then, becomes evident to them as deception because they already see deception.

They proceed, then, in the body of the *Letter* to make public the errors they have seen revealed through Hooker's style. They expose some seventeen points wherein they believe Hooker to deviate doctrinally from the Thirty-Nine Articles, and three more points of contention more generally conceived of as "Of speculative doctrine," "Of Calvin and the reformed churches," and "Schoolemen, Philosophie, and Poperie." Having seen and made public in the body of their *Letter* these points of deviation, the writers significantly turn once again to Hooker's "stile and maner of writing" in the penultimate section of their *Letter* in order to suggest how Hooker might begin to set himself right with true faith and doctrine (Booty 48–71).

Where in their introduction they spoke of Hooker's seductive style, they now concentrate on his deviation from acceptable models and in so doing provide a picture of their system of stylistics, a system of complex comparisons predicated on prior valuing of texts. Style is always relational. The most fundamental text is of course Scripture, the style of which is already endorsed because it is the word of God. With other texts, there is also a similar a priori endorsement of style that derives from the orthodoxy of the writers rather than from some abstract set of stylistic principles. The principles act as descriptors or labels of an already valued object: in a sense that is the process by which Aristotle developed his rhetoric, to describe an already valued object—Sophocles's Oedipus cycle, or an orator's address—and label what is valued. Those labels subsequently were abstracted as rules, but their complex and contextualized referents from which their meanings derived were necessarily lost (to be later replaced by newly endorsed referents). For the writers of the *Letter,* the referents are ready to hand in the Scriptures and in the fathers of the English church.

The writers see Hooker's writing as "farre differing from the simplicitie of holie Scripture, and nothing after the frame of the writinges of the Reverend and learned Fathers of our church, as of *Cranmer, Ridley, Latimer, Jewell, Whitgeeft, Fox, Fulke, etc.*" (Booty 71). The operating principle here seems to be that if, necessarily, one has only the fallen letter, not the naked truth, then one can only compare that fallen letter to words already officially designated as true. Style would then derive not from an abstract principle or a set of formal rules but from a process of comparison that is dependent upon truth claims.

Certainly, precisian writers consciously made use of systems of rules, particularly Ramist rhetoric (Lake 101), but that rhetoric was usable in part because it could be and, in fact, had been aligned with Protestant scriptural exegesis. Lisa Jardine suggests that for the Ramist in sixteenth-century Cambridge "the rules of dialectic [were] supposed to correspond directly to the rules of natural reason." Again and again in Ramist writings, Ramism is said to describe "the way in which all natural discourse is constructed" and thus would be taken as applying universally (Jardine, "Place" 58). In following the Ramist method, then, a writer believed himself to be following a body of impersonal rules that, though they derived from the best that had been written in all time ("Place" 58), transcended the limitations of time and place, allowing him to overcome the limitations of his own subjective response (Lake 101), in a way anticipating Francis Bacon's later attempts to provide "helps" (albeit man-made) that would somehow transcend the limitations of man's mind.

Jardine argues that the simplified, naturalistic lines of Ramism helped to displace the already eroded place of grammar and rhetoric in the university ("Place" 59), helping to make Aristotelian rhetoric appear an unnatural contrivance. Concomitant with the privileging of Ramist naturalism over Aristotelian contrivance was the religious alignment of the two systems of thinking and writing. For the writers of the *Letter*, Aristotle was inextricably linked, via the schoolmen, with popery. They cite Martin Luther as having "discovered" how the schoolmen with the help of Aristotle had caused to banish "from us the true and sincere divinitie" (Booty 65). Aristotle is to divinity, they argue, as darkness is to light. Thus, when they find that despite "manie good things, many truethes and fine pointes bravelie handled," Hooker favors Aristotle and the "ingenuous schoolemen," they see him as in error, as setting up reason more highly than holy Scripture, of valuing reading more highly than preaching. And they link this privileging of Aristotle to Hooker's "tedious and laborious writings" (Booty 67). Hooker is seen as favoring Aristotle not only in citing him but in writing like him. Thus, the writers propose that Hooker would show himself "another *Aristotle* by a certain metaphisicall and crupticall [cryptical] method to bring men into a maze, that they should rather wonder at your learning then be able to understand what you teach in your writinge" (Booty 72).

The writers would have preferred that Hooker had written following the example of "that most learned and reverend Father

D. *Whitgift,"* who had followed a question and answer format common among controversialists of the time. The writers—strategically—praise Whitgift for "judicially" setting down the question, answering "sensibly," and providing reasons either from "holy scripture, from Fathers or new writers, without all circumferences and crooked windings, directly applied, so as such poore men as wee be may beare away what hee saith and what hee intendeth" (Booty 73). This is the closest the writers come to what might be called an analytical description of style, but they deal here only in the largest structural terms: Hooker did not follow the question and answer format typical of the period. But the question and answer format could not of itself distinguish among the various parties in the religious disputes of the time, since most writers observed the convention. Once again, then, the significance of the formal description is predicated on some a priori valuing.

The significance of Hooker's deviation seems to hinge on the apparent transparency of the convention. Most writers in a sense announced their works as works of controversy by employing the convention. Whitgift in "The Defence of the Answer to the Admonition Against the Reply of T.C." quoted a disputed point from his opponent's work, in this instance, Thomas Cartwright, and then addressed the point directly using Scripture or the works of the approved fathers of the English church (Whitgift 2 ff.). The disputants and the issues are explicitly named. Hooker, in not following the format, would seem to be trying to suggest that his is not a work of controversy—trying, that is, from the writers' perspective, to mislead. But the writers of the *Letter*—as they put it—recognize a "brier tree" when they see one even if it be "all blowen over with . . . flowers" (Booty 72). Hooker, in failing to write as others have written, has compounded his separation from the fold: he deviates from acceptable models that would have certified the truthfulness of his work, but his very deviation is itself an attempt to hide that separation.

The culmination of the *Letter*'s critique of Hooker's style is a request that he conform, that he write as others of the church have written, not for style's sake but for the sake of truth. It is one of the striking aspects of the *Letter* that Hooker's style is designated as that which first reveals the possibility of error—style, therefore, reveals a kind of truth, the truth of error. Style is also the means by which Hooker can signify his correction of error and his clearer conformity to true doctrine. And yet throughout the *Letter* the writers have shown that style alone cannot signify truth, that style is dependent upon some anterior truth claims. A reader is necessarily left, then, with having to judge the truth of a work by something that exists apart from the work itself, something prior to the work.

W. Speed Hill has argued that Hooker's lifework "was conceived as an attempt to cleanse of every ambiguity and to ground in all possible certainty [a] fundamental truth of human experience" ("Doctrine" 193). He cites as support Hooker's expressed desire that he "make this cause so manifest, that if it were possible, no doubt or scruple concerning the same might remayne in any mans cogitation" (*Laws* 1: 156). What Hill does not note is what Hooker must urge of his readers in order that they can accept "this cause" as manifest. Hooker asks his audience, those zealous believers in the "Lords Discipline," that they approach his work with "that gracious humilitie which hath ever bene the crown and glorie of a christianlie disposed mind" (*Laws* 1: 2–3). This is powerful rhetoric in persuading many a reader of Hooker's moderation, of his judiciousness, of his tolerance. But what he is asking of his readers is that they lift the words out of the controversy of the moment and consider the words "for themselves." Indeed, the writers of *A Christian Letter* have shown in their criticism of his style the impossibility of taking his word for it. Hooker's words have meaning for the writers only through a system of complex intertextual comparison. The writers share with Hooker a belief in a realm of truth independent of man's fallen word and share with him a belief that Scripture comes as close as man can to approximating zero degree rhetoric. But Hooker's work is not Scripture, nor has it been certified as Scripture-like, as the writers imply Whitgift's works have been. Thus, Hooker's work calls for an exegetical practice attentive to the workings of fallen words, attentive to style. And such attention confirms for the writers that what they have before them is not a work that is "moderate" but a work in which the writers hear "the lowde outcryes and noyce of them which pursue their enimies in battell" (Booty 73–74).

The sixty or so years intervening between Hooker's death and the Restoration "demonstrate" for strife-weary men of the church the extent to which Hooker was a prophet in fearing that the established church might indeed pass away as in a dream (*Laws* 1: 1). During these intervening years, interest in Hooker's work continued. John Earle, for example, an early seventeenth-century writer of Theophrastian "characters," began a translation into Latin (Novarr 207). Jeremy Taylor, a contemporary of Earle's and an Anglican divine, made frequent reference to Hooker in his sermons and treatises (Wall). But there was no general interest or strong enough official interest sufficient to insure that the full eight books would be made available to readers until the Restoration, when a different system of intertextual comparison was developing, Hooker's opponents had been defeated, and Hooker could emerge as prophet, voice of reason, and exemplar of a moderate style.

II

If Hooker comes to represent moderation in religious discourse after the Restoration, Bacon comes to represent moderation in scientific discourse. Thomas Tenison offered his *Baconiana, Or Certaine Genuine Remains of Sr. Francis Bacon* in 1679, in part to reclaim Bacon from radical Protestants for a more explicitly latitudinarian view of learning, asserting that "his Lordship was for pacifying Disputes, knowing that *Controversies of Religion* would hinder the Advancement of Sciences" (57). *Baconiana* went through several printings and was included in the libraries of both prominent men (John Locke, for example, owned a copy) as well as the "ordinary readers" to whom Tenison explicitly addressed himself (Harrison 78). In choosing to write in English, Tenison was making available to less well-educated readers Bacon's "Philosophy, Mechanic inventions, and Writings" (6), not because editions were not already available, but because Tenison, archbishop of Canterbury, wanted to correct what he viewed to be misleading versions of Bacon's work. The particular misleading version Tenison had in mind was Gilbert Wats's translation of Bacon's *De Augmentis Scientiarum*, which was itself a Latin revision of *The Advancement of Learning* and likely not exclusively Bacon's Latin.

Tenison does not mention the fact that Wats was associated with reformist Protestants. Rather, he focuses on more formal defects:

> But some there were, who wished that Translation had been set forth, in which the Genius and Spirit of Lord *Bacon* had more appeared. And I have seen a letter, written by a certain Gentleman to Dr. *Rawley* [Bacon's amanuensis and later executor], wherein they *thus* importune him for a more accurate Version, by his own Hand. "It is our humble sute to you,—to give your self the Trouble, to correct the too much defective Translation of *de Augmentis Scientiarum*, which Dr. Wats hath set Forth. It is a thousand pities, that so worthy a Piece should lose its Grace, and credit by an ill Expositor; since those Persons, who read that Translation, taking it for Genuine, and upon that presumption not regarding the *Latine* Edition, are thereby robbed of that benefit which (if you would please to undertake the Business) they might receive. This tendeth to the dishonour of that Noble Lord, and the hindrance of the *Advancement of Learning*." (Tenison 26–27)

There are clear differences between Wats's translation and the still standard, nineteenth-century Spedding version: Brian Vickers notes several instances, for example, in which Wats "tones down or removes an image" (*Francis Bacon* 297, n. 2). But accuracy of translation or faithfulness of translation is less the issue for Tenison than the way in which Wats's edition had been used by Puritans during the interregnum to argue for particular educational reforms. To the extent that education was blamed in the post-Restoration period for the turmoil of civil war and the Commonwealth, Wats's "celebrated edition" (Webster 128), used by other reformers to claim Bacon as their own, was clearly suspect.

Toward the end of book 2 of the *Advancement of Learning*, Bacon considers "a kind of culture of the mind that seemeth yet more accurate and elaborate than the rest, and is built upon this ground; that the minds of all men are at some times in a state more perfect, and at other times in a state more depraved." The end of study should be to "fix and cherish the good hours of the mind, and to obliterate and take forth the evil" (175). There are two avenues toward such "obliteration": "some kind of redemption or expiation of that which is past," which is a sacred and religious office; and an "inception or account *de novo*, for the time to come," which is more rightly the aim of human philosophy (*Advancement* 175–76). It is to this latter that Bacon turns, opening out his understanding of charity: "If these two things be supposed, that a man set before him honest and good ends, and again, that he be resolute, constant, and true unto them; it will follow that he shall mould himself into all virtue at once. [The] divine state of mind, which religion and holy faith doth conduct men unto, by imprinting upon their souls charity, . . . is excellently called the bond of perfection, because it comprehendeth all virtues together" (*Advancement* 176–77).

Radical Protestants found in such ideas inspiration for their idealist and prophetic writings urging the reform of learning. Indeed, Christopher Hill argues that "significant outward evidence of Bacon's influence" dates from only after 1640 (*Intellectual Origins* 96), beginning, in other words, in the turbulent years just prior to and including the civil wars and marked by, among other events, the publication of the Wats translation.

Gilbert Wats, friend of continental Calvinists, undertook the translation as a way to promote puritan concerns. His interest in Bacon seems to have been spurred at least in part by his reading of John Amos Comenius, the Czech Calvinist who had expressed his enthusiasm for Bacon's instauration, that plan for a return to and renewal of true learning. Comenius thought the translation of the *De Augmentis* an auspicious event and wrote to the English reformer, Samuel Hartlib, that he hoped the publication would "prepare the ground" for the construction of a "universal college" to be founded in London (Webster 49). While this group of reformers is sometimes seen as one precursor of the Royal Society (cf. Kearney, Webster, and Christopher Hill, *Intellectual Origins*), the generally more latitudinarian members of the later Royal Society set out to dissociate themselves from both the religious enthusiasm and the reformist zeal characteristic of the earlier group (Kearney 95).

Wats's edition was important in playing a part in the efforts of men in and outside the universities to promote new learning. Lawrence Stone argues that between 1640 and 1660, "the puritan zeal to spread knowledge of God's words and to develop the study of protestant theology coalesced with the anxiety of the Baconians to change the classically oriented curriculum to something more practical and scientific" ("Literacy in Education" 72). Capping almost a century of educational expansion under the Tudors and the first Stuart monarch, a number of projects were proposed to further extend access to education and to more fundamentally reform educational institutions from the roots upward. A general, if uneven, increase in literacy was sponsored by and in turn helped to support Protestant interests.

In 1641, the puritan party in the Long Parliament invited Comenius to visit England. Comenius drew from Ramist and Baconian thought to argue for a universal schooling that would improve the moral and religious rather than the economic and social conditions of humankind. "If any ask," Comenius writes, " 'What will be the result if artisans, rustics, porters, and even women become lettered?' I answer, If this universal instruction of youth be brought about by the proper means, none of these will lack the material for thinking, choosing, following and doing good things . . . and, by the constant reading of the Bible and other good books, will avoid that idleness which is so dangerous to flesh and blood" (qtd. in Cressy, *Education in Tudor and Stuart England* 102). The "proper means" involved a simplified approach to the study of languages, following Ramus, and an emphasis on what would be most directly useful in daily life—a concern for the practical that Comenius found supported by Bacon's writings. The advancement of learning for this group, as Hugh Kearney points out, was not the advancement of "understanding for its own sake"—what Bacon called the "light" to be derived from learning—but a science that could be applied to agriculture and the crafts—what Bacon called the "fruit" of learning (Kearney, "Puritanism" 96). Science was perceived as "praxis" and Bacon's work provided a vision of a new science that could serve as a model of all kinds of learning, including learning about the injustice and abuses of established churches and governments (Jacob 67).

It is precisely with the "fruit" in this full sense that Wats's translation is concerned. In addressing the Favourable Reader, Wats urges that one ought not concern oneself with what is already done, nor with abilities of past agents or the capacity of their instruments, but with "propagation and Advancement of Knowledges; the improvement, and not the conservation only, of the Patrimony of our Ancestors" (n.p.). Thus, as readers we are invited to start afresh with Bacon's text, to follow him as architect. To make it more likely that readers will read the architect's blueprint correctly—Bacon is thus constructed as the *architectura scientiarum*—Wats offers marginal notation in order to "point to the mines from which Bacon dug his ore"; "a platform Analytique table" or chart showing the partitions of the various branches of knowledge; and divisions for the work, which Wats admits are "contrary to the mind of the author." Wats justifies this last contrary intervention by redeploying Bacon's language from the essay, "Of Building," using the architectural language to explain the structure of Bacon's works and Wats's relation to that structure. Dividing the work is warranted because "profit is to be preferred before artificial contrivance," that is, reader's ease in reading is to be preferred to the mere reproduction of the work for the sake of conservation.

Like the "toning down and removing" of images noted by Vickers—one might say to make the work plainer—this restructuring of Bacon's work suggests an important relationship to style. Unlike the editorial work of Bacon's executor, William Rawley, which had as its expressed aim the preserving of Bacon's spirit through the exact preservation of his style (since style was standing in for the man), Wats aims to take Bacon at his word; that is, one ought to work toward a transparent style that makes matter available for use:

Were the Author alive and his vast Designes going on, this alteration had been somewhat bold: but the inimitable Architect now dead, having perfected little more than the outward Courts, as it were, of his magnificent instaurations; and the whole summe of Sciences, and the stock of Arts in present possession not able to defray the charges of finishing this Fabrique; I thought fit by compartitions and distributions into several rooms, to improve what we have, to our best advantage, so it might be done without prejudice to the Authors procedure, and apt coherence, which I hope it is: Having respect . . . rather to accommodation than decoration; for Houses (as our Author saies) are built to live in and to look on, and therefore use is to be preferred before uniformity (n.p.)

Wats reads Bacon's concern that men have too long studied words and not matter as an invitation to restructure Bacon's text so that the matter is readier to hand. Clearly neither Wats nor Bacon could be free of style. Until readers were "manumissed from a servile" dependency on the opinions of others—too corrupted they were by nature and by bookish learning—they would require help in understanding something as remarkable as Bacon's works (n.p.). That help would be supplied by changing Bacon's text to make it more easily read, to make his meaning plainer. Bacon's writing was thus less a stylistic model to copy than the vehicle through which one moved closer to zero degree rhetoric. The purpose of style, then, was to educate readers past needing style—to manumiss them from authority epistemologically and stylistically.

Radical Protestants could and did find other sources of support for their interests in reforming language—in Ramus, as we have seen, for example—but in Bacon they found in one place support for several of their concerns—not only language reform, but also educational reform, the grounds for a new and especially *fruitful* learning and, for some republicans among the Protestants, a general leveling—in his emphasis on collecting data "which 'any man' could carry out." The act of reading Bacon could thus serve as a sign of one's distance from the state church, from the monarchy, and from the residual scholasticism of the universities (Perez-Ramos 13).

After the Restoration, Bacon had to be rehabilitated or rescued from revolutionaries and low church advocates if his work was to be put at the service of consolidating the rising middling classes. This process was so successful that, rather than marking one's distance from established church and Crown, affiliation with Baconian ideas came to serve as a "demarcation criterion," marking "the exclusion of metaphysical, theological, and political controversies from the realm of rational scientific discussion" (Perez-Ramos 15–16; 40, n. 19). Rather than being read in radical Protestant terms as providing the blueprint for a religiously grounded philosophic discourse, Bacon came to be read as making room for a science that would not be in conflict with religion (even though science would eventually come to displace religion as the dominant discourse).[8]

This shift is perhaps most readily apparent in John Wilkins and his interest in the development of the Real Character, a system that promised to more nearly express not words but things through assigning a distinct (and arbitrary) sign to every conceivable referent. Wilkins found in medieval speculative grammar and in Bacon's *Advancement of Learning* the inspiration for a universal philosophical language system that would provide a means to communicate across national boundaries, a system free of the ambiguities and corruptions of rhetoric (Salmon 68, 99). In the Real Character, Wilkins and others hoped to find the ideal of a zero degree rhetoric—not a plain style, but no style at all.

Through early training and patrons, Wilkins was associated with Puritans, but like other men who would later form the core of Royal Society membership, he had his doubts about the civil war and gradually came to support the restoration of monarchy. He was wary of religious factionalism, disliked the perceived lower-class leanings of many of the more radical Protestant sects, and saw their mysticism, excessive fervor and, in particular, their literal interpretation of the Bible as undermining reason and the orderly course of learning. Religion was not incompatible with the new learning, and Scripture did not have to prevent the acceptance of new findings in astronomy and the other branches of the new learning, but for Wilkins the Bible was written figuratively so as to be understood by the rude and unlearned and hence could not be taken literally. The general emphasis of religious study, he argued, should be on morality as directing one to live life in a Christian manner and on natural theology as revealing God's plan in nature (Shapiro 9, 66, 51).

Along with Robert Boyle and John Evelyn, Wilkins was, in the 1640s, not so far removed from Wats and his party in seeing Bacon as offering the beginning of a new and glorious age of learning. The difference, however, came in what in Bacon's work each group emphasized. For Wats it was the blueprint for universal learning, improvements in medicine, a "physical regeneration of the nation," and new mechanical philosophies that would improve people's living conditions. For Wilkins and his group, the emphasis was on experimentation. They were "convinced that order and design pervades the 'world natural' as well as the 'world politick.' If men would only embark upon a programme of experimental learning—in other words apply the work ethic to nature— then Bacon's dreams will be realised beyond his greatest expectations" (Jacob 71). Experimentation, work, disciplined education, and mutual communication all would occur under the guidance of Providence. But what for Wats was a social vision of scientific learning became, especially after the Restoration, more and more an entrepreneurial and politically conservative view of scientific work—isolated work whose benefits to trade and commerce would make possible expanding the empire and material prosperity for only some at home (Jacob 71, 74).

In his Epistle Dedicatory to the *Essay Towards a Real Character,* Wilkins not only saw a universal character as facilitating mutual "Commerce, amongst the Nations of the World, and the improving of all Natural knowledge," but in addition, he contended that it would "contribute much to the clearing of some of our Modern differences in Religion, by unmasking many wild errors, that shelter themselves under the disguise of affected phrases" (n.p.). The need for "mutual communication" across party lines and across national boundaries had little to do with mass communication as we might think of it now—in the sense of making learning generally available. Rather, because natural languages had evolved to meet the needs of vulgar capacities they were inadequate to the new scientific age. The need then was for a technical language that would allow for efficient communication among the cognoscenti. Wilkins cites Bacon as source for his plan to develop a system that brings language, thought, and reality together under a single sign. Bacon had described two kinds of grammar in the *Advancement:* one popular for learning languages and understanding authors, the other philosophical for examining "the power and nature of words as they are the footsteps and prints of reason" (138). Wilkins picks up this latter kind as justification for a "character" or sign that would "signifie not *words*, but *things* and *notions*" (qtd. in Salmon 99). Such a system would save time, Wilkins contends: the time formerly spent in learning words would be devoted instead to the study of things (Shapiro 47).

Jonathan Swift literalizes Wilkins's plan in the Laputa section of *Gulliver's Travels* through the the image of the sack of *things* that must be carried in order to communicate *ideas:* one pulls out some particular object from the sack to represent itself in order to communicate with another person who must also carry another weighty sack. While Wilkins's system—represented in a remarkable fold-out chart in his folio volume of the 1668 *Essay Towards a Real Character and Philosophical Language*—is comprised of ciphers, like hieroglypics, rather than *things*, Swift has nonetheless captured the unwieldiness of a system that would require a discrete (entirely denotative) sign for every idea, thing, notion, and feeling in the universe. But, however impractical (and in Swiftian terms, *silly*) the actual plan ends up being, it represents in extremity the repression of political and social affiliation that infects normative styles more generally. What is intended as a transparent system of denotation acts as mask to blot out class interest, religious affiliation, and (dis)loyalty to Crown and nation.

Wilkins's transparent, styleless language system is the logical extreme of the close, naked, natural style desired by the Royal Society. Bacon held up as a goal the possibility of communicating knowledge in the same form that it had been discovered, but this so-called natural form of communication is hardly easy. In the *Valerius Terminus*, he remarks on the difficulty one inevitably encounters in trying to convey the ideas of one man's mind into that of another "without loss or mistaking" (Bacon, *Works* 3: 248). Language of whatever kind will always be inadequate to the task. For man to come to read the book of nature aright, he has to, in Charles Whitney's perceptive phrase, "tell the truth with a plainness unconceived hitherto" (143); but the vexing paradox of it is that such plainness cannot be achieved through attention to style but only through attention to truth, and the truth is never simply available to the naked eye.

The Bacon that comes down to us is in many ways more the product of Royal Society appropriation than puritan religious vision. The tradition that gives us both Bacon and Hooker was thus born in the antirevolutionary, antisectarian moment of the Restoration. While this moment marks the return of the hereditary monarch, it also marks, paradoxically, the beginning of the end of the strong monarchs, a shift in economic structure toward a consolidation of market capitalism, and the consequent concentration of political power in a group increasingly conscious of itself as comprising a middle class (cf. Nussbaum). As part of this shift in power, the consolidating middling classes contributed to regularizing and codifying cultural values, among them what would count as knowledge and what kind of language would serve as the acceptable vehicle for that knowledge, a language of moderation, transparency, objectivity, and control. Such a workmanlike language, apparently free of party interest, promised peace and prosperity. If one considers Foucault's reminder that power does not merely oppress or repress, that it also enables, one can see post-Restoration discursive practice as producing writing and reading for information's sake—"the style of the clerk"—on a fairly radical scale. Such practice does not deny creativity, in Leavis's sense, but sets it aside, making a separate space for it: a style for information's sake at the center to do the world's business and a style for pleasure's sake on the periphery, set aside for those with leisure, means, and a certain privileged education. Creativity is produced as a commodity available to the few. It is excess, surplus that plays on the edge of sensible, natural, native easiness.

For the men of the Royal Society, a plain style was a rhetorical and therefore political choice from other still available options. Archbishop Tenison, for example, remarks in his introduction to the *Baconiana* that he will be more prolix, using a looser, more "Asiatic" style than might otherwise be required because he wants "to serve the more effectually, *ordinary Readers*, . . . whose Capacities can be no more reach'd by a close and strict Discourse, than Game can be taken by a Net unspread" (4). Built into such a decorous appreciation for audience needs is the presumption of the writer's superior relationship to the clearly inferior audience, a stylistic relationship that is assumed to be a sign of relative social position and cognitive capacity. Throughout the literature on normative style such a relationship is evident, from the Royal Society to twentieth-century American schooling, where the plain, basic language—what has come to mean *functional literacy*—has been not only the language of primary education but the language for those not privileged enough to experience the full stylistic repertoire, or what has come to mean *literature*.

The complexity of the literacy/literature nexus was and is rarely acknowledged in debates about who gets schooled how. Perhaps Gramsci's recognition of the importance of "vocational" and "classical" education for all citizens comes the closest. Even though literature has the potential to deconstruct the premises on which a transparent, functional prose rests (as Richard Lanham has argued), to make problematic any simple understanding of language as transparent on the world is not in itself liberatory. Because literature has come to signal privilege, in its very positioning as useless and excess, its potential to serve as a countervoice has been compromised (though it is not incapable of being reanimated). Similarly, literacy as basic skill is also hardly a guarantee of anything liberatory. The functionalist view of language presumes the learner to be less capable and presumes a life for the learner that will require little more than the narrowly functional. When Gramsci suggests that a classical education should be available to the ordinary woman or man, he is recognizing that literature has been historically constructed as the literacy of the elite. To be literate in that sense is to be schooled in the languages of power.

The linguistic reform of the post-Restoration period was not in itself essentially oppressive. Indeed, it made room for and was itself a product of new intellectual and social work. But the normalizing of that discourse into a pedagogical standard has emphasized orderliness over dexterity, limit over range, and has led to a bifurcated literacy—literature for the culturally entitled, and plain, functional language for the letter-blind millions. Leavis's dichotomizing—to see the villain as utilitarian functionalism that stifles spirit and creativity, versions of which are written all over the nineteenth-century debates concerning the institutionalization of English—is hardly sufficient critique, and yet we have not moved far from such dichotomizing, as will be evident in the next chapter on the contemporary discourse constructing a present-day literacy crisis.

5

The National Prose Problem

> I have been led from basic writing to Shakespeare by what
> seems to me an unbroken chain of implication.
>
> *E. D. Hirsch, "Culture and Literacy"*

> All of us who teach about words find ourselves, nowadays,
> caught up in three overlapping perplexities: a literacy crisis
> so widespread it has shaken our national self-esteem as an
> educated democracy; a school and college curriculum that
> no longer knows what subjects should be studied or when;
> and a humanism so directionless, unreasoned, and senti-
> mental that it seems almost to quest for Senator Proxmire's
> Golden Fleece.
>
> *Richard Lanham,* Literacy and the Survival of Humanism

> The independence of liberal arts education from establish-
> ment values is an illusion.
>
> *Anthony Grafton and Lisa Jardine,* From Humanism to the Humanities

Almost daily, news reports remind us that we are in the midst of a "literacy crisis." Literacy makes the headlines with warnings about how little young people know, how little they read, how little they write (and when they do write, how abysmal are the results). As the historian Karl Kaestle notes, "in the past few years measurement experts have documented low functional-literacy skills among young adults, educators have decried falling test scores, humanists have argued about the need for more 'cultural literacy,' books by reformers have warned us of an 'illiterate America,' and legislators have submitted bills to 'eliminate illiteracy.' Television networks, newspaper chains, business councils, and prominent political figures have joined the campaign" (xiii). Underlying the often heightened rhetoric is the assumption that somehow things have gotten worse. Students somehow cannot read or write as students once could. The average citizen appears less able to handle written language than citizens in the past. While social historians in the last twenty-five years—Kaestle among them—have challenged any simple picture of a golden age of literacy, documenting, for example, an expansion rather than a decline in literacy and in access to literacy education since the turn of the century, educators and politicians continue nonetheless to write and lecture and legislate as if that national literate culture we were supposed to have enjoyed in the past was seriously threatened.

One could argue about definitions of literacy, about how the ante has been upped, about how what counts as literate behavior now is something more or at least other than it was at the turn of the century. One could consider how the United States has been "welcoming" new immigrants in increasing numbers, an estimated 562,000 people in 1985 (excluding refugees and illegal aliens)—less than the high in 1910 of 1,041,570, but more than at any other time in this century—and how such an increase in primarily non–English speaking residents strains an already overburdened and undersupported educational system (Melville 14). One could consider the changing nature of the workplace and changing requirements for educating an employable citizenry (Sarmiento and Kay). The social, political, and economic factors that intersect with literacy, shaping in fact what it is and what it is good for, are numerous and complex. But few of the most public discussions of the so-called literacy crisis deal with that complexity and, in fact, cannot deal with it and still maintain a crisis rhetoric. It is crisis rhetoric that, while presumed to generate federal and state support, obscures the extent to which literacy campaigns can be both well-meaning and in the service of hegemonic structures.

In this last chapter I return to E. D. Hirsch, whose version of readability I discussed briefly in chapter 2, and consider him together with Richard Lanham as two influential writers who have attempted to confront the literacy question in some of its complexity as it impacts specifically on higher education. For both Hirsch and Lanham, literacy is situated in the American context in relation to particular social, economic, and political forces. Hirsch, for example, begins *Cultural Literacy: What Every American Needs to Know* with the assertion that the sort of literacy he advocates is the "only reliable way of combating the social determinism that now condemns [disadvantaged children] to remain in the same social and educational condition as their parents" (xiii). Hirsch explicitly connects literacy learning with social goals, with racial equality, with economic advantage. Similarly, in *Literacy and the Survival of Humanism* Lanham places literacy in the midst of the changing needs of a "multiracial and multilingual America" (115). He ties literacy to the changing cultural character of America and to the needs of a democracy.

Each writer sees before him a literacy crisis, and each believes that to address that crisis is also to address other social ills. What they do not do, however, is interrogate that causal equation; they do not explore the extent to which literacy may not be the primary causal factor in bettering the human condition; they presume that literacy (as they define it) is good for you, will lead to better jobs, greater self-esteem, greater capacity to live in a complex world, and more active involvement in the democratic process, despite considerable and readily available evidence to the contrary.[1] Ultimately, each acknowledges something of the complexity of the literacy question in late twentieth-century America only to shut down the question, to put the complexity out of play. And (significantly) for each writer, style operates as a detour around that complexity.

For Hirsch, style is initially the primary site for solving the literacy crisis, but in later work it becomes the sign of the "doctrine of educational formalism" that he condemns. Educational formalism is, in his terms, an attempt to evade the interestedness of educational decisions: a "spirit of neutrality" misleads us into thinking that literacy is mere skill rather than "political decision" ("Cultural Literacy" 161–62). But Hirsch does not mean "political" (or "cultural," for that matter) in a contestatory or fluid sense of negotiated meanings, and he certainly does not mean that the classroom itself is one of the places where political decisions are constantly being negotiated (Hirsch says very little about pedagogy, in fact). Rather, he means that schools have to decide what will count as requisite cultural knowledge—not once and for all and not exclusively as the province of the schools, but largely as within teachers' control as culture makers ("Cultural Literacy" 166) and with relative stability because cultural knowledge rests primarily on traditional materials (*Cultural Literacy* 137). What might have served as a needed critique of the ideology of style (and through it, a critique of English studies), ends up being (despite Hirsch's disclaimers) fodder for a reactionary turn in American educational debate.

Richard Lanham also yokes style to literacy, beginning as does Hirsch with the problem of teaching composition at the university level and moving to the larger issues of educating citizens in a democracy. His first target and, to some extent, his perpetual nemesis is C B S style—a normative style promoting the three god terms, Clarity, Brevity, and Sincerity, at the expense of play. "America's current epidemic verbal ineptitude comes on two levels," he argues in *Revising Prose* (1979). There is the rudimentary level and that is a matter of "simple functional literacy" ("students on this level make mistakes from ignorance . . . they don't know the rules") and there is the stylistic level and that is a matter of having available a greater range of stylistic options ("you are not so much making 'writing errors' as trying . . . to imitate a predominant [normative] style") (vii). Someone else will have to be responsible for functional literacy (elementary and high school teachers presumably). Lanham concentrates instead on promoting a greater stylistic range by teaching us how to bring to wholeness the two halves of human nature, *Homo sapiens* (the Platonic principle) joined to *Homo ludens* (the Ovidian principle)—uniting, one might say, both Hirsch's "communicative efficiency" and Bakhtin's "*carnivale.*"

This binary system evolves through the course of Lanham's writing to encompass a rather remarkable range of activity. In an address to the 1988 conference, Liberal Arts Education in the Late Twentieth Century: Emerging Conditions, Responsive Practices—a conference that received rather unusual media coverage because of its purportedly radical agenda—Lanham shifts from his earlier "motives of eloquence" to an "essential bistable alternation between the contingent and the absolute." It was precisely this bistable alternation, Lanham argues, upon which "the educational system that was invented to sustain democracy" was built in the first place—a base we need to return to if the humanities are to survive.

> If you want to teach citizenship in American democracy, you don't build your educational system on Hirsch's collection of canonical facts, or [William] Bennett's collection of canonical texts—or on Allan Bloom's collection of rancid Platonic pieties either. You build it . . . upon this essential bistable alternation between the contingent and the absolute. The only true absolute, in such a secular democratic education, is the obligation to keep that oscillation going, preserving a bistable core for the Western tradition which is not timeless but forever in time. The ways to do this are as infinite as the particular courses such a curriculum would create, but the center remains the same. ("Extraordinary Convergence" 51)

Although Lanham clearly distinguishes his notion of oscillation from Hirsch's infamous list, there are nonetheless rather striking similarities in their projects. Lanham, like Hirsch, understands the educational crisis in terms of binaries, and like Hirsch he argues for favoring one member of the binary pair over the other in order to right what is perceived to be the present imbalance. Each looks for a core, a center that will keep in check the centrifugal forces that threaten the liberal arts. Lanham's core is a return to rhetoric as the mother system, as the integrative heart, the common language of a liberal arts education, giving back to the lower-division courses the breadth that he believes has been eroded by increased pressure to specialize coming from the upper-division tendency toward "reductive specialized inquiry" ("Extraordinary Convergence" 49, 53). That common language is not so far removed from (though perhaps less literal-minded than) Hirsch's notion of cultural literacy as a national vocabulary or lexicon. Both men say that they are *not* proposing a static curriculum but rather a kind of antidote to perceived chaos. Like the post-Restoration move to find stability after the English civil wars and the nineteenth-century efforts to both accommodate and contain reform, Lanham and Hirsch represent a liberal desire to make room for learning by checking a cultural decentering whose most immediate origins might be located in the sixties but whose roots might be seen as planted more deeply in the promise of radical democracy.

Paul Feyerabend has argued that "liberal intellectuals are also 'rationalists.' And they regard rationalism (which for them coincides with science) not just as one view among many, but as a basis for society. The freedom they defend is therefore granted under conditions that they are no longer subjected to. It is granted only to those who have already accepted part of the rationalist (i.e. scientific) ideology" (77). This has meant *"equality of access to one particular tradition"* (77). While Lanham in particular wants to make room for the ludic, for what might be viewed as other than scientific, he (like Hirsch and Fred Newton Scott before him) nonetheless remains a rationalist, wary of extremes, wanting to admit more learners to a single tradition, rather than altering the fundamental grounding ideology. While both Lanham and Hirsch say they want to protect democracy, they register in their very concern for core/center/stability a fear of the consequences of a democracy unchecked. They embody, therefore, many of the conflicts I have traced in the course of this book and help to make visible what is at stake in the convergence of literature, literacy, and the ideology of style.

Hirsch and Lanham in their professional careers have straddled the institutional divide between literary study and the teaching of composition. Both have written about literature and both have directed composition programs—the institutionalized home for literacy instruction at the post-secondary level. In the not too distant past, this was not an unusual pattern. In fact, the Conference on College Composition and Communication (CCCC), the primary professional organization in composition studies, was founded in 1949 by men whose scholarly training was in literature but whose teaching and service obligations led them to reflect on the rather daunting task of managing often large freshman English programs.[2] Rather than keeping tidy and separate the two spheres of their professional lives—the scholarly and the service sectors—Hirsch and Lanham have drawn from the scholarly, from their literary study in their efforts to develop composition programs and, conversely, have found in composition a key to the salvation of the humanities. For Hirsch, this means drawing on the philosophy of language that underpins his literary theory (which hinges on the notion that the same thing can be said in different ways) and on a history of prose style (which he reads as revealing the progressive tendency toward ever greater communicative efficiency), to posit first a program for teaching writing and more recently a program for reforming all of education from elementary to post-secondary. Lanham also draws on a philosophy of language (more Wittgenstein, Kenneth Burke, and I. A. Richards than Hirsch's dyadic linguistics) and a history of prose from which he builds a theory of complex human motive (an explicitly Burkean term) to argue first for a composition program and more recently for a program by which composition can save English studies.

E. D. Hirsch had already published *Wordsworth and Schelling, Innocence and Experience,* and *Validity in Interpretation* when he stepped down from the departmental chairmanship at the University of Virginia in 1970 to direct composition. He refers to this move as a "conversion experience": "I write as one converted from aestheticism to the more practical side of an English teacher's responsibilities" (*The Philosophy of Composition* xii). Starting from the presumption of a divided field (theory as opposed to practice, literature as opposed to composition, the aesthetic as opposed to the practical), and having engaged in "an intensive study" of research in composition, Hirsch concludes that his previous literary studies had very little to do with this "more practical side." Hirsch's confession makes sense historically: nineteenth-century aestheticism arose in part in opposition to a rhetorical understanding of how texts work in the world; and, certainly, the ties that bound composition and literature together earlier in this century have been largely severed through increasing specialization, greater emphasis placed on graduate education and educating majors rather than on general education, and a devaluing of teaching more generally. But his confession also makes sense in terms of his own theory. His earlier work may not have appeared to him to have much to do with "practical" composition, but his philosophy of language and his theory of interpretation lead directly to his philosophy of composition and its later revision into cultural literacy.

In *The Philosophy of Composition* (1977), Hirsch argues for a particular kind of literacy on the basis of his construction of a history of prose style. The history of prose as he sees it reveals an "irresistible tendency" toward ever greater "communicative functionality" (*Philosophy* 52–53); and to resist such "progressive" tendencies, he warns, would lead not only to "logical and practical incoherence" but to (an unnamed) "social harm as well" (4). One could deconstruct Hirsch's argument to show that the concept *communicative functionality*—or what he calls later "intrinsic communicative effectiveness" ("Measuring" 196)—at the heart of his theory operates as an ahistorical term and thus cancels out his claim to be making a historical argument. Or, one could charge him with stacking the deck, with having premised an historical imperative, chosen his facts such that his history would support his pedagogy, thereby leaving no room but for the teacher to accept as inevitable that pedagogy. But Hirsch is too visible both within the academy and without to be dismissed so easily at the textual level.

Hirsch had committed himself to developing a theory that would make it possible to argue for validity in interpretation. His desire for certainty in the face of modern tendencies toward relativism is evident in his several articles on literary theory in *Critical Inquiry* and in his books *The Aims of Interpretation* and *Validity in Interpretation*. But that desire is evident as well in *The Philosophy of Composition* and in the subsequent series of revisionary articles in which Hirsch modifies his style-centered philosophy of composition to incorporate a cultural content. Certainty, for Hirsch, pivots on the principle that "meaning is unchanging" (*Validity* 214), which is an attempt, as David Hoy rightly observes, to counter what Hirsch considers "radical historicism" (Hoy 13–14). Thus for Hirsch, the reader can understand the (unchanging) meaning of the text independent of the interpretive context in which understanding takes place. The importance of a work may vary over time, in different contexts, but the meaning of the text remains the same, available to any reader.

In Hirsch's writings on literary theory, this theoretically determinate meaning is tied to a concept of author intentionality; put simply, the text's meaning is that meaning intended by the author (Literary Criticism Conference [Georgetown] 1985). In his work on composition, the principle of unchanging meaning is incorporated into the history of language and prose as underpinning the possibility of establishing a progressive history: if the meanings of texts stay the same, as Hirsch posits, we can then place them with certainty in relation to one another and evaluate their communicative functionality relative to other fixed texts. Unchanging meaning is further augmented in this argument by the corollary principle that the same meaning can be communicated through different combinations of words. It is just that some combinations are more efficient than others. Thus, in his early work, Hirsch could argue that not only can we place texts in a *certain* (in the sense of established) order, but we can evaluate the efficacy of each text against an ahistorical, acultural standard of relative readability (see chapter 1, above).

Hirsch's theory of certainty in composition and literature generated ample opposition within the academy (cf. Hoy, Doherty, Douglas). But there is a very real sense in which none of the critiques seems to account for the strength or persistence of Hirsch's agenda. A clue to that strength is not to be found so much in theoretical consistency but in relation to an ideological climate in which what Hirsch argued—first with author intentionality and stability of meaning and later with the importance of cultural knowledge—appears to any reasonable man (to borrow the lawyer's phrase) as common sense. I would argue that Hirsch has given theoretical voice to what many of our students believe about reading, writing, language, and meaning; what their parents (and our parents) believe; what writing teachers in their gut understand when they ask students to "say the same thing, but in different words," and what literature teachers mean when they "get" students to "see" the text (or say to colleagues, "But *Antigone* is not about civil disobedience; it is about . . .”). Hirsch has given voice to the fundamental theoretical ground for what common law honors in the concept of the objective standard; what strict constructionist jurists such as former Attorney General Edmund Meese or Chief Justice William Rehnquist assert; what much of Protestant exegesis rests on; what William Bennett had striven for in his call for a national education policy. Even though Hirsch personally distances himself from the political Right, his philosophy of language and of meaning, in so markedly opposing “historical relativism” (which in Hirsch is equated with Marxism), lends itself to rightist readings.

Hirsch is neither villain nor hero in this piece. But he has been a remarkably vocal and public player whose ideas are embedded in the common life of most people inside and outside the academy. The fact, however, that one needs to argue for common sense, to build bulkheads around it against the rising tide of historical relativism, suggests that there is something more at stake here than the simple, innocent (however ironic) “desire to be right,” as Hirsch has put it. It does have to do with an “ideology of truth”— again, his language—but not in the neutral, nonideological sense in which Hirsch attempts to use that phrase (“Politics of Theories of Interpretation” 235–36). Like the nineteenth-century advocates for the teaching of English before him, Hirsch has offered, in *Philosophy of Composition* and more recently in *Cultural Literacy,* a version of literacy that aims to increase access, a laudable goal, at the same time that it staves off more radical cultural critique, a critique that may be necessary before larger cultural structures are changed to make other than token access a reality. I am thinking here, for example, of Anthony Sarmiento’s call for changes in the workplace that would create a more hospitable, more democratic home for the exercise of more complex literacies.

If the *Philosophy of Composition* is the product of one conversion experience, *Cultural Literacy* is the product of another. After spending some time researching the “actual effects of a piece of prose as compared to its potential optimal effects on a competent audience” in order to determine “intrinsic communicative effectiveness” (see, for example, “Measuring the Communicative

Effectiveness of Prose"), Hirsch in 1980 reported his "shock of revelation" in discovering that what he calls the "craft of writing," coherence, organization, syntax, and so on, is not all there is to writing. Style is not everything. It is only half the story. The other half of the story is the "cultural aspect of writing." But it is apparent that that "cultural aspect" becomes visible only when composition—the "practical side"—threatens the humanist heart of English studies.

In a telling move, Hirsch ties his revelation to the job market and to funding:

> I hope you will be tolerant if, still reeling from my newest conversion, I speak with some of the one-sidedness that new converts are all too apt to exhibit. Such one-sidedness may be just what is needed at the moment, since the craft approach to writing is so powerfully in the ascendant. Specialists in the craft of composition are in great demand for teaching posts. Money for composition research is easy to come by. And even now, as I write, Yale University is pondering ways of spending a grant of 1.25 million dollars to improve the writing abilities of Yale undergraduates. ("Culture and Literacy" 27–28)

As long as the heart of English studies remains unthreatened, composition can be treated as the teaching of craft—in fact it would appear the less threatening as long as it is just the teaching of craft (important but not prestigious in the way teaching art would be, in this dichotomized discursive arena). Hirsch gallantly can offer to straighten out the compositionists' ideological muddle, to "uncover ever more efficient ways to teach [writing as craft]." But when real money and real jobs seem to validate the practical side of what we do in such a way that the practical side threatens the heart, it appears to be time to reconsider. Humanist values have to be brought back into view as the controlling center of the enterprise.

The problem here is not with Hirsch's claim that there is more to writing than craft. A number of critics of Hirsch have granted him the importance of knowledge, of *knowing about* (cf. Bartholomae, "Released into Language" 87). Indeed one might make a far more radical argument than has Hirsch about the capacity of composition, because of its apparent contentlessness (its very uncenteredness), to more readily make space for previously subjugated knowledges. But Hirsch's is no radical project. He does not construct a pedagogy that concerns itself with working on or producing knowledges—either of which might allow him to reconceptualize the relationship between writing and reading, between composition and literature. Instead, in commenting on the institutional allocation of resources he makes clear what is at stake: his dichotomized view of the field requires a practical side to be responsible for basic literacy, in contradistinction to the more highly valued, theoretically and aesthetically privileged domain of cultural content. It is particularly troubling to have the positivist-convert Hirsch claim that all work in composition has been as narrowly conceived as his own in order to disclaim such work so that the cultural-literacy-convert Hirsch can reclaim space for an embattled humanism.

Hirsch came across the importance of "extra-linguistic knowledge of the subject matter" while conducting a series of experiments measuring reading comprehension. Subjects were given both a well-written essay and the "same" essay "stylistically degraded." Hirsch expected that the "stylistically degraded" version would pose more difficulties for readers (assuming that clarity is exclusively a stylistic feature). But this turned out not to be the case. Hirsch found instead that style alone did not determine reading ease ("Culture and Literacy" 38). As he reports in a later article, "good style contributes little to our reading of unfamiliar material because we must continually backtrack to test out different hypotheses about what is being meant or referred to. . . . Style begins to lose its importance as a factor in reading unfamiliar material" ("Cultural Literacy" 163). This, it should be noted, is something that critics of readability have been saying for some time, but Hirsch is really not interested in abandoning altogether the formulaicism that informed his earlier work.

One may still refer to a text as having a "good style," but familiarity with the topic seemed to be the stronger determiner of reading ease. Hirsch deduced from this finding that there is "an unbroken continuum from cultural literacy, to literacy in reading, and thence to competence in writing." How could anyone write better than they read, he asks. If there is such a strong connection between reading and writing, it is reasonable to assume that training in writing skill alone will not lead to "advancement in general literacy." Indeed, Hirsch extends his argument to say that not only will training in basic skills alone not advance general literacy, but training in the writing process by itself is also inadequate: "This (for me) newly-won insight fosters a certain skepticism about the practical importance of new researches into the writing process. I am strongly in favor of this research. We can never learn too much about the most efficient and successful methods of teaching the skills of writing. On the other hand, we also need a reminder that even in the domain of writing skill per se, the cultural element always obtrudes" ("Culture and Literacy" 38–43).

In this early article, Hirsch ties his new insight to the Ann Arbor court case in which African American parents argued that white teachers should learn the language conventions of the African American community. Hirsch reads this case ("behind the ideological rhetoric") as confirming his sense that standardized methods of teaching writing cannot meet the diverse needs of diverse populations, an insight that seems to get lost in his later work, *Cultural Literacy: What Every American Needs to Know,* and that has certainly been lost on readers who have found in Hirsch support for the imposition of a national curriculum ("Culture and Literacy" 43–44). As long as culture is a content and writing is a skill, the possibility of thinking of language as always already cultural stays safely out of play. To really think of culture as fundamentally informing would mean that one could not simply add cultural content to the pedagogical pot without also changing the pot.

But culture as content preserves a place for the liberal arts, for a humanism that is threatened by a technological (practical) world. This is not a new story, as the history of nineteenth-century practice makes clear. The question, as Hirsch puts it, has been how to negotiate between "two equally American traditions of unity and diversity" ("Cultural Literacy" 161) or, put more politically explicitly, how to negotiate between cultural difference and cultural protectionism. In a 1983 essay in *The American Scholar,* Hirsch offers a brief history of the problem. The schools have been the place where the American culture was shaped by trying to "harmonize the various traditions of the parent cultures" but also by attempting to create what was uniquely American. The former celebrates pluralism; the latter, unity. We have resisted "narrow uniformity," Hirsch suggests, at the same time that we have striven for a "national culture." But now, in the late twentieth century, the balance has been tipped: in English courses—along with history, the subject closest to "culture making"—"diversity and pluralism now reign without challenge." Hirsch believes that such extreme diversity and pluralism threaten efforts to achieve a more literate culture. To correct the imbalance "we shall need to restore certain common contents to the humanistic side of the school curriculum" ("Cultural Literacy" 160–61).

Proposing something between the hyperbolic extremes of "lockstep, Napoleonic prescription of texts on the one side, and extreme laissez-faire pluralism on the other," Hirsch suggests that it would be useful to have "a lexicon of cultural literacy" available as a "guide to objects of instruction" ("Cultural Literacy" 166, 168). The choice of what should be this shared information is, he grants, a political one—not to be decided by "educational technicians" (an undefined phrase) but perhaps by a National Board of Education on the model of the New York State Board of Regents, "an imposing body of practical idealists" or, short of that, given our national suspicion of anything resembling a "ministry of culture," perhaps a consortium of universities or foundations or associations ("Cultural Literacy" 167–68). *Political* thus does not mean anything approximating democratic or even representative. And given recent controversies over such national ministries of culture as NEA and NEH and their political vulnerability, Hirsch now might modify his stance. The point, however, is to note how balance between unity and diversity in educational policy making is to be achieved through central control that on the face of it, tips the balance rather heavily toward unity (or order).

Unfortunately, what gets lost in all the talk about a national lexicon (the list) and a centralized board of education is any consideration of pedagogy, by which I mean not Hirsch's diminished sense of process or method but a reflective praxis that is itself a refusal of the theory/practice dichotomy (a dichotomy sustained as much by composition teachers as literature teachers). Given Hirsch's dichotomized view of things, he has to think either form or content, process or product, writing or reading, craft or art.[3] And such dichotomized thinking allows pedagogy to be trivialized into mere method. One might grant Hirsch his point that too much of schooling is so frightened of offending *somebody* that curricula has been constructed (and the passive construction is appropriate here) as if it were culturally neutral ("Cultural Literacy" 169), as if we could achieve that Royal Society ideal of pure knowledge. But to think differently about literacy, and schooling more generally, requires that we read the politics even of what purports to be politically neutral, not by maintaining the binaries that sustain such ideological disingenuousness but by deconstructing them. Because Hirsch is so invested in one half of the binary equation, however, even when he has the insight to see the limitation of such bifurcation, he has to reinscribe it in order to maintain his own privileged position. The answer, as he poses it— and Hirsch is hardly unique here—is to alter instrumentalist pedagogies by simply inserting a controlled content, rather than reimagining the classroom, reimagining the relationship between content and form, ideology and style. When Hirsch discovered that readers had to backtrack in order to make sense of unfamiliar material, he might have reimagined writing/reading pedagogy as providing the occasion for students to take such backtracking as the opportunity to learn. Instead of preteaching, to call up James Moffett's insightful term, instead of, that is, prereading texts for students so that they learn a lexicon *in order to* read or write, one might approach backtracking as precisely that process by which all of us learn to teach ourselves how to make sense of a text, generating questions that lead us to read more, to talk with others, to write it out, to *make* it make sense.[4]

The lack of any real attention to the classroom might alert us to the extent to which Hirsch is not really interested in changing very much. Neither laboratory experiments with cooked texts nor a canned lexicon gets us very far toward understanding the complex arena of the classroom. Changing what we teach without theorizing more fully a pedagogical dialogics—how the way we teach has the potential to reshape the content and how the content pressures how we teach—changes very little. To theorize a pedagogical dialogics, however, would require that one abandon the philosophy of language on which Hirsch's project works—one *cannot* in fact say the *same* thing in different words—and that one deconstruct the dichotomies that keep literacy and literature institutionally separate.

Richard Lanham's work rests on a more explicitly playful sense of language and of style, leading him to try to reshape more than just content. From *Style: An Anti-Textbook* (1974) to his more recent work on the relationship of technology to the humanities, Lanham has offered not so much blueprints for change as sometimes gleeful inspiration for rearranging everything from academic structures to the very heart of civilization. But even in the midst of his talk of "oscillation" and playfulness and a homo ludens that can counter the stuffed shirts in and outside the academy, Lanham looks for a controlling center, less narrowly conceived than Hirsch but still protectionist in its desires. In *Literacy and the Survival of Humanism* (1983), Lanham suggests the need for "homeostatic social regulators which will allow us, with our vast numbers and our lethal new toys, to survive." Such social regulation will have to come not from Marx or Mao—or even from Sir Thomas More and his utopian vision—but from something more like Castiglione's sense of *sprezzatura:* "the spontaneous affectation that self-consciously chooses to harmonize the various parts of our human nature and then pretends that this harmony is as natural as breathing." Human nature is prone to artifice, Lanham believes, and that artifice is the "generative concept of civility, of sociality itself" (12–13).

The old humanism, "which tried to repudiate stylistic motive," will not work anymore. For a uniquely American context— "America is the only country in the world rich enough to have the leisure, and democratic enough to have the inclination, to teach its whole citizenry not merely to write, but to write well" (*Style* ix)—and coming to the end of the culture of the book ("From Book to Screen"), a new (electronically informed) humanism that restores balance to human motive is needed. In a 1992 review of several books addressing the impact of electronic technology on the liberal arts, Lanham posits a rhetorical *paideia* or encultura- tion that might help accommodate (center) pedagogically and ad- ministratively a "non-hierarchical, non-canonical, interactive, un- stable medium" such as the electronic text ("From Book to Screen" 206). Rhetoric—and more recently, the machine together with rhetoric—stand for order, not the stiffly serious order that Lanham describes variously as Newtonian, utopian, Edenic, Ramist, or Socratic, or the bureaucratic order represented in the C B S style, but a dynamic order more akin to the stylistic deco- rum of the early Renaissance as he reconstructs it but brought into a new electronic age. "Stylistic decorum measures how we look alternately at and through a text" and should stand at the center of the composition course and at the center of the liberal arts "more largely conceived" ("Extraordinary Convergence" 50).

Lanham had already written on Sidney's *Arcadia* (1965), *Tris- tram Shandy* (1973), and Renaissance rhetoric before turning in 1974 to a series of books on prose style intended for student and teacher use—all of which address what he sees as a "national prose problem." He has remarked that some of his friends thought that in this move he was "deserting" literature for compo- sition—"as if a moderately well-established orthopedic surgeon had decided to abandon his practice and open an inner-city clinic in chiropractic acupuncture" (*Literacy* 2). Despite his friends' fears that his turn toward composition was akin to academic slumming, he saw his combined interests as making perfect sense. After all, the current literacy crisis as he read it paralleled in important features that of the Renaissance: "When the first hu- manist revival came to Europe in the Renaissance, it came as a re- sult not only of a scholarly revolution—the rediscovery of classi- cal texts—but also from a crisis of public literacy as hydra-headed as our own, one that comprehended the unsettling dangers of a Bible in English, the decay of church education following the Ref- ormation, and an unprecedented social need for effective vernac- ular communication which would serve a plethora of new social, political, and economic purposes" (*Literacy* 177). The worldly and the scholarly came together in "a study of the word, a study of style." The present literacy crisis has the potential to become similarly centered.

In his version of the development of English as a discipline, Lanham explains the irony that we are now, after nearly a hundred years of practice, in a rather fine position to educate that society—"white, literate, and at least middle-class"—that was there at the founding of the Oxford English School in 1894:

> [The] process of disciplinary growth has now reached full self-conscious maturity: practitioners in the field are reflecting self-consciously on the boundary conditions of their own activity, anatomizing it into its careerist, gamelike, and creative aspects. The maturation was accelerated by the two go-go decades of academic prosperity from 1955 to 1975, a flood of students and money that released English studies not only from composition instruction, until then its historic base in America, but also from routine instruction in the lower division. The discipline was thus freed to draw in upon itself, become graduate- and professional-centered, and sponsor meta-level reflections upon literary texts and inquiry—upon, that is, itself. ("One, Two, Three" 15–16)

Despite brief distractions from the social upheaval of those years, Lanham contends that English studies developed in self-enclosed fashion. This allowed for a theoretical blossoming, but without much attention to the "social base": the "society in which English studies must function, in America at least, is no longer predominantly middle and upper middle class, nor is the dwindling white segment of it any longer reliably literate." Thus, "English studies, like so many armies in the past, now stands superbly equipped to fight the last war" ("One, Two, Three" 16). In this version of history, the foot soldiers—the composition teachers—may not know much theory but they have a better sense than the generals of the enemy they face. They can see more clearly from the trenches the "enormous social need for instruction in language" ("One, Two, Three" 16).

Given the fact that graduate students and part-timers make up the bulk of composition teachers and that, in some institutions, few faculty see their students or their students' writing up close,

Lanham can be said to register a disturbing truth. One might object that he oversimplifies institutional history—some theorists have been paying rather extraordinary attention to sociopolitical dimensions of English studies (if not until lately and with rather minimal impact on pedagogy), and composition has hardly been a theoretically virgin field (even if its tendency toward eclecticism may disturb theoretical purists). But Lanham is not so much interested in offering a messy materialist history of current practice as he is in constructing a fable with a particular moral. He makes a point of tweaking the theorists' noses for spending too much time examining their disciplinary navels and yet he does not give over the hero's place to the composition Marthas set on theory-free foot washing. Instead, this fable requires a new—or, more accurately, a newly reformed—hero who will give social meaning and coherence to English studies. Lanham proposes that we bring back to center stage the liberal humanist, newly *pixilated*.

By rethinking what is at the center of both literature and composition study and teaching, Lanham hopes to preserve not only English studies as a discipline but the humanities more generally. "The literacy crisis presents literary studies with an enormous problem. We can of course ignore it, draw our wagons into a circle, and hope for the best. But if we do this, I think that sooner or later the problem will kill us. If we try instead to solve the crisis, dangerous as the trying will be, we may find that the crisis has redeemed us, both our teaching and our research—put literary study back in the center of modern humanism where in our hearts we know it belongs" ("One, Two, Three" 29). Having a big problem to solve—Lanham compares the literacy crisis to the problem faced by atomic physics during World War II—would give life to an English studies that may be at the end of an "exhausted paradigm." Literature faculty interesting themselves in composition might force a return to an earlier way of conceiving of the humanities— the Renaissance play of mixed motives with literature at the heart.

Some idea of what this might look like can be found in Lanham's *Motives of Eloquence* (1976). Lanham "synthesizes a generic portrait" of "homo rhetoricus," one member of a binary opposition that Lanham constructs to characterize "Western man," the other member being "homo seriosus." The "Western self," Lanham posits, is a constantly shifting combination of these two members.[5] The function of literature is "to keep man in the rich central confusion of the mixed self . . . in the mixed middle, a self by turns central and social." That literature is best which neither veers too far toward seriousness nor too far toward play (32). Western man might wish to take himself seriously but, Lanham argues, "actual Western practice" suggests the extent to which Western man has trained himself rhetorically. Lanham does not cite "actual practice" but offers, instead, instructions for creating the rhetorical man: teach him young "a minute concentration on the word, how to write it, speak it, remember it. . . . Teach a taxonomy of impersonation. Drill the student incessantly on correspondences between verbal style and personality type, life style" . . . and so on. The student is urged to be forever "rehearsing," trying on different arguments, different stances, different selves. Rhetorical man is thus always an actor, "his reality public, dramatic" (2–4).

Our present literacy crisis is at least in part caused by our collective abandonment of such a (playful) rhetorical education, and that abandonment, Lanham argues, is sustained by a deep-seated suspicion of style: "The way we have trivialized the teaching of composition is exactly the way we have trivialized the liberal arts themselves. We teach comp only as the art of transparent expression of pure, apolitical, extrahuman truth. We remove the rhetoric, the human interest, from it." We have aspired to a pure utopian language; the "basic rhetorical impulses of competition and play are outlawed in favor of plain Edenic purpose." In such an Eden, style must give way to "an insubstantial something we have learned to call 'substance' " ("Extraordinary Convergence" 49–50). Lanham blames this turn from style and rhetorical richness variously on Newtonian seriousness ("From Book to Screen" 202), Ramus's sense that "moral and formal judgments can never mix" ("Extraordinary Convergence" 47), and American pragmatism and American Puritanism (*Style* 10). Again, the rhetorical weight (whatever the historical slipperiness) of such shifting blame is to suggest how science, Puritanism, and pragmatism converge to push style, play, and ultimately humanism off center stage.

To restore humanism, and with it style and play, to their rightful position promises, in Lanham's fable, benefits for everyone from the individual student to the whole of western civilization. To the extent that "writing is a way to clarify, strengthen, and energize the self, to render individuality rich, full and social," a modern redeployment or appropriation of the Renaissance ideal of mixed motive has a kind of moral imperative: "What the act of writing prose involves for the writer is an integration of his self, a deliberate act of balancing its two component parts. It represents an act of socialization, and it is by repeated acts of such socialization that we become sociable beings, that we grow up. Thus the act of writing models the presentation of self in society, constitutes a rehearsal for a social reality" (*Revising Prose* 105). The moral ingredient, as Lanham poses it, works not on the message but on the sender. One should write well, then, "to invigorate and enrich [one's] selfhood, to increase, in the most literal sense, [one's] self-consciousness. . . . It makes [one] more alive" (*Revising Prose* 106). The style is thus the man himself, but "sometimes as he is, sometimes as he wants to be, sometimes as he is palpably pretending to be, sometimes, as in comedy, both as he pretends to be and as he is" (*Style* 124). Not the Emersonian ideal, Lanham instead offers the self-fashioned courtier (or the Horatio Alger), the man of his own making, not class-marked, social but not socially or politically situated. A man, in other words, who does not live in this world.

This style-centered pedagogy, having its origins in the education of an elite, is stripped of its sociopolitical situatedness and offered up as an answer to American (classless) education. Despite his acknowledging the importance of political truth, Lanham's work rests on the assumption that transculturally, transhistorically, human motive is bistable. He does not look to see how social situation defines the nature of linguistic choosing. He stays, if not in the land of Clarity-Brevity-Sincerity, nonetheless in a land of ahistorical human nature. Lanham's playfulness, though appearing more flexible (and frankly more fun) than Hirsch's list making, cannot seem to acknowledge what Hirsch notes (if fails to fully understand): the determinative relationship between language and social status, the relationship between what jobs beckon what workers

with what linguistic skills, the relationship between the kinds of literacies available to what students, and the relationship between
what we know and what we can say. Who is deemed ready to play
with language, after all? Who has the social right or luxury and the
leisure to play? And why don't all kinds of language play count?

Too much of writing pedagogy, Lanham argues, has attempted
to ban the expression of personality and social relationship
through the imposition of an Official Style, with its moralizing,
rule-centered pedagogy and its "simplistic static conception of self
and society" (*Revising Prose* 115). The Renaissance ideal, however,
is not without its own version of order. If we choose to resist the
Official Style, Lanham makes clear, we will have to make room for
expressions of personality and social relationships, but we will
also have to *"try to control them"* (emphasis added; *Revising Prose*
113). Without control, we become a mob, represented most vividly
for Lanham in the "tantrum prose" of political extremism (*Style*
126). One might hear in this an echo of Fred Newton Scott's fear of
the Billy Sundays, earlier nineteenth-century fears of the illiterate
rabble, and the Restoration fear of enthusiasm.

Stylistic decorum supplies the needed control. In describing
the UCLA Writing Programs, Lanham suggests that because the
"At/Through oscillation" is a natural outcome of a polyglot, multilingual university, teachers do not need to ask students to try on
various styles as suggested in *Style: An Anti-Textbook;* rather, they
have attempted to "reinvent a Drydenian middle style" (*Literacy*
175). Students, thus, do not in fact play with multiple styles, as
Lanham earlier proposed, but work toward developing a "common
language" to counter the centrifugal forces operating in the modern university. Leavis rather archly tagged Dryden with wanting to
establish what was "correct" ("and what does 'correct' mean?" 95),
but Lanham sees in the middle style hope for a common language.
For all the celebration of oscillation, of stylistic play, when it
comes down to conceptualizing a large writing program, Lanham
opts for common language. Oscillation and play must be checked
by commonality in terms remarkably like Hirsch's.

In much of his work, Lanham argues for a new pedagogy that is
a return to a Renaissance model, modernized through technology

and controlled so that it does not get out of hand. In its liberal lines, in its desire to control, it is in the direct line of descent from the nineteenth-century pedagogues. In a 1976 review of *Style,* Patrick Strong reads Lanham as a high Victorian liberal humanist "a la Mathew Arnold." Certainly Lanham is writing out of a tradition familiar to John Churton Collins, a pedagogy that situates itself in relation to some conception of an ideal past and sees itself as rescuing a version of liberal education that is perceived to be in peril. In Lanham's case, as in Leavis's and Eliot's, the ideal past is the style-conscious Renaissance (colored, in the case of the plan for the writing program, by a post-Restoration ethic). In order to oppose the utilitarians, foes we inherit from the nineteenth century (and before, if as Lanham views it they are aligned with Puritans [*Style* 10]), Lanham returns to the Renaissance to find a model for a "richer and more humane" pedagogy. At the same time, this more humane pedagogy has, as at least part of its aim, an opposition to what is read as extremism in terms similar to those used in the post-Restoration reaction to radical Puritanism.

Brian Doyle has remarked that "English and education both tend to carry the sense of an unproblematic national cultural heritage" (18). "Style" seems to operate in much the same way for Lanham, Hirsch, and the nineteenth-century pedagogues. But it is as evident in "disinterested" twentieth-century accounts of "style" as in earlier readings of "style" that (again to use Doyle's language) "style," like "English" and like "literature," represents a "ratification[] of a selective sense of culture and history" (18). The move that many academics make to try to clear themselves of the charge of bias (or, in its strongest form, the charge of cultural imperialism) is to argue in terms of a literary history that is simply factually there. As Lanham uses them, historical styles are simply there, already described for us like recipes to follow to produce new prose. Even when there is apparently some awareness of interconnections between "style" and "snob values" (*Motives* 3), such awareness does not serve to complicate the general presentation of "style" as classless. Neither Hirsch nor Lanham shies from the necessity of disseminating cultural value, but neither examines critically whose interest such values serve, assuming in fact that such values will serve all equally well.

The issue here, it should be stressed, is not that disseminating cultural values is necessarily bad, or that one could in fact teach in such a way that a course would be value-free. Rather, the problem is the refusal (perhaps the inability) to acknowledge the level to which any language learning is necessarily ideologically laden, and the reluctance to make that an explicit part of teaching (not by simply *telling* students how particular language forms are ideologically laden—not, that is, by playing the theoretical snake in the garden—but by engaging them in the question of how language in various forms works and has worked in the world).[6]

Indeed, the ideology of style—like the ideology of formalism more generally—directs us away from history and politics and complexity. The centripetal tendency to construct normalizing discourse inevitably involves constructing a vision of extremism, disorder, and mobbishness as the rhetorical counterweight to commonality, harmony, and rationality. I have been suggesting that we need to critically reread those terms in their material context in order to see how other cultural values—such as democracy and difference—may be lost in the recentering of normative discourse.

A study of style needs to pay attention to what has been and what continues to be at stake in struggles for cultural authority. This would mean—to paraphrase the quotation from Batsleer with which this book began—not simply adding names to the roster, or deleting canonical figures, or playing with styles supplied by the teacher, but rereading and rewriting the collective cultural heritage with our students. In the present circumstance, the purported literacy crisis or the national prose problem tend to define the terms under which those of us who teach English operate. And those terms tend to derive from fairly unproblematized notions of reading, writing, and texts and generally unexamined notions of cultural heritage—much of which we inherit from the beginnings of the academic study of English in the nineteenth century. *Style* as used by Hirsch or Lanham offers no possibility for rethinking literacy, operating as it does as a detour to direct attention away from political or social issues. The study of style suggested here is not a solution to the so-called literacy crisis. But such studies of the implicatedness of language learning should lead us to question the ostensibly depoliticized discourse that dominates the present debate.

Postscript
Classroom Dialogue

"Jack Kemp's argument is more persuasive because it's clearer."

"What makes it clearer as you read it?"

"Well, he uses reasons. Jesse Jackson uses emotions."

"What kind of reasons? What are you noticing in particular in that speech?"

"Well, see here where he gives a story, about his father? That supports his idea about capital, about investing."

"I see. And this story about his father working hard doesn't appeal to your emotions?"

"No, it's just straightforward. Fact. He doesn't try to whip the audience into action. He just says he knows about poverty, because he's been there."

"Okay, how about Jackson? He uses the story about the women in that factory in the South, how the working conditions were unlawful. How's that not the same kind of story?"

"Because it isn't straightforward. It tries to play on your emotions, to try to make you feel sorry for those women so you'll vote Democratic. He just isn't as clear and rational."

I began a recent course in writing the argument with two speeches from the 1992 national political party conventions. Jack Kemp and Jesse Jackson used remarkably similar textual strategies in their speeches—both attempted to define their audience broadly in order to make their respective parties seem more inclusive; each relied heavily on repetition, anecdote, historical reference, and the occasional ad hominem aimed at some representative member of the other party, and both drew from cultural commonplaces—sports, religion, bootstrap stories, and the like.

Despite these formal, textual similarities, I expected that students would see the speeches as radically different, because the students would be responding more in terms of their own a priori assumptions, party loyalties, or preconceptions about the issues or the men than on the shape of the respective arguments. I wanted class members early on in the semester to complicate the commonplace rap that good arguments rested simply and solely on something called sound reasoning. Indeed, how one defined *sound reasoning* would depend on much more than formal textbook characteristics. Once argument was complicated, the investigation of fuller, richer approaches to argumentation would come more naturally. Or so I hoped.

Of course, students defy—thankfully—any tidy plan. My argument class was no exception. On one level, the idea that our response to argument rests on many factors prior to and outside the text was old news. Virtually every student granted without even a hint of reservation that they knew whose speech they would prefer before they read either, and most found nothing troubling about the fact that they had no expectation that they could be persuaded by reason or anything else to see another point of view. Almost all the students in the class were juniors and seniors, almost two-thirds of whom expected to go on to law school. The other third planned to go to graduate school in the humanities, social sciences, or education. They were thoroughly skeptical about the political process, few voted in the election, and fewer still had watched either political convention. One young man, who plans on entering a seminary, suggested that none of us were in fact the intended audience for the speeches. Rather, the very word *party* suggested that the speeches were addressed to members only, and the media were only eavesdropping. We, then, were eavesdropping on the eavesdropping. The student went on to say that our class could certainly go ahead and analyze such speeches—presumably since school activities often asked one to do strange and useless things—but we would have to *pretend* that we were being addressed; we would role-play party members. No one in class voiced an objection to this student's view.

Written response to the two speeches was clearly schooled response, as I have characterized it in earlier chapters. Students offered fairly lengthy explanations of how, despite their already established preferences for one candidate rather than the other, they could nonetheless weigh each speech objectively, and to a person—even among those who actually stated they personally liked Jesse Jackson—Kemp's was judged the stronger speech because it was "rational" rather than "emotional." Later in the semester they might have been more wary of the either/orness and circularity of the arguments they mounted and might have had more ways of describing similarities in the structures of the two speeches, but for this first response paper, most students when pressed to support the differences they were reading fell back on writing commonplaces—the plainer, more straightforward speech was the more honest-sounding, the more rational. When one student raised the possibility that the class just wasn't as familiar with the kind of reasoning Jackson was employing—that it might just be different reasoning rather than absent reasoning—another student patiently explained that it was fine for Jackson to speak that way; there was nothing wrong with appealing to the emotions; it just wasn't good argument because it wasn't objective.

My own study should have taught me not to be so surprised at these responses, especially early in the semester. The students were demonstrating for me the extent to which style—normative plain style and its equation with objectivity and truth—continues to operate as a way to deflect us from having to talk about what might well divide us ideologically. We don't have to confront the possible racism of our responses to Jesse Jackson, for example—that the very form of an African American minister's speech (or the very fact that Jackson is African American) labels him, before he has begun, as irrational. We don't have to confront the extent to which neither Kemp nor Jackson felt obligated or believed it possible to talk more reflectively, to elaborate, to complicate—to honor their audience with the expectation that the audience might actually be patient enough to listen to complex and complicated argument. We don't have to confront our own cynicism that would have it that such speechifying makes little if any difference, that, as one student put it, we are not the audience intended, that we are not engaged in any real way in a public discourse that might help shape our public culture.

The present study of the institutional practices that have helped shape a normative style does not point in any simple way to a better pedagogy that will somehow cure what ails us, because there is no simple cure. Histories complicate our understandings of any simple cause-and-effect relationships and therefore cannot dictate future practices. What such history can do is raise our awareness of the ways we perpetuate (unknowingly) values, practices, and institutions that we (at least consciously) do not mean to support. To reflect more critically on the disjuncture between what various postmodernisms open up as possibilities and what our institutional practices shut down is to begin a process of rethinking what English studies might be and what role such studies might take in helping to shape (or thwart) postmodern democratic institutions.

Appendix
Notes
Bibliography
Index

Appendix

Collins' English Composition Exercise Book (1877) comes in three parts, each separately bound in marbleized covers, priced at three and four pence, with ruled blank pages. Part 1 includes only instruction in simple sentences; parts 1 and 2 together offer simple sentences and letter writing; parts 1, 2, and 3 bound together include simple sentences, letter writing, and composition. On the inside cover of each volume are two columns, one with "Directions for Pupils," the other "Suggestions for Teachers" as reproduced below.

Directions for Pupils

1. Choose a subject about which you know something, or in regard to which you have opportunities of acquiring information.

2. Select your subject at least a week before writing your composition.

3. Read whatever you can find bearing on the subject, and take notes.

Suggestions for Teachers

1. Composition writing should receive as constant attention as reading or spelling. Ask pupils to write only what they know, and assist them in each new and difficult step. Pupils will consider the work as pleasant as any school task if it receives the same attention.

2. Encourage pupils to gather information before attempting to write. Tell them what to read. Talk with them about their subjects, and give them thoughts. Insist on the necessary quotation marks, but attach no disgrace to their use.

3. It will not be of much advantage to the pupils if the rules of punctuation and the use of capitals are simply committed to memory. Each should be made the subject of special instruction, and illustrations should be collected by the pupils, or original ones com-

posed. The figures of rhetoric should be studied in the same way.

4. Talk about the subject with your teachers and friends, and note their opinions and suggestions.

4. The method of correcting compositions will, if followed, lessen the drudgery of the teacher, and discipline the pupils.

The system of signs for rhetorical errors are intended more especially for advanced classes. The principles given should receive careful attention.

5. Think about the subject, and make memorandum of such thoughts as you intend to put in the composition. It is the only sure way of keeping them.

5. First attempts at composition-writing should be made in the teacher's presence and with his assistance. The suggestions given in connection with the lists of subjects will assist in grading the work. In the more advanced classes pupils may be referred to the directions in the previous column, which give the method pursued by most writers in preparing essays, orations, sermons, etc.

6. Write an analysis of your subject; that is, determine how you will treat it, and arrange the headings in their proper order. Hand the analysis to your teacher for criticisms, suggestions, or revision.

6. There are advantages in writing both the original and the copy in this book on adjacent pages. Reserve the first page for an index of subjects. Write the original compositions on the left hand pages. This enables the teacher to determine by a glance from one page to the other whether the pupil has made the necessary corrections.

7. Write your composition. Express your thoughts in simple language, following the heads of the analysis, and developing each in turn.

8. Revise your composition, and strive to improve it.
   a. Cut out all superfluous words and sentences.
   b. Rewrite all sentences that are awkwardly expressed.
   c. See that each paragraph follows in logical order.
   d. Read over your composition carefully with reference to spelling, capital letters, and punctuation.

9. Copy your composition
   a. Select paper of the same size as this book.
   b. Rule fine lines with a pencil from top to bottom.
   c. Title the page.
   d. Indent.
   e. Proofread.

10. Fold your composition

In the third volume follow three pages on capitalization (fifteen rules), three pages on punctuation, one on forms of letters, one on envelope forms, two on correcting, one on figures of speech, and two on subjects for composition, including the following:

1. Familiar objects (mosquitoes, clouds)
2. Amusements (croquet)
3. Imaginary sketches (a trip to the moon)
4. Reproductions
   — Restating ideas of a passage read orally by the teacher
   — Reproduce the substance and style of a work studied
   — Compare reproduction with original and revise (to instruct in concise and grammatical language)
5. Translation of poetry to prose
6. Interpretation of proverbs
7. Descriptions
8. Letter writing
9. Imaginary sketches based on historical events
10. Historical or biographical sketches

11. Arguments
    — One side of a question
    — Both sides of a question
    — Dialogue between two students, one answering the other
12. Essays
    — Writing compositions
    — Ambition
    — The ideal and the real
    — No and yes
    — Honor
    — Make hay while the sun shines
    — Has civilization been more effectually promoted by war, commerce, or missionary enterprise?

NOTES

Introduction: Style as Cultural Capital

1. In the chapter "Cultural Capital and Pedagogic Communication" from *Reproduction,* Pierre Bourdieu explains that "the educational process of differential elimination according to social class (leading, at every moment, to a determinate distribution of competences within the various categories of survivors) is the product of the continuous action of the factors which define the positions of the different classes with regard to the school system, i.e. *cultural capital* and *class ethos.*" (87). Henry Giroux's gloss on "cultural capital" is useful here: "Just as a country distributes goods and services, what can be labeled as material capital, it also distributes and legitimates certain forms of knowledge, language practices, values, modes of style, and so forth, or what can be labeled as cultural capital" ("Rethinking the Language of Schooling" 5).

2. Nan Johnson has examined the "perceived role of the study and practice of rhetoric" more generally as it contributes to "the maintenance of social and political order" (4).

3. I have used *appropriation* in the two senses discussed by Roger Chartier: as the "social appropriation of discourse" in the sense that Foucault has used it in *The Order of Things,* that is, "one of the primary procedures for gaining control of discourse, subjecting it, and putting it beyond the reach of those who through limited competence or inferior position were denied access to it," but also in a more comprehensive sense, as all those "conditions and . . . processes that quite concretely bear the operations of the construction of meaning (in the reading relation but in many other relations as well)" (Chartier 13).

4. Edward Said has used the term *interference* in ways I take as parallel to the sense in which I am using *interested.* He argues that, currently, "the particular mission of the humanities is, in the aggregate, to represent *noninterference* in the affairs of the everyday world," which is the result of what he sees to be a "historical erosion in the role of letters" (22). Noninterference means for Said that academics, particularly in the humanities, operate as if their domains were free from interference from the everyday world and as if academics were free from having to interfere themselves: "Very broadly stated, then, noninterference for the humanist means *laissez-faire:* 'they' can run the country, we will explicate Wordsworth and Schlegel" (23). But, as Said argues, noninterference is part of

the more general workings of culture—culture, that is, that "works very effectively to make invisible and even 'impossible' the actual affiliations that exist between the world of ideas and scholarship, on the one hand, and the world of brute politics, corporate and state power, and military force, on the other" (2). Thus, noninterference or disinterestedness, in signifying the possibility of inquiry free from the everyday world, help to cover over but also perpetuate affiliations academics often ignore and some would choose to deny.

5. I am indebted to Margaret Ferguson for clarifying Leavis's solidifying of Eliot's rather more fluid term.

6. Susan Miller traces a nineteenth lineage for the cleanliness fetish in American pedagogy. She observes that the "obsession with mechanical correctness . . . participated in a broadly conceived nineteenth-century project of cleanliness. As Stallybrass and White explain this project, it was undertaken in all good as well as bad faith to convince the masses of their dirtiness while saving them from it." Hygienic prose, as Miller suggests, might hold out the hope of a kind of anonymous writing that would allow those otherwise barred by social class to enter into public conversation. But she also notes the cost of such practice: "The embarrassments that students were meant to feel after corrections . . . placed them well within the range of shame that idiosyncratic speech, or the body, can evoke" (57).

7. Michael Halloran and Merrill Whitburn have noted not only government regulation legislating "plain English," but a movement in industry to develop a computer-compatible "plain language." They distinguish two dominant but conflicting arguments for "plain English": the "mature" style argument, based on the work of Kellog Hunt, John Mellon, and Francis Christensen, among others; and the "communicative efficiency" model or "maximally readable" style, growing out of the work of readability researchers such as Rudolf Flesch and Robert Gunning and more recently advocated by E. D. Hirsch (58–59). This latter movement will be treated in chapter 2. Halloran and Whitburn see the "recent thinking about plain language [to be] rooted in the same simplistic positivism as seventeenth-century views on the plain style and [believe] that this positivistic view of the universe is even less appropriate in our own time than it was in the seventeenth century" (60). While Halloran and Whitburn are helpful in their rereading of Cicero as a way to reclaim a "symphonic" rather than "generic" understanding of style, my concern is not to trace a history of ideas or to recuperate a lost rhetorical understanding but to construct a cultural, material history of style.

8. Kurt Spellmeyer notes the irony of the teacher who endorses Strunk and White maxims even when the teacher's experience fails to support those maxims (3).

1. *Prosa Oratio:* "All Men's and Every Man's Best Style"

1. Rosewell Graves Lowrey was another sentence counter, publishing *The English Sentence in Literature and in College Freshman Composition* (1928), in which he compared the writing produced by women at Blue Mountain College in Mississippi with that produced by the "Great Masters." He wanted to figure out what forms and constructions were most common among literary masters in order to provide guidance to the college freshmen who had no facility with what he called the display of individual style. Lowrey analyzed the prose of canonical figures from four periods in English literature in order "to determine sentence length; classification of sentences as simple, compound, complex, or compound-complex; frequency of use of prepositional phrases, verbals, absolute constructions, appositives, and compound predicates; and frequency of use of certain types of inversions" (7–8). He concluded that the freshmen were already plenty modern enough in the brevity of their sentences but needed work on prepositional phrases, verbals, appositives, and absolute constructions (25)—a conclusion that might please a present-day sentence combiner.

2. It might be noted that Gunning continues to be quoted favorably not only in journalism classes but also in composition texts and journals. In a review of a textbook, for example, Waddell asserts that "aspiring technical writers should at least be aware of Robert Gunning's 'Fog Index.' Anderson and Cox [the editors of the textbook] have prudently included a six page excerpt from Gunning's *The Technique of Clear Writing*" (496).

3. Harry Zeitlin has suggested that, early in Roosevelt's administration, educators saw considerable congruence between their own progressive aspirations and New Deal policies even though the administration tended not to turn for guidance in policy making to school administrators or professors from schools of education (288). Roosevelt felt that when educational needs arose that affected national welfare, the federal government had an obligation to create programs outside the educational establishment to meet those needs (311). Hence the strong educational mission of the Civilian Conservation Corps and the Works Progress Administration and the more general support for "experimentation and innovation" (336). *Access* to a wide range of educational programs was a key component of the New Deal, and such access Zeitlin credits as having helped to prevent any "effective or large revolutionary movement" in a time of considerable social, economic, and political distress (335). Indeed, progressive aims are very explicitly yoked to the need for social control in New Deal rhetoric and in the scientific management movement.

4. Flesch (*Marks of a Readable Style*) cites an essay by Richards, "What is Involved in the Interpretation of Meaning?" included in a

volume edited by William Gray, *Reading and Pupil Development*, published in 1940.

5. I determined frequency of inclusion in anthologies by reviewing all twentieth-century high school and college texts—anthologies, readers, rhetorics—in the University of Pennsylvania's Pennington Collection of educational materials in order to augment my count from a sample of texts in the University of Pittsburgh collection.

6. Hirsch refers at several points to Herbert Spencer's *The Philosophy of Style*, first published in 1852. E. Digby Baltzell has noted how popular Spencer's various books were in the last three decades of the nineteenth century, selling some four hundred copies in America (*The Protestant Establishment* 99–100). Spencer is perhaps best known for his Social Darwinism, but like many other Victorian scholars, he did not define his interests narrowly. His treatise on style is of a piece with his *Essays on Education* and his evolutionary sociology. It might be noted along these lines that Spencer does not hold out much hope for instruction in composition. He does value practice but observes that "no amount of instruction will remedy" what he calls mental idiosyncracies or defects (*The Philosophy of Style* 167–78). Hirsch makes use of Spencer's concept of a progressive history but finds his single maxim for good style to be too general: Spencer omits giving students practical help. What Hirsch fails to note is that, because Spencer's progressive history is connected to his notion of Social Darwinism, he has no desire to give practical help. Those who are able will "get it"; those who are "defective" would not "get it" with any amount of instruction.

2. The Charmed Circle, Part 1: Literature and Literacy as Instruments of Culture

1. Gauri Viswanathan has argued persuasively that "English literature appeared as a subject in the curriculum of the colonies [she is speaking specifically about India] long before it was institutionalized in the home country" (3).

2. Assessing how such materials were used is more difficult than describing what they contain. One must inevitably reconstruct the actual literacy event through indirect sources—through student papers, as JoAnn Campbell has been doing, or student marginalia and commonplace books, as in Grafton and Jardine's and William Reese's work. My interest here, however, is in how literacy was constructed through the materials of institutionalization. It should also be noted that I am moving transatlantically, not to minimize differences between the American and British cultures but to emphasize the material commerce of pedagogical materials that helped shape the teaching of English in both countries *despite* those differences. It was not at all unusual for manuals

and handbooks intended to prepare students for examinations in England to be revised for a general readership and published as reference books in the United States. Austen Dobson's *Civil Service Handbook of English Literature*, for example, a "popular work for self-instruction" first published in 1874, was revised and published in 1897 in New York in "an attempt to extend the utility of the book as a work of reference" (preface).

3. Horace Mann on examinations quoted in Louis Fish, p. 25.

4. The London schoolmaster is identified in the British Library catalogue as William Dodds.

5. The various sources recommended by the schoolmaster suggest the eclecticism of such manuals, mixing and matching work from writers of rather different pedagogical and political orientation: Robert Gordon Latham (1812–1888), philologist, succeeded to Chair in English Language and History at University College in 1839; J. D. Morrell, inspector of schools, who adopted the German approach to analysis of sentences (Bain, *Autobiography* 275); Richard Chenevix Trench (1807–1886), archbishop of Dublin, whose *On the Study of Words* was taught extensively in England and America; Charles Knight (1791–1873), publisher for Brougham's Society for the Diffusion of Useful Knowledge; Alexander Reid (1802–1860), *Rudiments of English Composition*, 1839; James Cormwell (1812–1902), *The Young Composer; or Progressive Exercises in English Composition*, 1844.

6. As Court has noted, Brougham was concerned with the value of literary study for social communication rather than as a means to teach cultural history (*Institutionalizing* 45).

7. Sanderson has remarked that the "conflict between generalism and specialism . . . lay between . . . two different traditions within liberal education itself—those of England and Scotland" and that the Scottish arts degree, while being nonvocational, was in some sense wider in scope than the classical English curriculum, "comprising variously English, classics, mathematics, natural philosophy (physics), logic, moral philosophy and some branch of natural science." The Scottish universities also tried to provide an education for a lower social class and more multidisciplinary study. Despite English disdain for what seemed to be a superficial education, English universities did move "in the direction of neo-Scotticism" in the course of the nineteenth century (8).

8. John Keble's edition of Hooker's work was part of a larger effort on the part of clergymen academics associated with the high church Oxford Movement to assert an Anglo-Catholic rather than a reformist lineage for the Church of England. Explicitly aimed at rescuing Hooker from radical and nonconformist interests, Keble's edition corrected ideological "errors" evident in the earlier 1830 edition of Hooker's works produced by

Benjamin Hanbury, who had read Hooker as supporting disestablish-
ment, or the separation of church and state.

9. Kenneth Cmiel observes that freshman English late in the century
hid its close ties to English literature: "Most composition teachers emphasized daily writing drills over cultivating a literary sensibility" (240).

3. The Charmed Circle, Part 2: The Pedagogues

1. Nan Johnson, in her study of nineteenth-century rhetoric, names
Bain among the eleven or so influential rhetoricians whose work was frequently used in the academy or cited as a source or theoretical influence
in the period (267, n. 3).

2. In *The Teaching of English*, Scott, Carpenter, and Baker give some
sense of what such cultivation might look like. They consider, among
other things, whether students should be assigned topics for writing or
given free rein. Current advocates for expressivist pedagogy—those who
have a stake in reclaiming Fred Newton Scott as a progenitor for alternative teaching practice—would opt for the latter. Scott, however, sounding
very much like Bain, suggests that that is not good pedagogy. Allowing
the student to choose his topic is a false kind of freedom and inefficient
teaching. While granting that in the "school of life there will be no
teacher at [the student's] side to choose his subject for him," Scott points
out that much of the mental effort involved in choosing a topic is "of no
practical value." Students leave the decision until the last minute and
have little time to spend on writing. Further, free choice in "real life" is
rather the exception than the rule. Reporters are given assignments; novelists and essayists are "pursued relentlessly by ideas which cry for utterance." It is better to choose for students topics that meet the students'
needs and are responsive to their individual personalities, provide a common topic for discussion, and cover a broad range of subject matter (320,
323). What is clear here is that Scott has a particular pedagogical end in
mind: cultivating in the student the ability to produce formal prose. And
he understands that to do so requires harnessing students' interests and
capacities. *Harnessing* is an apt metaphor—on the order of harnessing a
great river but also, of course, harnessing a workhorse—in contrast to the
reading that is sometimes given Scott's position, that of releasing the student to his or her own creativity.

4. "Eliot's 'Axe to Grind'": Locating Origins

1. I want to reiterate here that my concern is not with claiming that a
change as defined by formal, stylistic analysis in fact took place. Paul
Arakelian exposes such a claim as the "myth of a Restoration style shift."
Rather, I'm concerned with the reality of a shift as it is constructed by contemporaries and later writers to make rhetorical and therefore political

claims about particular ideological projects. Robert Adolph, while not giving up the possibility of describing what he takes to be the empirical reality of a "great stylistic shift," nonetheless concludes that "more interesting" is the question of why the shift occurred and how styles "reflect extralinguistic concerns" (4–5). I would push his argument further to say that what is most interesting is the *interaction* of linguistic and extralinguistic forces.

2. Richard William Church refers in 1884 to Bacon's manner of composing with some sense of the craftedness of "ease": "Easy and understated as his writing seems, it was . . . the result of uninterrupted trouble and varied modes of working" ("Easy," OED).

3. All references to *A Christian Letter* and Hooker's marginal notes are to John Booty's edition, *Of The Laws of Ecclesiastical Polity: Attack and Response.*

4. *A Christian Letter* was printed without official approval by Richard Schilders at Middleburgh in the Lowlands. Schilders, probably himself a Calvinist, was a "famed printer of Puritan tracts," including Thomas Cartwright's *A Brief Apologie* (1596). John Booty speculates that the authors of the *Letter* retained Schilders to hide their identities, but also because other Puritans who were not separatists—including Cartwright—had patronized him (xxv). The issue here is that the authors identify themselves in the opening lines of the *Letter* as "unfayned favourers of the present state of Religion." They claim to be, in other words, not separatists, but loyal members of the Church of England, members, however, who oppose the stance taken by Hooker.

5. It is clear that without Sandys's financial support, the first four books would not have found a printer. In testimony for a Chancery suit over assets from the sale of Hooker's work, printers contended that books such as the *Laws*, "books of that argument . . . were not saleable" (Edelen xiv). Printers were fearful that books "of a reverend man being then newly printed were badly sold" (Sisson 138). And according to one of Hooker's supporters, "no assistance was forthcoming . . . from 'the eminent persons whom the cause did most specially concern' " (Sisson 52). It is generally assumed the "eminent persons" included the archbishop of Canterbury, Whitgift, who had himself undertaken to defend the established church against presbyterian Thomas Cartwright's criticisms and had supported Hooker in the controversy with Travers (Sinfield, *Literature* 13–14; Sisson 49; Almasy 252). But whether Whitgift, a Calvinist, actively sought out Hooker, an anti-Calvinist, to be champion of church polity or no, neither Whitgift nor any other prelate helped to see that the work was printed. The work did pass the censors' inspection and received the necessary license from the bishop of London (McKerrow xi–xv; Booty 231, n. 69, 13–14), but only with the publication of the fifth book in 1597 does the work bear any official sign of more than ordinary approval for

printing—that in the form of a dedication to Whitgift in the printed copy and Whitgift's endorsement on Hooker's own longhand copy written out by his amanuensis (W. Speed Hill, Preface xv).

The printers' suspicions that such a work would be a financial liability was borne out by the publishing record. Georges Edelen reasons that the maximum size of the 1593 edition was probably eight hundred copies in contrast to a "normal" run of from twelve hundred to twelve hundred and fifty copies (*Laws* 1: 370). But even so, the small folio sheets of the 1593 edition were not sold out until 1604. Sheets from the 1597 edition of the fifth book combined with the 1604 paginary reprint of the first four books remained unsold in 1611, when a newly set, more elaborate edition was published by William Stansby, who had acquired rights to the books. It was only after 1611 that the *Laws* proved a publishing success, going through five editions between 1611 and 1639 (Edelen xx–xxii). It might help to compare this sales record with another work of "moderate puritan" persuasion (Lake 10), William Perkins's *Golden Chair,* which was reprinted twelve times between 1591 and 1600 (Sinfield, *Literature,* 13–14). In a way rather like the early eager reception of Bunyan's *Pilgrim's Progress,* in contrast to minimal interest in Milton's *Paradise Lost,* popular interest focussed most heavily on such Puritan works as Perkins's, while Hooker's *Laws* had to wait on future generations for any measure of popularity.

6. Christopher Hill has argued that Presbyterians—probably the most immediate target of Hooker's polemic—"had no more wish to abolish the Church of England than had Henry VIII and Cranmer" but wished to change its government "in a further (and final) instalment of national reformation" ("Occasional Conformity" 203). William Perkins, Thomas Cartwright, or other precisian writers of prominence, many of whom held positions of some importance in the church and in the universities, were as fearful of the rabble as Hooker. Where he argues against Calvinist activities as leading to schism incendiary to social order, many precisian writers argued for further reform as a way to avoid the rise of "socially subversive sectaries" (Hill 207).

7. Christopher Hill argues that Hooker's *Laws* played a part in driving some of the supporters of the classis movement—Presbyterians, often of a more moderate bent—into separatism and into appealing for popular support ("Occasional Conformity" 203–04). Interestingly enough, William Covel in 1603 said something rather similar. Hooker's friend, Covel addresses the reader by saying that Hooker's *Polity,* "that . . . might have contented all, was in divers, a spurre to a more violent choler" (n.p.).

8. Other appropriations of Bacon's work from the same period—less scholarly than Wats's and designed more specifically for didactic purposes—also emphasized the extent to which style should be in the service

of wisdom and God's glory. In 1654, Thomas Blount published *The Acad-emie of Eloquence containing a compleat English Rhetorique, exemplied, with common-places, and formes, digested into an easie and methodical way to speak and write fluently, according the mode of the present times.* This popular rhetoric and guide to letter writing intended for the young of both sexes purports to draw on Bacon's precepts. On the frontispiece are engraved four portraits arrayed around a Mercury figure (in the 1656 edition, the messenger of the gods is replaced by a picture of what is la-beled as the Academie of Eloquence). Bacon appears with Demosthenes, Cicero, and Sir Philip Sidney, suggesting less a break with the past, as Wats's edition presents it, but rather a continuity with ancient and mod-ern figures who represent eloquence. The Baconian element in this rhetoric In addition to a collection of Bacon's letters to various corre-spondents, including Queen Elizabeth and King James—is the emphasis on an "easie and methodical way" and the yoking of eloquence to God's glory. Blount instructs his young (and likely not so young) readers that eloquence is chiefly grounded upon wisdom, and offers, following Bacon, a guide to the compiling of commonplaces as a means to strengthen judg-ment. But given the audience—presumably young people in need of in-struction or adults lower in the social order without access to traditional education—Blount does not "clear the way" so Bacon's matter can be heard, as Wats purports to do. Instead, as compilers of rhetorics before and after him, Blount offers Bacon as a dispenser of precepts and exem-plar of style. Also note Thomas Bushell's *Abridgement* and such later di-dactic collections as Knox's *Elegant Extracts* and Coppee's *Select Acade-mic Speaker.*

5. The National Prose Problem

1. Work in literacy studies since the 1970s has complicated our un-derstanding of literacy. Earlier research had started from the premise that literacy represented a cognitive and cultural break from an oral (and savage) past: educational (and missionary) work concentrated on elimi-nating "illiteracy" locally and internationally; histories of the book and of printing presumed a Gutenberg revolution; and anthropological studies investigated what they took to be a radical break from "oral" to "literate" cultures. Thanks to the work of Harvey Graff, Natalie Zemon Davis, Brian Street, John Ogbu, Shirley Brice Heath, Sylvia Scribner and Michael Cole, and others who draw from crossdisciplinary (anthropo-logical, educational, literary, linguistic, historical) culture studies, the literacy/illiteracy, civilized/savage sorts of dichotomies have been decon-structed—at least theoretically. But for various reasons that have not been adequately explored, such deconstruction has had relatively little impact on public policy makers, literacy workers (who must appeal for

funds to the policy makers who do not do well with complex arguments), or the general public that supports (or fails to support) the policies and programs proposed and implemented by those policy makers and literacy workers.

2. A critical history of CCCC has yet to be written. The National Council of Teachers of English (NCTE) archives are underutilized, and Nancy Bird's dissertation, "The Conference on College Composition and Communication: A Historical Study of Its Continuing Education and Professionalization Activities, 1949–1975," while quite useful, focusses on organizational processes rather than institutional practices.

3. Gail Hawisher has critiqued Hirsch's content/process split, pointing out how disciplinary divisions exaggerate a false divide. But Hawisher, like Hirsch and Lanham, concludes that we should be seeking a balanced perspective—"a perspective that seeks not only to unite binary oppositions into productive synthesis but also seeks to preserve the rich diversity of knowledge among us" (16).

4. Mariolina Salvatori addresses the problem of a diminished sense of pedagogy in "Pedagogy: From the Periphery to the Center" and also the limitations of Hirsch's hermeneutic for the classroom in " 'Cultural Literacy': Critical Reading" and "Reading and Writing a Text."

5. Jonathan Crewe offers cogent criticism of Lanham's approach to the "problem of rhetoric," which he calls a "short cut": "Lanham's solution is to settle all the outstanding questions by begging them. Within an idealized Western order of things, the two principles oscillate without apparent cause or consequence, except that in doing so they maintain an exemplary balance" (5).

6. What is needed is the articulation of a postmodern rhetoric not as a globalizing pedagogy but as contingent, various, and local interventions, something Terry Eagleton hints at in the last pages of his *Literary Theory: An Introduction* and which I find versions of in Donahue and Quandahl's *Reclaiming Pedagogy;* in Paul Bove's "Theory as Practice, or How One Studies Literature and Culture"; in Jerry Harste and colleagues' *Creating Classrooms for Authors* (aimed at teachers of young children but of potential interest to any teacher); and in Bartholomae and Petrosky's *Facts, Artifacts, Counterfacts.*

BIBLIOGRAPHY

Abrams, M. H., et al., eds. *The Norton Anthology of English Literature.* Rev. ed. 2 vols. New York: Norton, 1968.

———. *The Norton Anthology of English Literature.* Rev. ed. 2 vols. New York: Norton, 1986.

Adolph, Robert *The Rise of Modern Prose Style.* Cambridge: MIT P, 1968.

Almasy, Rudolph. "The Purpose of Richard Hooker's Polemic." *Journal of the History of Ideas* 39 (1978): 251–70.

Altick, Richard D. *Victorian People and Ideas.* New York: Norton, 1973.

Applebee, Arthur N. *Tradition and Reform in the Teaching of English: A History.* Urbana: NCTE, 1974.

Arakelian, Paul G. "The Myth of a Restoration Style Shift." *Eighteenth Century* 20 (1979): 227–45.

Bacon, Alan. "Attempts to Introduce a School of English Literature at Oxford: The National Debate of 1886 and 1887." *History of Education* 9 (1980): 303–13.

———. "English Literature Becomes a University Subject: King's College, London As Pioneer." *Victorian Studies* 29 (1986): 591–612.

Bacon, Francis. *The Advancement of Learning.* Ed. G. W. Kitchin. Totowa: Dent, 1973.

———. *A Harmony of the Essays of Francis Bacon.* Ed. Edward Arber. English Reprints 7. New York: AMS, 1966.

———. *The New Organon.* Ed. Fulton H. Anderson. Library of the Liberal Arts. Indianapolis: Bobbs, 1960.

———. *The Twoo Bookes of Francis Bacon. Of the Proficience and Advancement of Learning, Divine and Humane.* London: Henrie Tomes, 1605.

———. *The Works.* Ed. James Spedding, Robert Ellis, and Douglas Heath. 14 vols. London: Longmen, 1857–1874.

Bain, Alexander. *Autobiography.* New York: Longmans, 1904.

———. *Education As a Science.* New York: Appleton, 1886.

———. *English Composition and Rhetoric.* New York: Appleton, 1866.

———. *On Teaching English with Detailed Examples and an Enquiry into the Definition of Poetry.* New York: Appleton, 1887.

———. *Practical Essays.* London: Longmans, 1884.

Bakhtin, M. M. *Rabelais and His World.* Trans. Helene Iswolsky. Bloomington: Indiana UP, 1984.

Balibar, Renée. "An Example of Literary Work in France: George Sand's 'La Mare Au Diable'/'The Devil's Pool' of 1846." *1848: The Sociology of Literature*. Proc. of the Essex Conference on the Sociology of Literature, July 1977. Ed. Francis Barker et al. Essex: U of Essex P, 1978. 27–46.

Baltzell, E. Digby. *The Protestant Establishment: Aristocracy and Caste in America*. New York: Vintage, 1964.

Barker, Francis. *1642: Literature and Power in the Seventeenth Century*. Proc. of the Essex Conference on the Sociology of Literature, July 1980. Essex: U of Essex P, 1981.

Barlet, Stephane. *London University Matriculation Papers with Translations, Answers, and Solutions*. London: Percy Young, 1882.

Barnes, James J. *Authors, Publishers, and Politicians: The Quest for an Anglo-American Copyright Agreement, 1815–1854*. Columbus: Ohio State UP, 1974.

Bartholomae, David. "Inventing the University." *When a Writer Can't Write: Studies in Writer's Block and Other Composing Problems*. Ed. Mike Rose. New York: Guilford, 1985. 134–65.

———. "Released into Language: Errors, Expectations, and the Legacy of Mina Shaughnessy." *The Territory of Language: Linguistics, Stylistics, and the Teaching of Composition*. Ed. Donald McQuade. Carbondale: Southern Illinois UP, 1986. 65–88.

———. "Writing on the Margins: The Concept of Literacy in Higher Education." *Sourcebook for Basic Writing Teachers*. Ed. Theresa Enos. New York: Random, 1987. 67–83.

Bartholomae, David, and Anthony Petrosky. *Facts, Artifacts, and Counterfacts: Theory and Method for a Reading and Writing Course*. Upper Montclair: Boynton, 1986.

Batsleer, Janet, et al. *Rewriting English: Cultural Politics and Gender and Class*. New York: Methuen, 1985.

Bauman, Richard. *Let Your Words Be Few: Symbolism of Speaking and Silence among Seventeenth-Century Quakers*. Prospect Heights: Waveland, 1990.

Bennett, Tony. *Formalism and Marxism*. New York: Methuen, 1979.

———. "Texts, Readers, Reading Formations." *Bulletin of the Midwest Modern Language Association* 16 (1983): 3–17.

Berlin, James A. *Rhetoric and Reality: Writing Instruction in American Colleges, 1900–1985*. Carbondale: Southern Illinois UP, 1987.

———. *Writing Instruction in Nineteenth-Century American Colleges*. Carbondale: Southern Illinois UP, 1984.

Bird, Nancy. "The Conference on College Composition and Communication: A Historical Study of Its Continuing Education and Professionalization Activities, 1949–1975." Diss. Virginia Polytechnic and State U, 1977.

Blake, Marion. *Plain Language and the Law: An Inquiry and a Bibliography.* Ottawa: Department of Justice Canada, 1986.

Blount, Thomas. *The Academie of Eloquence containing a Compleat English Rhetorique.* London, 1654.

Booth, Wayne C., and Marshall W. Gregory. *The Harper and Row Reader.* New York: Harper, 1984.

———. *The Harper and Row Rhetoric: Writing As Thinking/Thinking As Writing.* New York: Harper, 1987.

Booty, John E., ed. *Of the Laws of Ecclesiastical Polity: Attack and Response.* Vol. 4. Cambridge, Mass.: Harvard UP, 1982.

Bourdieu, Pierre. *Reproduction in Education, Society and Culture.* London: Sage, 1977.

Bové, Paul. "Theory as Practice, or, How One Studies Literature and Culture." *Works and Days* 8 (1990): 11–28.

Brewster, William T., ed. *Representative Essays on the Theory of Style.* New York: Macmillan, 1928.

Briggs, John C. *Francis Bacon and the Rhetoric of Nature.* Cambridge: Harvard UP, 1989.

Brougham, Henry Peter. *Practical Observations on Popular Education.* 20th ed. Boston: Office of the Massachusetts Journal, 1826.

Bryson, Lymon. Foreword. *The Art of Plain Talk.* By Rudolf Flesch. New York: Harper, 1946. ix–xi.

Bushell, Thomas. *Mr. Bushell's Abridgement of the Lord Chancellor Bacon's Philosophical Theory in Mineral.* London: 1659.

Butler, Marilyn. "Against Tradition: The Case for a Particularized Historical Method." *Historical Studies and Literary Criticism.* Ed. Jerome J. McGann. Madison: U of Wisconsin P, 1985. 25–47.

Chall, Jeanne S. *Learning to Read: The Great Debate.* Rev. ed. New York: McGraw, 1983.

———. *Readability: An Appraisal of Research and Application.* Columbus: Ohio State UP, 1958.

Chartier, Roger. *Cultural History: Between Practices and Representations.* Trans. Lydia G. Cochrane. Ithaca: Cornell UP, 1988.

Church, Richard William. *Bacon.* New York: Harper, 1884.

Clark, Aubert J. *The Movement for International Copyright in Nineteenth Century America.* Washington: Catholic U of America P, 1960.

Cmiel, Kenneth. *Democratic Eloquence: The Fight over Popular Speech in Nineteenth-Century America.* Berkeley: U of California P, 1990.

Collins' English Composition Exercise Book. London: Collins, 1877.

Collins, John Churton. *The Study of English Literature: A Plea for Its Recognition and Organization at the Universities.* New York: Macmillan, 1891.

Connors, Robert J. "The Textbooks and the Evolution of the Discipline." *College Composition and Communication* 37 (1986): 178–94.

Coppee, Henry. *The Select Academic Speaker; Containing A Large Number of New and Appropriate Pieces, for Prose Declamation, Poetical Recitation, and Dramatic Readings . . . Best Authors, American, English, and Continental.* Philadelphia: Butler, 1860.

Corbett, Edward P. J. *Classical Rhetoric for the Modern Student.* 3rd ed. New York: Oxford UP, 1990.

Court, Franklin E. *Institutionalizing English: The Culture and Politics of Literary Study, 1750–1900.* Stanford: Stanford UP, 1992.

———. "Reply to Donald Greene." *PMLA* 104 (1989): 222.

———. "The Social and Historical Significance of the First English Literature Professorship in England." *PMLA* 103 (1988): 796–807.

Covel, William. *A Iust and Temperate Defence of the Five Books of Ecclesiastical Policie . . . Against an Uncharitable Letter.* London: P. Short for C. Knight, 1603.

Cox, George Bede. *London Matriculation Papers in English for Twelve Years.* London: Stewart, [1882].

Cressy, David. *Education in Tudor and Stuart England.* London: Arnold, 1975.

———. *Literacy and the Social Order: Reading and Writing in Tudor and Stuart England.* New York: Cambridge UP, 1980.

Crewe, Jonathan V. *Unredeemed Rhetoric: Thomas Nashe and the Scandal of Authorship.* Baltimore: Johns Hopkins UP, 1982.

Croll, Morris. "Attic Prose in the Seventeenth Century." *Studies in Philology* 18 (1921): 79–128.

———. *Style, Rhetoric and Rhythm: Essays by Morris W. Croll.* Ed. J. Max Patrick et al. Princeton: Princeton UP, 1966.

Curtis, Mark. *Oxford and Cambridge in Transition: 1558–1642.* Oxford: Clarendon, 1959.

Davidson, Donald. *Twenty Lessons in Reading and Writing Prose.* New York: Scribner's, 1955.

Davis, Natalie Zemon. *Society and Culture in Early Modern France: Eight Essays.* Stanford: Stanford UP, 1975.

Dawes, Richard. Preface. *Manual of Educational Requirements Necessary for the Civil Service.* Report of the Commissioners, The Right Hon. Sir Edward Ryan and John Shaw Lefevre, Esq. London: Groombridge, 1856.

Dickerson, Reed. "Should Plain English Be Legislated?" Audiotape. A Gathering on Plain English in a Complex Society. Indianapolis: Indiana U School of Law, 1980.

Disraeli, Isaac. *Amenities of Literature: Consisting of Sketches and Characters of English Literature.* Ed. Benjamin Disraeli. 2 vols. Paris: Baudry's European Library, 1842.

Dobson, Austin. *Civil Service Handbook of English Literature.* London: Lockwood, 1874.

Dodds, William. *What to Read, and How to Read It; or Hints to Candidates for the Government Civil Service.* London: Edward Stanford, 1858.

Doherty, Paul C. "Hirsch's *Philosophy of Composition:* An Evaluation of the Argument." *College Composition and Communication* 33 (1982): 184–95.

Donahue, Patricia, and Ellen Quandahl, eds. *Reclaiming Pedagogy: The Rhetoric of the Classroom.* Carbondale: Southern Illinois UP, 1989.

Douglas, Wallace W. Rev. of *The Philosophy of Composition,* by E. D. Hirsch, Jr. *College English* 40 (1978): 90–99.

Dowden, Edward. *New Studies in Literature.* London: Kegan Paul, [1895].

Doyle, Brian. "The Hidden History of English Studies." *Re-Reading English.* Ed. Peter Widdowson. London: Methuen, 1982. 10–42.

Eagleton, Terry. "Ideology and Scholarship." *Historical Studies and Literary Criticism.* Ed. Jerome McGann. Madison: U of Wisconsin P, 1985. 114–25.

———. *Literary Theory: An Introduction.* Oxford: Blackwell, 1983.

"Easy." *Compact Edition of the Oxford English Dictionary.* 1971.

Edelen, Georges, ed. *Of the Laws of Ecclesiastical Polity: Preface, Books I to IV.* By Richard Hooker. Vol. 1. Cambridge, Mass.: Harvard UP, 1977.

Eliot, T. S. *For Lancelot Andrewes: Essays on Style and Order.* Garden City: Doubleday, 1929.

———. "The Genesis of Philosophic Prose: Bacon and Hooker." *The Listener* 26 (June 1919): 907–08.

———. "Prose and Verse." *The Chapbook* 22 (April 1921): 9.

———. "What is a Classic?" *On Poetry and Poets.* London: Faber, 1969. 52–74.

Epstein, E. L. *Language and Style.* London: Methuen, 1978.

Fakundiny, Lydia. *The Art of the Essay.* Boston: Houghton, 1991.

Feyerabend, Paul. *Science in a Free Society.* London: New Left Books, 1978.

Fish, Louis. *One Hundred Years of Examinations in Boston.* Dedham: Transcript, 1941.

Fish, Stanley. *Is There a Text in This Class? The Authority of Interpretative Communities.* Cambridge: Harvard UP, 1980.

Fitch, Joshua. *Thomas and Matthew Arnold and Their Influence on English Education.* New York: Scribner's, 1897.

Flannery, James L. "The Stanford-Binet Intelligence Tests and the Lippmann-Terman Debate." Unpublished paper. Indiana U, 1990.

Flesch, Rudolf. *The Art of Plain Talk.* New York: Harper, 1946.

———. *The Art of Readable Writing.* New York: Harper, 1949.

———. "Let's Face the Facts about Writing: A Look at Our Common Problems." *College English* 12 (1950): 19–24.

———. *Marks of a Readable Style: A Study in Adult Education.* Contributions to Education 897. New York: Teachers College, 1943.

———. *Why Johnny Can't Read.* New York: Harper, 1955.

———. *Why Johnny Still Can't Read: A New Look at the Scandal of Our Schools.* New York: Harper, 1981.

Fortune. "The Language of Business." *Toward Liberal Education.* Ed. Louis G. Locke et al. 3rd ed. New York: Rinehart, 1957. 133–37.

Foucault, Michel. *Discipline and Punish: The Birth of the Prison.* Trans. Alan Sheridan. New York: Vintage, 1979.

———. *The Order of Things: An Archaeology of the Human Sciences.* New York: Pantheon, 1971.

Gauden, John, ed. *The Works.* Richard Hooker. London, 1662.

Gibson, John. *The London Matriculation Course: Being a Complete Guide to the London Matriculation Examination.* London: Reeves, 1883.

Gillespie, Gerald. "Scientific Discourse and Postmodernity: Frances Bacon and the Empirical Birth of 'Revision.' " *boundary 2* 7 (1979): 119–48.

Giroux, Henry A. "Rethinking the Language of Schooling." *Teachers As Intellectuals: Toward a Critical Pedagogy of Learning.* Granby, Mass.: 1988. 1–42.

Goodman, Kenneth. *Language and Literacy: The Selected Writings of Kenneth S. Goodman.* Boston: Routledge, 1982.

Goody, John. *The Domestication of the Savage Mind.* Cambridge: Cambridge UP, 1977.

Graff, Gerald. *Professing Literature: An Institutional History.* Chicago: U of Chicago P, 1987.

Graff, Harvey Jr., ed. *Literacy and Social Development in the West: A Reader.* New York: Cambridge UP, 1981.

———. *Literacy in History: An Interdisciplinary Research Bibliography.* New York: Garland, 1981.

Grafton, Anthony, and Lisa Jardine. *From Humanism to the Humanities: Education and the Liberal Arts in Fifteenth- and Sixteenth-Century Europe.* Cambridge: Harvard UP, 1986.

Gray, William, and Bernice Leary. *What Makes a Book Readable.* Chicago: U of Chicago P, 1935.

Great Britain Board of Education. *Teaching of English in England.* London: HMSO, 1921.

Green, Mary Anne Everett, ed. *Calendar of State Papers: Domestic Series, of the Reign of Elizabeth, 1591–1594, Preserved in Her Majesty's Public Record Office.* 1867. Nendeln, Liechtenstein: Kraus Reprint, 1967.

Gunning, Robert. *The Technique of Clear Writing*. New York: McGraw, 1952.

Hall, Donald. *The Contemporary Essay*. New York: Bedford, 1984.

Hall, Donald, and D. L. Emblen. *A Writer's Reader*. Boston: Little, 1979.

Halloran, S. Michael, and Merrill D. Whitburn. "Ciceronian Rhetoric and the Rise of Science: The Plain Style Reconsidered." *The Rhetorical Tradition and Modern Writing*. Ed. James J. Murphy. New York: MLA, 1982. 58–72.

Harrison, John, and Peter Laslett. *The Library of John Locke*. Oxford: Clarendon P, 1971.

Harste, Jerome, Kathy Short, and Carolyn Burke. *Creating Classrooms for Authors: The Reading-Writing Connection*. Portsmouth: Heinemann, 1988.

Hartley, Alan J., ed. *Sketches of Contemporary Authors, 1828*. By F. D. Maurice. Hamden: Archon, 1970.

Havighurst, Walter. *The Miami Years: 1809–1959*. New York: Putnam, 1958.

Hawisher, Gail. "Content Knowledge versus Process Knowledge: A False Dichotomy." *On Literacy and Its Teaching*. Ed. Gail Hawisher and Anna Soter. Albany: State U of New York P, 1990. 1–18.

Hayles, Katherine. *Chaos Bound: Orderly Disorder in Contemporary Literature and Science*. Ithaca: Cornell UP, 1990.

Heath, Shirley Brice. *Ways With Words*. New York: Cambridge UP, 1983.

Hill, Adams Sherman. *Our English*. New York: Chautauqua P, 1891.

Hill, Christopher. *Intellectual Origins of the English Revolution*. Oxford: Clarendon, 1965.

———. "Occasional Conformity." *Reformation, Conformity, and Dissent: Essays in Honour of Geoffrey Nuttall*. Ed. R. Buick Knox. London: Epworth, 1977. 199–220.

Hill, W. Speed. "Doctrine and Polity in Hooker's *Laws*." *English Literary Renaissance* 2 (1972): 173–93.

———. Preface. *Studies in Richard Hooker: Essays Preliminary to an Edition of His Works*. Cleveland: P of Case Western Reserve U, 1972.

———. Textual Introduction. *Of the Laws of Ecclesiastical Polity: Book V*. By Richard Hooker. Vol. 2. Cambridge: Harvard UP, 1977.

Hirsch, E. D., Jr. *The Aims of Interpretation*. Chicago: Chicago UP, 1976.

———. "Cultural Literacy." *The American Scholar* 52 (1983): 159–69.

———. *Cultural Literacy: What Every American Needs to Know*. Boston: Houghton, 1987.

———. "Culture and Literacy." *Journal of Basic Writing* 3 (1980): 27–47.

———. Literary Criticism Conference. Georgetown University, June 1985.

———. "Measuring the Communicative Effectiveness of Prose." *Writing: The Nature, Development and Teaching of Written Communication*.

Ed. Carl Fredriksen and Joseph Dominic. Vol. 2. Hillsdale: Erlbaum, 1981. 189–208.

———. *The Philosophy of Composition*. Chicago: U of Chicago P, 1977.

———. "The Politics of Theories of Interpretation." *Critical Inquiry* 9 (1982): 235–47.

———. *Validity in Interpretation*. New Haven: Yale UP, 1967.

Hollander, John, and Frank Kermode, eds. *The Literature of Renaissance England*. New York: Oxford UP, 1973.

Hooker, Richard. *Of the Laws of Ecclesiastical Polity: Attack and Response*. Gen. Ed. W. Speed Hill. The Folger Library edition. 4 vols. Cambridge: Harvard UP, 1977–.

Hoskin, Keith. "Examinations and the Schooling of Science." *Days of Judgement: Science, Examinations and the Organization of Knowledge in Late Victorian England*. Ed. Roy Macleod. Driffield: Nafferton, 1982. 213–36.

Houck, Raymond, ed. *Hooker's Ecclesiastical Polity: Book VIII*. New York: Columbia UP, 1931.

Hoy, David Couzens. *The Critical Circle: Literature, History, and Philosophical Hermeneutics*. Berkeley: U of California P, 1982.

Hunter, John, ed. *The Essays of Lord Bacon, with Critical and Illustrative Notes, and an Example, with Answers, of a University Middle-Class Examination Paper on the Essays*. London: Longmans, 1875.

Jacob, Margaret. *The Radical Enlightenment: Pantheists, Freemasons, and Republicans*. London: Allen, 1981.

Jardine, Lisa. "The Place of Dialectic Teaching in Sixteenth-Century Cambridge." *Studies in the Renaissance* 21 (1974): 31–62.

Johnson, Nan. *Nineteenth-Century Rhetoric in North America*. Carbondale: Southern Illinois UP, 1991.

Jones, Richard F. "The Attack on Pulpit Eloquence: An Episode in the Development of the Neo-Classical Standard of Prose." *Journal of English and Germanic Philology* 30 (1931): 188–217.

———. "The Moral Sense of Simplicity." *Studies in Honor of Frederick Shipley*. Language and Literature 14. Washington U P, 1942. 267–73.

———. "Science and English Prose Style in the Third Quarter of the Seventeenth Century." *The Seventeenth Century: Studies in the History of English Thought and Literature from Bacon to Pope*. Stanford: Stanford UP, 1951, 75–110.

———. *The Triumph of the English Language: A Survey of Opinions Concerning the Vernacular from the Introduction of Printing to the Restoration*. Stanford: Stanford UP, 1953.

Jonson, Ben. *Timber: Or, Discourses Made Upon Men and Matter. Seventeenth-Century Prose and Poetry*. 1963. Ed. Alexander Witherspoon and Frank Warnke. 2nd ed. New York: Harcourt, 1982.

Kaestle, Carl F. *Literacy in the United States: Readers and Reading since 1880*. New Haven: Yale UP, 1991.

Kearney, Hugh. "Puritanism, Capitalism and the Scientific Revolution." *Past and Present* 28 (1964): 81–101.

Keble, John, Ed. *A Library of the Fathers of the Holy Catholic Church, Anterior to the Division of the East and West*. Vol. 4. Oxford: Parker, 1839.

———, ed. *The Works of That Reverend and Judicious Divine, Mr. Richard Hooker*. 3rd American ed. from last Oxford ed. New York: Appleton, 1854.

Kenner, Hugh. "The Politics of the Plain Style." *New York Times Book Review* 15 Sept. 1985, 1, 39–40.

Kitzhaber, Albert R. *Rhetoric in American Colleges, 1850–1900*. Ed. John Gage. Dallas: Southern Methodist UP, 1990.

Klare, George R. *The Measurement of Readability*. Ames: Iowa UP, 1963.

Kliebard, Herbert. *The Struggle for the American Curriculum, 1893–1958*. Boston: Routledge, 1986.

Knox, Vicesimus. *Elegant Extracts in Prose Selected for the Improvement of Young Persons*. London: Rivington, 1816.

Kranidas, Thomas. *The Fierce Equation: A Study of Milton's Decorum*. The Hague: Mouton, 1965.

LaCapra, Dominick. Madame Bovary *on Trial*. Ithaca: Cornell UP, 1982.

Lake, Peter. *Moderate Puritans and the Elizabethan Church*. Cambridge: Cambridge UP, 1982.

Lanham, Richard A. "The Extraordinary Convergence: Democracy, Technology, Theory, and the University Curriculum." *The Politics of Liberal Education*. Ed. Darryl J. Gless and Barbara Herrnstein Smith. Durham: Duke UP, 1992. 33–56.

———. "From Book to Screen: Four Recent Studies." *College English* 54 (1992): 199–206.

———. *Literacy and the Survival of Humanism*. New Haven: Yale UP, 1983.

———. *The Motives of Eloquence: Literary Rhetoric in the Renaissance*. New Haven: Yale UP, 1976.

———. "One, Two, Three." *Composition and Literature: Bridging the Gap*. Ed. Winifred Bryan Horner. Chicago: U of Chicago P, 1983. 14–29.

———. *Revising Prose*. 2nd ed. New York: Macmillan, 1987.

———. *Style: An Anti-Textbook*. 1974. New Haven: Yale UP, 1978.

Larkin, Philip. "Church Going." *Chief Modern Poets of Britain and America*. Ed. Gerald Sanders et al. London: Macmillan, 1970. 411–413.

Latham, Henry. *On the Action of Examinations: Considered As a Means of Selection*. Boston: Willard Small, 1886.

Leavis, F. R. *English Literature in Our Time and the University: The Clark Lectures, 1967*. London: Chatto and Windus, 1969.

Lee, Sidney. *The Place of English Literature in the Modern University: An Inaugural Lecture Delivered at East London College on October 2, 1913*. London: Smith, Elder, 1913.

Levine, Philip, and Henri Coulette. *Character and Crisis: A Contemporary Reader*. New York: McGraw, 1966.

Lewis, Henry, ed. *The Essays (XXXII–LVII) or Counsels Civil and Moral of Francis Lord Verulam*. Collins' School and College Classics 1. London: Collins, 1879.

Lowrey, Rosewell Graves. *The English Sentence in Literature and in College Freshman Composition*. Nashville: George Peabody College for Teachers, 1928.

Macaulay, Thomas Babington. "Lord Bacon." *Critical, Historical and Miscellaneous Essays*. Vols. 3–4. New York: Armstrong, 1860. 336–495.

McDiarmid, John Fergus. "Language: System to Act to Report. The Development of English Linguistic Thought in the Sixteenth Century." Diss. Yale U, 1980.

MacDonald, Duncan. "Should Plain English Be Legislated?" Audiotape. A Gathering on Plain English in a Complex Society. Indianapolis: Indiana U School of Law, 1980.

McGann, Jerome. *A Critique of Modern Textual Criticism*. Chicago: U of Chicago P, 1983.

McKerrow, Ronald B. *The Treatment of Shakespeare's Text by His Earlier Editors: 1709–1768*. Proceedings of the British Academy, Vol. 19. London: Humphrey Milford, 1933.

Macleod, Roy, ed. *Days of Judgement: Science, Examinations and the Organization of Knowledge in Late Victorian England*. Driffield: Nafferton, 1982.

McMurtry, Jo. *English Language, English Literature: The Creation of an Academic Discipline*. Hamden: Archon, 1985.

Marvil, Jonathan. *Trials of Counsel: Francis Bacon in 1621*. Detroit: Wayne State U P, 1976.

Maurice, Frederick Denison. *Has the Church, Or the State, The Power to Educate the Nation? A Course of Lectures*. London: Rivington, 1839.

———. *Queen's College, London: Its Objects and Method. A Lecture Delivered in the Hanover Square Rooms, on Weds., March 29th, 1848*. London: Rivington, 1848.

Melville, Keith. *Immigration: What We Promised, Where To Draw the Line*. National Issues Forums. Dubuque: Kendall/Hunt, 1987.

Miller, Perry. *The New England Mind: The Seventeenth Century*. Boston: Beacon, 1961.

Miller, Susan. *Textual Carnivals: The Politics of Composition*. Carbondale: Southern Illinois UP, 1991.

Mirrour of State and Eloquence. London, 1656.

Moffett, James. *Teaching the Universe of Discourse*. Boston: Houghton Mifflin, 1968.

Montagu, Basil. *Selections from the Works of Taylor, Hooker, Barrow, South, Latimer, Brown, Milton, and Bacon*. 3rd ed. London: Pickering, 1829.

———. *The Works of Francis Bacon*. Philadelphia: Carey and Hart, 1842.

———. *The Works of Francis Bacon, Lord Chancellor of England*. London: Pickering, 1825.

Montgomery, R. J. *Examinations: An Account of Their Evolution As Administrative Devices in England*. Studies in Comparative Education 6. Pittsburgh: U of Pittsburgh P, 1965.

Mukarovsky, Jan. *Aesthetic Function: Norm and Value as Social Facts*. Trans. Mark E. Suino. Ann Arbor. U of Michigan P, 1970.

Mumford, Terry. "Should Plain English Be Legislated?" Audiotape. A Gathering on Plain English in a Complex Society. Indianapolis: Indiana U School of Law, 1980.

Neale, J. E. *Queen Elizabeth I: A Biography*. New York: Doubleday, 1970.

New Jersey Statutes Annotated. Title 56: "Trade Names, Trade-Marks and Unfair Trade Practices," 12–1 et seq.

Newman, John Henry. *Essays: Critical and Historical*. Vols. 1 and 2. London: Longmans, 1891.

Novarr, David. *The Making of Walton's Lives*. Ithaca: Cornell UP, 1958.

Nussbaum, Felicity. *The Autobiographical Subject: Gender and Ideology in Eighteenth-Century England*. Baltimore: Johns Hopkins UP, 1989.

Ogbu, John. "Literacy and Schooling in Subordinate Cultures: The Case of Black Americans." *Perspectives on Literacy*. Ed. Eugene Kintgen, Barry Kroll, and Mike Rose. Carbondale: Southern Illinois UP, 1988. 227–42.

Ohmann, Richard. "Use Definite, Specific, Concrete Language." *College English* 41 (1979): 390–97.

Ong, Walter J. *Ramus: Method and the Decay of Dialogue. From the Art of Discourse to the Art of Reason*. Cambridge: Harvard UP, 1958.

Palmer, D. J. *The Rise of English Studies: An Account of the Study of English Language and Literature from its Origins to the Making of the Oxford English School*. London: Oxford UP, 1965.

Penrose, Stephen. "The Reputation and Influence of Francis Bacon in the Seventeenth Century." Diss. Columbia U, 1934.

Perez-Ramos, Antonio. *Francis Bacon's Idea of Science and the Maker's Knowledge Tradition*. Oxford: Clarendon, 1988.

Pollard, Arthur. *Richard Hooker*. London: Longmans, 1966.

Potter, Stephen. *The Muse in Chains: A Study in Education*. London: Jonathan Cape, 1937.

Rawley, William, ed. *Certaine Miscellany Works of the Right Honorable Francis . . . Viscount St. Alban.* By Francis Bacon. London, 1629.

——, ed. and trans. *History Natural and Experimental of Life and Death or the Prolongation of Life.* By Francis Bacon. London, 1638. Prefatory material unpaginated.

——, ed. *Manes Verulamiani.* By Francis Bacon. Trans. E. K. Rand. Boston: privately printed, 1904.

——, ed. *Resuscitatio, or, Bringing unto Publick Light Several Pieces of the Works . . . of . . . Francis Bacon.* By Francis Bacon. London, 1657. Prefatory material unpaginated.

——, ed. *Sylva Sylvarum or A Natural History.* By Francis Bacon. London, 1626. Prefatory material unpaginated.

"Reasonable." *Compact Edition of the Oxford English Dictionary.* 1971.

Reese, William. "Knowledge of the Most." Unpublished manuscript. Indiana U, 1991.

Reynolds, Samuel Harvey, ed. *The Essays or Counsels, Civil and Moral.* By Francis Bacon. Oxford: Clarendon, 1890.

Richards, I. A. *Practical Criticism: A Study in Literary Judgment.* New York: Harcourt, 1929.

Ricketson, Sam. *The Berne Convention for the Protection of Literary and Artistic Works: 1886–1986.* London: Queen Mary College, 1987.

Ricoeur, Paul. *The Rule of Metaphor: Multidisciplinary Studies of the Creation of Meaning in Language.* Trans. Robert Czerny. Toronto: U of Toronto P, 1977.

Roach, John Peter Charles. *Public Examinations in England: 1850–1900.* Cambridge: U of Cambridge P, 1971.

Rudolph, Frederick. *The American College and University: A History.* New York: Knopf, 1962.

Said, Edward. "Opponents, Audiences, Constituencies, and Community." *Critical Inquiry* 9 (1982): 1–26.

Saintsbury, George. *A History of Elizabethan Literature.* New York: Macmillan, 1924.

Salmon, Vivian. *The Study of Language in Seventeenth-Century England.* Amsterdam: Benamins, 1979.

Salvatori, Mariolina. " 'Cultural Literacy': Critical Reading." *Correspondences Seven: Broadside Opinions and Conversations al Fresco.* Ed. Ann Berthoff. Upper Montclair: Boynton/Cook, n.d. n.p.

——. "Pedagogy: From the Periphery to the Center." *Reclaiming Pedagogy: The Rhetoric of the Classroom.* Ed. Patricia Donahue and Ellen Quandahl. Carbondale: Southern Illinois UP, 1989. 17–34.

——. "Reading and Writing a Text: Correlations Between Reading and Writing Patterns." *College English* 45 (83): 657–66.

Sanderson, Michael. *The Universities in the Nineteenth Century*. London: Routledge, 1975.

Sarmiento, Anthony, and Ann Kay. *Worker-Centered Learning: A Union Guide to Workplace Literacy*. Washington: AFL-CIO Human Resources Development Institute, 1990.

Scott, Fred Newton. "English Composition as a Mode of Behavior." *English Journal* 11 (1922): 463–73.

———. Introduction. *The Philosophy of Style*. By Herbert Spencer. Boston: Allyn, 1895.

———. "The Standard of American Speech." *English Journal* 6 (1917): 1–11.

Scott, Fred Newton, George Carpenter, and Franklin Baker. *The Teaching of English*. New York: Longmans, 1903.

Scott, Fred Newton, and Joseph Denney. *Composition-Literature*. Boston: Allyn and Bacon, 1902.

Scribner, Sylvia, and Michael Cole. "Unpackaging Literacy." *Perspectives on Literacy*. Ed. Eugene Kintgen, Barry Kroll, and Mike Rose. Carbondale: Southern Illinois UP, 1988. 57–70.

Shannon, Patrick. *The Struggle to Continue: Progressive Reading Instruction in the United States*. Portsmouth: Heinemann, 1990.

Shapiro, Barbara. *John Wilkins: An Intellectual Biography*. Berkeley: U of California P, 1969.

Sherman, Lucius Adelno. *Analytics of Literature: A Manual for the Objective Study of English Prose and Poetry*. Boston: Ginn, 1893.

———. "Some Observations upon the Sentence-Length in English Prose." *Nebraska University Studies* 1 (1888–1892): 119–30.

Sinfield, Alan. *Faultlines: Cultural Materialism and the Politics of Dissident Reading*. Berkeley: U of California P, 1992.

———. *Literature in Protestant England: 1560–1660*. London: Croom Helm, 1983.

Sisson, C. J. *The Judicious Marriage of Mr. Hooker and the Birth of* The Laws of Ecclesiastical Polity. Cambridge: Cambridge U P, 1940.

Slaton, Walter F., Jr. "The Characters of Style in Elizabethan Prose." *Journal of English and German Philology* 62 (1958): 197–207.

Smallwood, Mary Lovett. *An Historical Study of Examinations and Grading Systems in Early American Universities: A Critical Study of the Original Records of Harvard, William and Mary, Yale, Mount Holyoke, and Michigan from Their Founding to 1900*. Harvard Studies in Education 24. Cambridge: Harvard U P, 1935.

Spedding, James, Robert Ellis, and Douglas Heath, eds. *The Works of Francis Bacon*. 14 vols. London: Longman, 1857–1874.

———. *The Works*. By Francis Bacon. Vol. 1. Boston: Houghton, 1857–1874.

Spellmeyer, Kurt. *Common Ground: Dialogue and Composition.* Englewood Cliffs: Prentice Hall, 1992.

Spencer, Herbert. *Essays on Education.* New York: Dutton, 1911.

———. "The Philosophy of Style." *Representative Essays on the Theory of Style.* Ed. William T. Brewster. New York: Macmillan, 1928.

Sprat, Thomas. *History of the Royal Society of London. Complaint and Reform in England, 1436–1714.* Ed. William Huse Dunham and Stanley Pargellis. New York: Oxford U P, 1938. 733–72.

———. *From* The History of the Royal Society: *English Prose of the XVII Century.* Ed. Roberta Florence Brinkley. New York: Norton, 1951. 878–90.

Staffard, William, and Frederick Candelaria. *The Voices of Prose.* New York: McGraw, 1966.

Stevens, James. *Francis Bacon and the Style of Science.* Chicago: U of Chicago P, 1975.

Stewart, Donald C. "The Barnyard Goose, History, and Fred Newton Scott." *English Journal* 67 (1978): 14–17.

Stone, Lawrence. "Literacy and Education in England, 1640–1900." *Past and Present* 42 (1969): 69–139.

Street, Brian. *Literacy in Theory and Practice.* Cambridge Studies in Oral and Literate Culture. Cambridge: Cambridge UP, 1984.

Strong, Patrick. "Being and Writing." Rev. of *Style: An Anti-Textbook* by Richard Lanham. *College English* 38 (1976): 201–05.

Tanselle, G. Thomas. "The Editorial Problem of Final Authorial Intention." *Studies in Bibliography* 29 (1976): 167–211. Bibliographical Society of the University of Virginia.

Tenison, Thomas, ed. *Baconiana: Or Certaine Genuine Remains of Sir Francis Bacon.* London, 1679.

Terman, Lewis M. *The Measurement of Intelligence: An Explanation of and a Complete Guide for the Use of the Stanford Revision and Extension of the Binet-Simon Intelligence Scale.* Boston: Houghton, 1916.

Thorndike, Edward Lee. *A Teachers' Word Book of the Twenty Thousand Words Found Most Frequently and Widely in General Reading for Children and Young People.* New York: Teachers College, Columbia U, 1941.

Travers, Walter. *A Supplication Made to the Privy Counsel.* Oxford: Joseph Barnes, 1612.

Vaughan, Michalina, and Margaret Scotford Archer. *Social Conflict and Educational Change in England and France: 1789–1848.* London: Cambridge UP, 1971.

Verulamiana; or Opinions on Men, Manners, Literature, Politics, and Theology. By Francis Bacon. London: Dutton, 1803.

Vickers, Brian, ed. *Essential Articles for the Study of Francis Bacon.* Hamden: Alchon, 1968.

———. *Francis Bacon and Renaissance Prose.* Cambridge: Cambridge UP, 1968.

———. Introduction: "Hooker's Prose Style." *Of the Laws of Ecclesiastical Polity.* Abridged. By Richard Hooker. Ed. A. S. McGrade and Brian Vickers. New York: St. Martin's, 1977.

Viswanathan, Gauri. *Masks of Conquest: Literary Study and British Rule in India.* New York: Columbia UP, 1989.

Waddell, Craig. Rev. of *The Technical Reader: Readings in Technical, Business, and Scientific Communication,* ed. W. Steve Anderson and Don Richard Cox. *College Composition and Communication* 36 (1985): 495–96.

Wall, John N., Jr. "Jeremy Taylor and Richard Hooker's Contemporary Reputation." *Seventeenth-Century News* 35 (1977): 112.

Wallace, Karl R. *Francis Bacon on Communication and Rhetoric.* Chapel Hill: U of North Carolina P, 1943.

Walton, Izaak. *The Lives of Dr. John Donne, Sir Henry Wotton, Richard Hooker, George Herbert, and Dr. Robert Sanderson.* Ed. Thomas Zouch. Boston: Crosby, Nichols, Lee, 1860.

Wats, Gilbert, trans. *Of the Advancement and Proficience of Learning or the Partitions of Sciences.* By Francis Bacon. London, 1640. Prefatory material unpaginated.

Webster, Charles. *The Great Instauration: Science, Medicine and Reform, 1626–1660.* New York: Holmes and Meier, 1976.

Whately, Richard, ed. *Bacon's Essays: With Annotations.* 5th ed. 1861. Essay Index Reprint Series. Freeport: Books for Libraries, 1973.

———, ed. *Bacon's Essays: With Annotations.* With Notes and Glossarial Index by Franklin Fiske Heard. Boston: Lee and Shepard, 1884.

Whitgift, John. *The Works: The Third Portion.* Ed. John Ayre. Cambridge: Cambridge UP, 1853.

Whitney, Charles. *Francis Bacon and Modernity.* New Haven: Yale UP, 1986.

Wilkins, Gene. "Should Plain English Be Legislated?" Audiotape. A Gathering on Plain English in a Complex Society. Indianapolis: Indiana U School of Law, 1980.

Wilkins, John. *Essay Towards a Real Character and a Philosophical Language.* London: Gellibrand, 1668.

Williams, Raymond. "Base and Superstructure in Marxist Cultural Theory." *New Left Review* 82 (1973): 3–16.

———. *Keywords: A Vocabulary of Culture and Society.* Rev. ed. New York: Oxford UP, 1983.

Williamson, George. *The Senecan Amble: Prose Form from Bacon to Collier.* Chicago: U of Chicago P, 1951.

Willson, David Harris. *A History of England.* 2nd ed. Hinsdale: Dryden, 1972.

Wright, W. Aldis, ed. *Essays, and Colour of Good and Evil.* By Francis Bacon. Golden Treasury Series. Cambridge: Macmillan, 1862.

Young, Richard, et al. *Rhetoric: Discovery and Change.* New York: Harcourt, 1970.

Zeitlin, Harry. *Federal Relations in American Education, 1933–1943: A Study of New Deal Efforts and Innovations.* Diss. Columbia U, 1958. Ann Arbor: UMI, 1980.

INDEX

Academy. *See* Universities
Accessibility, 61, 131–32; of education,
    101, 165, 172, 211*n*3; of language,
    64, 162–63; in scientific manage-
    ment, 55, 61; social, 176, 183
Advancement of Learning, The
    (Bacon), 163–64, 170
American English, 122, 128–31
Analytics of Literature (Sherman), 33
Anglican church, 81–83, 95
Applebee, Arthur, 86, 102
Aristotle, 158–59
Arnold, Matthew, 119–20
Arnold, Thomas, 98
Art of Plain Talk, The (Flesch), 47
Ascham, Roger, 145
Audience, 111, 172; and literacy,
    58–59, 64; and plain style, 60, 65;
    for speeches, 199–200, 201–02
Authorial intent, 17–18, 53, 182

Bacon, Francis, 6–7, 88–91; and form
    vs. content, 11–18, 107–11, 142; se-
    lection of pieces by, 55–56, 59,
    68–69, 94, 126–27, 216–17*n*8;
    translations of, 162–63, 166; use of
    by educational reformers, 80–81,
    84–85, 140; use of in history of
    prose styles, 35, 38–40, 59–61; use
    of in plain talk movement, 33–34,
    51–53; use of style of, 17–18,
    103–04, 131–32; use of to promote
    values, 100–01, 141, 169–71
*Baconiana, Or Certaine Genuine
    Remains of Sr. Francis Bacon*
    (Tenison), 162–63, 172
Bain, Alexander, 78, 88, 101–13
Balibar, Renée, 8–10, 113
Barnes, James, 87
Bennett, Tony, 8

Bentham, Jeremy, 79
Berlin, James, 121
Blount, Thomas, 216–17*n*8
Books, 46, 49, 119
Booth, Wayne, 21–23
Booty, John, 147, 215*n*4
Brewster, William, 7–8
Brougham, Henry, 79–81, 111
Bryson, Lymon, 50
Business, 33–34, 41, 53–54, 169–70
Butler, Marilyn, 135

Calvinism, 148–51, 154–55, 164
Canonization/canonical figures, 8–18,
    34; and Bacon, 12–18, 39, 51–53,
    59–61; and Hooker, 12–18, 36; and
    pedagogy, 64–65, 88–91, 103–04;
    uses of, 53, 67–68, 132, 137–40
Cartwright, Thomas, 144
Catholicism. *See* Roman Catholicism
Christian Letter, A, 142, 143–44,
    146–48, 151–61, 215*n*4
Church, 102; and education, 95, 100,
    167–68; reform of, 138–40, 143–61
Church of England, 143–48, 147–61,
    216*n*6, 216*n*7
Clark, Aubert, 87–88
Classes, social: access to literature by,
    8–9, 43–44, 86, 112–13; develop-
    ment of middle, 168, 171; educa-
    tion for, 74–78, 83–84, 93, 95–101,
    119, 172–73, 191–92, 209*n*1; main-
    taining hierarchy of, 50–51, 69,
    120, 131–32, 194–95
Classical education, 74, 78, 83, 172;
    and English literature, 114–15, 117
*Classical Rhetoric for the Modern Stu-
    dent* (Corbett), 7
Cmiel, Kenneth, 65, 214*n*9
Collins, John Churton, 88, 113–20

Comenius, John Amos, 164, 165
Composition, 98, 122; in English studies, 184, 191–92; pedagogy of, 18–24, 27–28, 54–56, 60, 61–64, 72, 102–10, 121–22, 192–94, 212n6; scientific teaching of, 104, 106, 108; vs. literature, 82, 179–81, 185, 190, 214n9. See also Literature, teaching composition through
Composition Exercise Books, 105
Composition-Literature (Scott and Denney), 125
Consumers, 24–29, 58
Contemporary Essay, The (Hall), 18–21
Content: for compositions, 19, 21, 105, 125, 214n2; in literature selection, 56, 59, 86, 117–18; neutrality of, 16–17, 101; and unchanging meanings, 181–83. See also Form vs. content
Corbett, Edward, 7
Covel, William, 143, 147
Cox, George Bede, 72–73
Creativity, 171, 173
Croll, Morris, 54
Cultural capital, 3–4, 53, 75, 209n1
Cultural literacy, 61, 178, 187
Cultural Literacy: What Every American Needs to Know (Hirsch), 176, 183, 186
Culture, 10–11, 19, 209–10n4; defense of, 30, 132; gatekeeping of, 95–101, 120; and language, 22–23, 130–31, 186–87; and style, 6–7, 146; values of, 115–20, 176–77, 196–97
Curriculum, 78, 116, 186

Dawes, Richard, 71
De Augmentis Scientiarum (Bacon), 163, 164
Decorum, 96–97, 99–101, 190, 195
Democracy, 176–79, 202
Denney, Joseph, 125
Devil's Pool, The (George Sand), 9
Dickerson, Reed, 26
Dissociation of sensibility, 14–15, 133–34
Doyle, Brian, 196

Eagleton, Terry, 67
Earle, John, 162
Education, 86; and culture, 3–5; and English teacher training, 111, 113–14, 120–21, 127; failures in, 57–59; pedagogy of, 18–24, 27–28, 38, 60–65, 68–74, 88, 192–94, 196; and social hierarchy, 8–10, 29–30, 67–68, 74–78, 143–44, 163, 211n3; state in, 95, 100, 167–68. See also Composition, pedagogy of
Educational formalism, 176–77
Educational psychologists, 41–42
Educational reform, 71–72, 77–78, 137; and secularization, 79–83, 102; in U.S., 83–84, 178–79; use of Bacon to promote, 140, 163–65, 167
Efficiency: in literature selections, 61, 103; in scientific management, 55, 63, 64, 210n7
Eliot, T. S., 11–18, 133–34
Emblen, D. L., 60
English Composition and Rhetoric (Bain), 104–05
English departments, 54–55, 120, 179–80; Bain's influence on, 102, 104
English studies, 119, 132, 202; composition in, 102–13, 180, 184; development of, 66–74, 77–86, 92, 191, 212n1; teacher training in, 113–14, 120–21, 127; texts for, 88–91, 93–97
Essays, 5–6, 40, 52, 55–56; use of teaching composition, 20–21, 108
Essays (Bacon), 40, 89–90, 94, 100–01, 108–10
Essay Towards a Real Character (Wilkins), 169
Ethics, 26–27, 124–25
Examinations, 68–74, 75–77
Experimentation, 169
Extract books, 103–04

Feyerabend, Paul, 179
Fish, Stanley, 4
Flesch, Rudolf, 24–26, 47–50
Form vs. content, 20–21, 22–23, 144–45, 166–67; in Bacon and Hooker, 12–18, 13, 38–40, 141,

142–43, 156; in pedagogy, 104–09, 184–85, 186–89
Foucault, Michel, 70, 209n3
Francis Bacon and the Style of Science (Stevens), 39

Gauden, John, 138–39
Genealogy, 64–65, 67
Gibson, John, 73–74
Giroux, Henry, 3–4
Goldfarb, Ronald, 25–26
Grafton, Anthony, 14
Grammar, 170; teaching composition through, 72, 73; teaching of, 9, 127–28
Graves, Robert, 19
Gray, William, 44–47
Gregory, Marshall, 21–23
Gunning, Robert, 26, 41, 51–54, 64–65, 211n2

Hall, Donald, 18–21, 60
Halloran, Michael, 210n7
Harper and Row Rhetoric (Booth and Gregory), 21–23
Harvey, Gabriel, 145
Hegemony, 7, 10
Hildyard, Angela, 5–6
Hill, Adams Sherman, 69–70
Hill, Christopher, 164, 216nn6, 7
Hill, W. Speed, 17, 138, 161
Hirsch, E. D., 61–64, 110, 175–77, 178–80, 180–89
History, 135, 139; attempts to transcend, 5–6, 12–18, 40, 100, 141; and dehistoricizing, 18, 36–38, 161
History of the Royal Society of London (Sprat), 136–37, 140–41
Hollander, John, 39
Hooker, Richard, 213–14n8; controversy and, 36–38, 134; in history of prose styles, 11–18, 35–38, 84–85, 88–91; use of to promote values, 134, 141; use of style of, 103, 132, 138–40. *See also Laws*
Hoskin, Keith, 70–71
Houck, Raymond, 139, 146
Humanism, 14, 17, 144, 184–85, 186–87; and education, 91, 194;

and the humanities, 58, 178, 180, 192
Humanistic functionalism, 61–64

Ideology, 4–5, 29–30, 62–64, 196–97
Industrialization, 77–78, 86, 120
Information for the People series, 101–02

Jardine, Lisa, 14, 158–59
Jones, Richard Foster, 54, 145
Jonson, Ben, 55
Just and Temperate Defence of the Five Books of Ecclesiustical Policie, A (Covel), 143

Kaestle, Karl, 45, 174–75
Keble, John, 80, 81, 213–14n8
Kermode, Frank, 39
Kilduff, Edward, 57–58
Kitzhaber, Albert, 84, 121, 122
Kliebard, Herbert, 42

Lake, Peter, 147–48
Language, 78; American English, 122, 128–31; and culture, 13–14, 22–23; evolution of, 127–28, 169–70; gender in, 30, 96–98; and legislation, 24–30, 210n7; philosophy of, 180–81; in plain talk movement, 47–50, 57–59; and social hierarchy, 9–10, 43–44, 64, 93, 95–101, 194–95. *See also* National language and culture
Lanham, Richard, 175–76, 177–80, 189–96
Laws (Hooker), 138–39; availability of, 89, 215–16n5; controversy and response to, 141–42, 143–48, 149–52
Leary, Bernice, 44–47
Leavis, F. R., 14–15, 133, 135–37
Lectures, English, 11–16, 111
Legal language reform legislation, 24–29
Lewis, Henry, 68
Liberal arts, 118–19, 178, 190; vs. practical education, 74–78, 186–87, 213n7

Liberalism, 66–67, 132

Linguistic reform, 167, 173; by Royal Society, 137, 140–41

Literacy, 212–13n2, 217–18n1; crisis of, 54–55, 65, 174–76, 190–91, 192–94, 197–98; and culture, 23, 49–50, 67–68, 101; and democracy, 176–79; enlightenment rhetoric on, 45–46; functional, 57–59, 61, 172–73, 177; increase in, 10, 43–44, 79–81, 165; levels of, 45–46, 61, 74, 76; normative, 5–6, 91, 92; values of, 13, 29, 45–46

Literacy and the Survival of Humanism (Lanham), 176

Literary genealogy, 8, 52–53, 64–65, 67

Literary history, 11, 54, 57, 72–75, 76–77, 196–97

Literature, 39–40; and culture, 67–68, 93, 115–16, 132; as discipline, 78–79, 119; history of, 12–18, 110–11, 114, 122; in liberal education, 74–78; principles in English, 118; selection of for teaching, 55–56, 59, 107–09; and social hierarchy, 8–10, 96–97, 98–101, 112–13; teaching composition through, 54–56, 69, 86, 102–10, 125–27; vs. composition, 82, 179–81, 185, 190; vs. functional literacy, 57–59, 172–73

Lowrey, Rosewell Graves, 211n1

McDiarmid, John, 144, 145

MacDonald, Duncan, 26–27

McKerrow, Ronald, 89, 90–91

Manner/matter. *See* Form vs. content

Marks of a Readable Style: A Study in Adult Education (Flesch), 47

Marvil, Jonathan, 38–39

Masculine expression, 30, 96–97

Maturity: of language, 14, 210n7; stages of, 112–13

Maurice, John Frederick Denison, 88, 93–101

Meaning. *See* Content; Form vs. content

Mechanics Institution, 102

Middle class, 95–96

Mill, James, 101

Mill, John Stuart, 101

Moderation, 141, 155, 162; and Hooker, 36–38, 138–40, 147, 156, 161–62

Montagu, Basil, 89–90

Motives of Eloquence (Lanham), 192–93

Mumford, Terry, 27

National curriculum, 186

Nationalism, 8–18, 55, 106

National language and culture, 8–10, 13, 16, 178, 187; effects of on education, 67, 77–78; families and, 129–30; and grammar standards, 127–28, 129–30, 131

Nebraska University Studies (Sherman), 33

New Deal, the, 211n3

Newton, John Henry, 75

Normative style, 63, 113, 131, 202; criticism of, 97–98, 170–71, 172, 177; development of, 24; origin of, 60–61, 85. *See also* Plain style

Novum Organum (Bacon), 55–56

Objectivity, 4–7, 7, 201, 209–10n4

"Of Studies" (Bacon), 55–56

"Of Vicissitude of Things" (Bacon), 55–56

Ohmann, Richard, 4–5, 17

Olson, David, 5–6

Ong, Walter, 145

Organicism, 123, 124

Palmer, D. J., 77

Pedagogy. *See* Composition; Education

Penrose, Stephen, 38–39

Philology, 114, 117, 119

Philosophy of Composition, The (Hirsch), 61–64, 181, 183

Philosophy of Style, The (Spencer), 123–24, 212n6

Plain English legislation, 24–30, 210n7

Plain style, 24–29, 60–65, 172; of Bacon, 16–17, 60; criticism of,

57–59; origins of, 54, 140–41; and truth, 28–29, 40, 201. *See also* Normative style

Plain talk movement, 41, 47–50, 64–65, 210n7, 211n3

Playfulness, 189, 193

Pluralism, 187

Politics, 186–88; and education, 21, 93, 99–101, 175–77, 183; and language, 6, 16–17, 19–20, 28–29

Post-Restoration period, 136, 138–40; reform in, 137, 173

Practical Observations on Popular Education (Brougham), 79–80

Presbyterians, 139, 216n6, 216n7

Prose engineering, 54

Prose style, 12, 17, 18–20, 33–34; development of, 10, 14–16, 34–35, 110–11, 181

Protestants, 140, 148–50; and Bacon, 162–65, 167–68

Publishing, 94; of Hooker's books, 89, 138–40, 149, 215–16n5; and literacy, 79–80, 87–88

Puritans, 144–45, 147, 149–50, 163

Question and answer format, 159–60

Ramism, 17, 144, 158–59

Rationalism, 179

Rawley, William, 166

Raymond, James, 25–26

Readability, 57–59, 65, 185–86, 210; adult studies on, 44–45, 47–48; intelligence and, 41–45; relative, 61–64; studies on, 27, 33–34, 41–45, 46–51, 53, 57; vocabulary and, 42, 46–48, 51

Reading, 48–49, 79–81, 87–88, 111–12; and writing, 186, 188

Reading lists: for literacy, 80, 93–97, 116; for writing pedagogy, 55–56, 59, 88–91, 107, 108

Real Character, 168

Relative readability, 61–64

Relativism, historical, 183

Religion, 138–40, 144–45, 164–65, 168–69; and education, 79–83, 100, 102, 106. *See also* Church

Renaissance, 17, 190–91; style of, 8–14, 10–11, 195–96

Restoration, 14–15, 171; Bacon and Hooker used after, 134, 147, 168. *See also* Post-Restoration period

Revising Prose (Lanham), 177

Reynolds, Samuel, 90

Rhetoric, 19–20, 141, 158–59, 168, 190; defense as style of, 145, 143–44; flexibility and, 26; teaching of, 102 10, 121, 122, 178, 193; techniques of, 37–38, 199. *See also* Form vs. content

Rhetoric (Young, Becker, & Pike), 60

Roman Catholicism, 149

Royal Society of London, 5–6, 136–37, 140–41, 164–65

Saintsbury, George, 38

Sand, George, 9, 10

Sandys, Edwin, 149

Scholars, 95–96

Science, 39–40, 168; and education, 41–42, 165–66; in readability studies, 44–45, 57. *See also* Technology

Scientific management movement, 53, 55, 63, 211n3

Scott, Fred Newton, 88, 120–31, 214n2

Scriptures, 158, 161, 168

Self-expression, 122–23, 125, 130

Self-improvement, 111–12

Self-knowledge, 19, 194

Sentence length, 25–29, 33–34, 46–47, 211n1

Set books, 93–97

Sherman, Lucius Adelno, 33

Sincerity, 125–26, 128

Spedding, James, 40

Spencer, Herbert, 64, 101, 110, 123–24, 212n6

Sprat, Thomas, 136–37, 140–41

Standard style. *See* Style, formal

Stevens, James, 39

Stone, Lawrence, 165

Street, Brian, 5–7

Strong, Patrick, 196

Students, 70–72, 175; capacity of for language, 127, 129–30; children as, 9–10, 43–44
Style: An Anti-Textbook (Lanham), 189, 196
Style: colloquial, 29; and culture, 6–7, 146; economy of, 123–24, 125; formal, 21–23; functional, 171; genealogy of, 11, 60–61; history of prose, 34–35, 54, 61, 63–64, 180, 181; Hooker's use of, 103, 132, 138–40; middle, 195; modern, 13, 16, 54, 85, 133–34; official, 195; technical, 29; techniques of, 19, 22. *See also* Normative style; Plain style; Prose style; Renaisssance, style of
Stylelessness, 40, 142, 167–68, 170
Style talk, 5–8, 8, 11, 21, 24
Stylistic reform. *See* Linguistic reform
Sullivan Law, 24–25, 27
Swift, Jonathan, 170

Taylor, Jeremy, 147, 162
Technique of Clear Writing, The (Gunning), 41
Technology, 14–15, 58, 189–90
Tenison, Thomas, 162–63, 172
Terman, Louis M., 41–42
Textbooks, 8–9, 94, 144; for composition, 20, 21–23, 109; English and American, 87–88, 212–13n2; rhetoric and readers, 55, 56, 59, 125–27, 216–17n8; use of canonical figures in, 59–61, 64–65, 88–91
Texts, 34, 52, 53, 139; for teaching, 54–56, 59, 68–70, 86, 93–97, 103–04; valuing of, 98–99, 114–17, 158
Thinking, 6, 36–37
Thorndike, Edward, 42, 48
Timber (Jonson), 55
Tradition, uses of, 134–35
Travers, Walter, 144, 154
Truth/deception, 19, 145; and plain style, 16–17, 25, 28–29, 40, 171, 201; by style, 151–61
Twenty Lessons in Reading and Writing Prose, 55–56

Universal schooling, 164, 165
Universities, 57–59, 68–73, 82, 119, 143–44, 159; English studies at, 66–74, 83–84, 113–15; and readability studies, 53–54, 57
Utilitarianism, 78, 103; secular, 79–81, 140; and universal schooling, 165–66. *See also* Literacy, functional; Technology

Values, 21, 28–29, 64, 196–97
Vickers, Brian, 17–18, 37–38, 163
Viswanathan, Gauri, 91, 212n1
Vocabulary, 42, 46–48, 51

Walton, Izaac, 139
Wats, Gilbert, 163, 164–67
What Makes a Book Readable? (Gray and Leary), 44–45
What to Read, and How to Read It; or Hints to Candidates for the Government Civil Service, 72, 74
Whitburn, Merrill, 210n7
Whitgift, Archbishop, 148–49, 151, 159–60, 215–16n5
Whitney, Charles, 17
Wilkins, Gene, 27
Wilkins, John, 168
William Collins and Sons, 68, 105
Williams, Raymond, 9
Wright, W. Aldis, 90
Writer's Reader, A (Hall and Emblen), 60
Writing, 18–21, 22–23, 105, 125. *See also* Composition
Wydick, Richard, 25

Pittsburgh Series in

Composition, Literacy, and Culture

David Bartholomae and Jean Ferguson Carr, Editors

Academic Discourse and Critical Consciousness
Patricia Bizzell

Between Languages and Cultures: Translation and Cross-cultural Texts
Anuradha Dingwaney and Carol Maier, Editors

Eating on the Street: Teaching Literacy in a Multicultural Society
David Schaafsma

The Emperor's New Clothes: Literature, Literacy, and the Ideology of Style
Kathryn T. Flannery

Feminine Principles and Women's Experience in American Composition
and Rhetoric
Louise Wetherbee Phelps and Janet Emig, Editors

Fragments of Rationality: Postmodernity and the Subject of Composition
Lester Faigley

The Insistence of the Letter: Literacy Studies and Curriculum Theories
Bill Green, Editor

Knowledge, Culture, and Power: International Perspectives on Literacy as
Policy and Practice
Peter Freebody and Anthony R. Welch, Editors

The Labyrinths of Literacy: Reflections on Literacy Past and Present
Harvey J. Graff

Literacy Online: The Promise (and Peril) of Reading and Writing
with Computers
Myron C. Tuman, Editor

The Origins of Composition Studies in the American College, 1875–1925:
A Documentary History
John C. Brereton, Editor

The Powers of Literacy: A Genre Approach to Teaching Writing
Bill Cope and Mary Kalantzis, Editors

Pre/Text: The First Decade
Victor Vitanza, Editor

Reclaiming Rhetorica: Women in the Rhetorical Tradition
Andrea A. Lunsford, Editor

'Round My Way: Authority and Double-Consciousness in Three Urban
High School Writers
Eli C. Goldblatt

Word Perfect: Literacy in the Computer Age
Myron C. Tuman

Writing Science: Literacy and Discursive Power
M.A.K. Halliday and J. R. Martin